*TEX SMITH'S*
**Hot Rod**
**LIBRARY**

# HOW TO BUILD

*FORD, CHEVY, DODGE, GMC, IH, STUDE*

**By Jim Clark**

First produced in 1993 by co-publishers, CarTech, Inc., 11481 Kost Dam Rd, North Branch, MN,55056, and Tex Smith Publishing, PO Box 726, Driggs, ID 83422.

CarTech, Inc., and Tex Smith Publishing Company recommend you follow all safety procedures when working on your vehicle. Wear eye protection and respiration filter, especially when painting and around tools. Always dispose of hazardous fluids, batteries, tires and parts properly and safely to protect our environment.

CarTech, inc., and Tex Smith  Publishing Company books are also available at discounts in bulk quantity for industrial or sales-promotional use. For details, contact the marketing director at:

CarTech, Inc., 11481 Kost Dam Rd, North Branch, MN 55056, telephone (612)583-3471, fax (612)583-2023
 Tex Smith Books, PO Box  726, Driggs, ID 83422, telephone (208)354-8133, fax (208)354-8104.

Overseas distribution by:BROOKLANDS BOOKS LTD, PO Box 146, COBHAM, SURREY, KT11 1LG, ENGLAND, telephone  0932 865051 Fax:0932 868803.
BROOKLANDS BOOKS LTD. 1/81 DARLEY ST. PO Box 199, MONA VALE, NSW 2103, AUSTRALIA, telephone 2 997 8428   Fax: 2 452 4679

ISBN   1-884089-00-3

Printed and bound in the United States of America

| | |
|---|---|
| Author | **JIM  CLARK** |
| Publisher | **LEROI  TEX  SMITH** |
| Editor | **RICHARD  JOHNSON** |
| Art Director | **BOB  REECE** |

# CONTENTS

| **Publisher** | **Editor** | **Art Director** | **Circulation** |
| LeRoi Tex Smith | Rich Johnson | Bob Reece | Sierra Smith |

| **Author** | **Tech Editor** | **Copy Editor** | |
| Jim Clark | Ron Ceridono | Becky Jaye | |

# Foreword

## Look At What You Missed, Grandpa!

**G**randpa was a chicken rancher, with poultry spread out over half of northern Utah — or so it seemed to a little kid. Everything was bigger back then, and according to my kid's eye view of the world, grandpa had at least a zillion chickens and a spread to rival the Ponderosa. And that's where I learned to drive hot rod trucks.

Actually, there wasn't anything too hot about the old Ford flatbed that was used to haul egg baskets during the getherin' chores. (Getherin' is northern Utah chicken rancher lingo for sneaking eggs out from under hopeful hens.) But at least the truck had a 3-foot-high floor shift and made neat noises in granny gear, so that made us kids believe it was hot.

It was all I could do to sit on the seat and reach the pedals, but grandpa still let me and cousin Galen haul stuff around the farm. One day, we were out in the recently harvested wheat field seeing how much stubble we could run over

when we got the idea that the stubble on the far side of the irrigation ditch needed some flattening. So off we went, with me behind the wheel, in search of a way to get across the ditch. When we found the crossing it was nothing but a narrow metal culvert with dirt laid over it. I eyeballed the makeshift bridge and headed across. Galen was hung out the passenger side window giving me advice, when suddenly he said, "Oh no!" Unfortunately, I took that to mean the truck was too far over on his side, so I swung the steering wheel to the left. Immediately, the dual rear tires on my side fell off the bridge into the ditch, and there we hung.

All the driving technique I knew at the time failed me. I figured the truck was a total loss, and Galen was helpful enough to detail exactly what grandpa was probably going to do to me when he found out what I had done. Being short on courage and only marginal on wisdom, I high-tailed it for the chicken coop to hide out and ponder the purpose of life until I reached manhood (maybe another 12 years) and could face grandpa with the news that I had destroyed his truck and probably cost him the farm. It was a dismal day in the young life of a career truck driving egg getherer.

I'd still be hiding out in the coop, eating raw chickens and sucking eggs for nourishment, but somehow grandpa found me and applied a huge dose of love and understanding (along with a few well chosen words about driving trucks).

Years later, married and with a couple of kids, it was time to invest in a pickup of my own. Becky and I scoured newspaper ads, looking for the perfect (cheap) old truck to turn into a family project vehicle. When we spotted an ad for a '56 Chevy for only a couple hundred bucks, I knew this was it. So on a Saturday afternoon, we followed the directions given us over the phone to a rural farm. When I say the place was rural, I mean it was so far out of town that evolution still hadn't gotten all the way there. I'd swear the dog had feathers and scales instead of hair.

The farmer came out to look us over, and he tried to stifle a little grin that I have since come to identify with psychotic characters in Hitchcock movies. At the moment, the grin slipped past me because all I was seeing was this fantastic '56 Chevy pickup begging me to take it home. It was brown (mostly), with rust and dents only in insignificant places. It rode on four mismatched tires and wheels, which I figured would give us a variety of traction characteristics for all-season driving. Almost all six cylinders were firing, at least most of the time. The brakes didn't work very well, but then the truck wouldn't go fast enough to need brakes very much anyway. Double or triple clutching was usually sufficient for gear changes, and I was convinced that my legs could use the exercise. And to balance my lower body exercise with the upper body, the steering had stiffened up nicely.

I was nearly speechless at the thought of owning such a glorious truck. Becky, however, more than made up for my momentary loss of vocabulary. Nevertheless, being an excellent (patient, long-suffering) wife, she let me buy the truck on condition that I wouldn't make her drive it.

On the way home, I discovered that the steering had not only stiffened up, but it only turned one direction. Somehow I hadn't noticed that while driving it around clockwise circle in the farmer's field. Hmmm. Do you suppose the farmer planned it that way? But, no matter. As luck would have it, a friend was upgrading his 1/2-ton Chevy to 3/4-ton chassis stuff, and I knew I could talk him out of his old front axle and all the steering mechanism.

Two years later, having repaired a blown rear bearing that ate the axle shaft, and a spun main bearing that ate the crankshaft, we sold the brown (mostly) '56 Chevy pickup with rust and dents still in insignificant places, riding on a completely different set of mismatched tires and wheels. But at least it steered in both directions. I cried as I watched it drive away under new ownership, but in perfect counter-balance, Becky reacted with emotions that she felt were more appropriate for the occasion.

Between then and now, there have been many trucks in my life. It's a love affair that still hasn't ended, and likely never will. There is simply something about a truck that speaks to a man's heart. It doesn't much matter if the truck is old or new, restored, customized or hot rodded. If it's a truck, that's enough.

Detroit has recognized what a powerful product a light truck can be, and in recent years the automakers have turned a tremendous amount of styling and engineering emphasis toward their light trucks. In a time when factory hot rod cars were almost forgotten, some tire smoking pickups were rolling off the assembly lines, decked out with paint and graphics that stir the heart. The emphasis is on image. Trucks look muscular, tough, rugged, macho, sexy. All the things that make people want to have one.

Hot rods are image vehicles. The majority of mechanical and cosmetic alteration is more form than function. It has always been that way, and always will. Early hot rods were mainly stockers that had been relieved of fenders, hood and sometimes even the windshield so they could go faster at the dry lakes. The image spilled over to the street, and soon all the speed tricks started showing up on vehicles that would never be raced.

As racing technology progressed, new speed tricks showed up. Louvers, scoops, raking the suspension, bigs and littles, etc. Decades later, Detroit finally caught on to the race image, as evidenced by modern trucks with air dams, spoilers, and ground effects that serve no logical function until speeds beyond the capability of the powertrain are reached. But the image works, regardless of how well the cosmetic stuff works.

But hot rodding is more than just race equipment. Real hot rodding is applied ingenuity to solve automotive problems. Where speed events come into play is as a test bed for new equipment and techniques. If you work over the suspension for improved ride and handling, where better to put it to the test than on a race course? What works fine at 35 mph may be a mess at 85, and the race course is where the truth is discovered.

Chrome is not a prerequisite to real hot rodding, although a lot of neat vehicles are loaded with chrome goodies. But a fantastic hot rod truck can be built without any chrome on it. Likewise, it doesn't take a deep paint job and a million dollars worth of after-market glitter to make a hot rod truck. What it takes is ingenuity and craftsmanship, imagination and skill, patience and a love for things automotive.

Actually, the image of what makes a hot rod truck is defined more inside the heart of the owner/builder than by any set of standards that could be applied by another person. Some are wild, others are mild. A hot rod is whatever you want it to be.

Between the covers of this book, you'll find trucks of every vintage and description. And you'll learn from experts how hot rod trucks are built, and how to inject your own unique personality into such a project.

Man alive! If we'd had a truck like any of the ones in this book on the farm, we could have gethered eggs faster than the chickens could lay 'em, and looked good while we were doing it. Who knows, I might even have made it over the culvert. Miracles happen when you drive a hot rod truck.

Look what you missed, grandpa!

*Rich Johnson*

# WHAT TO BUILD

BY RICH JOHNSON

They're everywhere! Old dead trucks can be found hiding behind brush piles, tumble-down buildings, abandoned barns and in tall grass all across America. They're lying around wrecking yards begging for someone to come along and rescue them from oblivion, but they usually get overlooked because they're surrounded by cars that tend to get all the attention. And every one is an opportunity that is just waiting for a hot rod or custom truck enthusiast to come along and take advantage of it.

Rural areas of the country are prime hunting grounds because trucks routinely get used up and worn out then cast aside as useless, only to be replaced by newer equipment. You don't have to look very far to find every conceivable vintage and description of truck that has been put out to pasture, literally.

Old farm trucks sometimes get beat to death in the day-to-day business of agriculture. But it's not uncommon to find a great truck with very little body damage that has simply given up the ghost and been pushed out into the field to decompose. It's of absolutely no use to the farmer, and he will often gladly donate the "junk" to anyone willing to haul it off. Be aware that such a truck may require entirely new running gear (which is why we spend a significant amount of space in this book discussing chassis modifications and upgrades), but truck frames are usually stout enough to survive the rigors of rural life, so little if anything will need to be done in the frame department.

City-bound builders are in luck, too, but they need to keep their eyes open. Look around to see what the plumber and electrician are driving. They may be

getting ready to dispose of a perfectly good older truck that is simply worn out, but has seen relatively light duty on paved streets all its life.

Making the choice of what to build is often a matter of taste, rather than logic. You like a particular body style, so that's what you decide to build. We admire people who know exactly what they want and stick to the project until they've accomplished the goal. However, sometimes it's easier, cheaper or more convenient to just work with whatever you have. Elsewhere in this book, you'll see examples of excellent hot rod and custom trucks that were built simply because it was what the builder happened to have sitting in the backyard at the time. Or, he was able to pick the thing up for next to nothing. There's nothing wrong with making the decision based on economics or availability. It's the amount of skill, patience, and creativity applied to the project that counts, not the amount of money spent or the fact that the truck is a popular model.

The hot rod or custom truck builder has the benefit of nearly unlimited choices. Early or late vintage, restored or customized body, mild to wild hop-up of the powertrain. And working on a truck is significantly easier than a car, because the cab is separate from the cargo box or flatbed so it can be removed and worked on independently. The cargo box may be abandoned altogether in favor of a custom built flatbed. You may decide to build a late model chassis to take advantage of stuff like power steering, power disc brakes, and modern suspension, then transplant a vintage truck cab onto it. That's a great way to enjoy the best of today and yesterday at the same time.

If you're into early iron, sit back and enjoy looking at the photos on these pages, then dream about discovering a neat project truck that has been shoved aside behind an old barn. If newer trucks are your style, consider the late model pickup down the street that has a wasted engine and can be bought cheap. Late model trucks are easy to work on because wrecking yards are stuffed with replacement parts.

No matter where you are or what the budget looks like, there are trucks available that can be built into hot rods or customs. Part of the fun is finding the right one for you. Then comes the real adventure as you build the truck of your dreams. And that's what this book is all about.

# OPTIMUM VEHICLE HANDLING

**BY JIM CLARK**

Vehicle handling is a subject that requires dealing with a large number of variables. Attaining optimum vehicle handling requires the adjustment of these variables to achieve the desired result. Cars and trucks require the same techniques to achieve the optimum setup, but the moment that any loading takes place that balance is disturbed.

Trucks are more difficult subjects though. Their load bias (front to rear) shifts more radically than that of the average car because of the variable created when a load is placed in the rear of the vehicle. Original suspension design characteristics and tire selection will determine how the vehicle will react both loaded and empty, but some adjustments can be made to compensate for this.

To get an idea of what takes place under these conditions and what can be done to compensate for them let's look at the case in point presented by Bob Strange, advanced tire development engineer for BFGoodrich, regarding the classic example of widely varying vehicle loading—the pickup truck.

Because the changes in loading can be so great, and their effects on handling so large, it is very easy to see what goes on...and why. So let's consider an imaginary pickup truck like the one in Figure B.

First, we'll look at it in its unloaded state, with 1500 lbs on the front tires and 1200 on the rear. Remember that lateral acceleration is nothing more than the percentage of a vehicle's weight that the tires generate in lateral force. To find it, you just divide lateral force by weight.

If you look at the curve in Figure A, you'll see that each of the front tires has the capability of generating 600 lbs of lateral force when loaded at 750 lbs (half of the total weight on the front). So, by dividing the front tires' combined 1200 lbs of lateral force by their 1500-lb. combined loading, you'll see that they can generate 0.800 G of lateral acceleration (this can also be called cornering power or cornering capability). Following the same pattern, you'll see that the rears can generate 0.833 G.

In this example, the rear of the truck has 4.1 percent more cornering capability than the front. That indicates an understeer condition. In other words, the front would lose traction (break loose) before the rear.

Now let's put 600 lbs of additional weight in the truck's bed—right over the rear wheels, to keep the loading on the front tires the same.

Since nothing has changed up front, those tires can still generate 0.800 G. However, with the rears now loaded to 900 lbs apiece, they can generate 630 lbs of

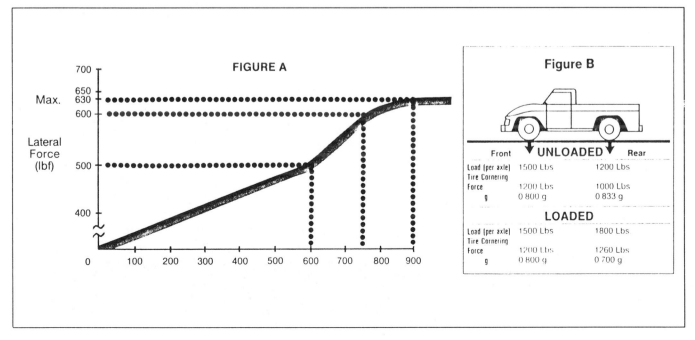

lateral force each (check the chart). By dividing 1260 lbs by 1800, you can see that the rear can now generate only 0.700 G. So our pickup has suddenly gone from having 4.1 percent more "bite" at the rear to 12.5 percent less.

Simply by loading this truck with an extra 600 lbs, we have turned what was a mildly understeering vehicle into one with a pronounced oversteer...that is, the back would lose traction well before the front. Adding still more weight would make things even worse. So what can realistically be done to remedy the situation? Stiffen the front springs, or anti-roll bars, or both? This would reduce the front cornering level and decrease the oversteer by forcing the outside-front tire to carry more of the load; but it would require adjustable springs and anti-roll bars. Not very practical for a pickup.

Put larger tires on the rear? That would increase the cornering forces and would decrease the loaded oversteer, but the truck would then understeer heavily when empty or lightly loaded. Not good.

Adjust air pressure? Since all tires gain cornering power with an increase in inflation pressure (up to a point), you could increase the lateral force that the rear tires can generate by boosting their inflation pressures. Not only is that the most convenient method, it also allows you to optimize the handling to the loading at any time. So that is the recommendation for this truck. (It is also the recommendation of most truck manufacturers).

This phenomenon of being able to modify handling characteristics simply by adjusting inflation pressure applies to any kind of vehicle that you're likely to encounter, and it is used extensively in racing to fine-tune a car's performance. So understanding the relationships of load, inflation pressure and tire cornering power can be extremely beneficial to you both on the race track and in day-to-day driving as well.

## INDEPENDENT FRONT SUSPENSIONS

There are three basic types of front suspension systems: coil spring, torsion bar, and strut. Coil springs and torsion bars were the traditional suspension used on American cars until the recent popularity of strut systems. Strut suspensions are lighter weight, which helps save gas; and they take up less space in the engine compartment, which is very important with the transverse-mounted engines used in most front-wheel drive cars. Most trucks are traditional front engine/rear drive and, with the exception of a few very light duty models, don't utilize the strut suspension.

All three types are independent front suspensions. When one wheel rolls over a bump or into a hole, the road shock is absorbed by that wheel's suspension. The other wheel is only minimally affected. This provides much greater stability and directional control than the old solid axle designs.

In all three suspension systems, each front wheel is connected to a steering knuckle and wheel spindle assembly.

### Coil Spring Suspension

In a coil spring suspension system, the steering knuckle and wheel spindle assembly is connected between upper and lower control arms. The control

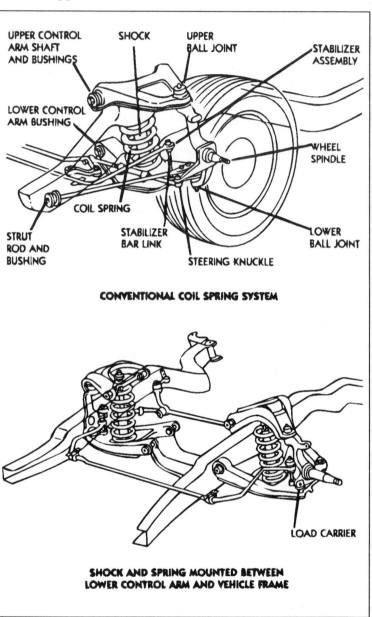

CONVENTIONAL COIL SPRING SYSTEM

SHOCK AND SPRING MOUNTED BETWEEN LOWER CONTROL ARM AND VEHICLE FRAME

arms are connected to the vehicle frame, and the coil spring is positioned either between the upper control arm and the vehicle's body or between the lower control arm and the vehicle frame. In either case, a shock absorber dampens the up and down oscillations of the spring. The weight of the front half of the vehicle rests upon the coil springs.

The ball joints connect the steering knuckle to the control arms, allowing the steering knuckle to pivot between the control arms when the vehicle is steered.

They also permit up and down movement of the control arm. One ball joint is called the load carrier and the other is called the follower. Which is which depends on the location of the shock and spring.

When the shock and spring are positioned between the lower control arm and the frame, the lower ball joint is the load carrier. When the shock and spring are connected between the upper control arm and the vehicle body, the upper ball joint is the load carrier.

In both cases, the weight of the vehicle is transmitted through the spring to the control arm at its bottom...and through the control arm to the load carrier ball joint. Load carrier ball joints bear approximately one-half of the total vehicle weight. They are subjected to severe wear and it is important to periodically inspect them.

Conventional shock absorbers, on the other hand, do not carry weight. The purpose of shock absorbers is to control spring action and hold tires firmly on the road.

Tires are really just an air spring. And, like any spring, they will continue to bounce until the bounce energy is absorbed. Springs dissipate some of this energy, but its the shock that absorbs excess energy from the spring. Shock absorbers turn this motion energy into heat energy and dissipate it into the atmosphere.

Like ball joints, shock absorbers require frequent inspection. When a shock stops dampening spring oscillations:

- Steering and handling become more difficult
- Braking action may be affected
- There is excessive bouncing after stops
- Springs can bottom out
- And, cupping can appear on tires.

Routinely inspect shock absorbers and replace them before these problems begin.

Other front suspension system components include the stabilizer bar and stabilizer links. The stabilizer bar and links join the two lower control arms to transmit cornering forces from the outside wheel to the inside wheel during a turn. This helps equalize wheel loads and prevent the vehicle from leaning or rolling outward when cornering. The stabilizer bar is also called the sway bar.

A strut rod is used in some systems to restrict the forward and backward movement of the lower control arm. It is attached between the lower control arm and the frame. Often, both ends of the strut rod are threaded to allow for the caster angle adjustment when performing a wheel alignment.

Stabilizer bars and strut rods do not wear out—they need to be replaced only when damaged or bent. Wear occurs at their connections, at the bushings. When the bushings wear, the connection is loosened. Vehicle handling gets a little sloppy and the wheels cannot remain in proper alignment. It is important to regularly inspect suspension system bushings.

## Torsion Bar Suspension

There are no coil springs in a torsion bar suspension system. Instead, a torsion bar supports the vehicle weight and absorbs the road shocks. While a coil spring performs these functions by compressing, the torsion bar acts by twisting.

The torsion bar is connected between the lower control arm and the frame. The bar can be connected either longitudinally or transversely. Torsion bars can

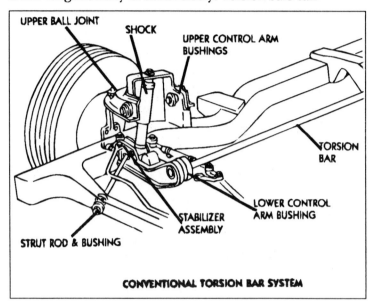

UPPER BALL JOINT    SHOCK    UPPER CONTROL ARM BUSHINGS
TORSION BAR
LOWER CONTROL ARM BUSHING
STABILIZER ASSEMBLY
STRUT ROD & BUSHING

**CONVENTIONAL TORSION BAR SYSTEM**

be used to adjust vehicle riding height. Not a way to lower the vehicle however, since ideally the lower control arm should be relatively parallel with the road surface when the vehicle is at rest. They are not interchangeable from side to side, because the direction of the twisting (or torsion) is different between the left and right sides.

Other than the difference between the torsion bar and the coil spring, this type of suspension is the same as the coil spring variety. Because the torsion bar is connected to the lower control arm, the lower ball joint is the load carrier. A shock absorber is connected between the lower control arm and the frame to dampen the twisting motion of the torsion bar.

## STEERING LINKAGE

Suspension system components couple to the steering linkage at the steering knuckles, and the condition of the suspension system affects steering capability. Worn shocks or struts, for example, contribute to front end wander.

Tie rod ends are bolted to the steering knuckles. A ball and socket joint in the tie rod end makes this a pivoting connection essential to steering.

In a parallelogram system, steering is transmitted to the linkage through a pitman arm, which converts steering wheel rotation into the back and forth motion of the linkage.

The two tie rods are connected to the center link and through adjusting sleeves to the tie rod ends. The sleeves are threaded to allow lengthening and shortening of the tie rod assembly when the toe angle is adjusted during a wheel alignment.

An increasingly popular type of steering system is rack and pinion. A pinion gear translates the rotary motion of the steering wheel into the linear motion of the rack. The rack acts like the center link, moving the tie rods back and forth to steer the vehicle. Rack placement varies from one car manufacturer to another and from model to model.

Rack and pinion steering provides easy turning and fast steering response because of its low gear ratio (8:1 to 10:1).

## REAR SUSPENSIONS

Rear suspension systems are as critical to ride control, as front end systems. A vehicle must be in optimum pitch and balance to ride right. There are two types of conventional rear suspension systems: coil spring and leaf spring.

### Coil Spring Suspension

On a coil spring suspension, the spring is mounted between the axle housing and frame. A lower control arm connects the axle housing to the frame. Some vehicles use an upper control arm for added stability.

### Leaf Spring Rear Suspension

Control arms are not required on leaf spring suspensions. The leaf spring is connected to the axle housing with U-Bolts, and to the frame by bolts in the front and by a shackle assembly in the rear. The shackle assembly allows spring movement.

In both applications, shock absorbers connect between the axle housing and the frame and absorb excess energy from the system. If the vehicle is being used to carry heavy loads or tow trailers, load-assist shock absorbers are recommended.

## WHEEL ALIGNMENT

An important part of vehicle ride control is directional control. Will the vehicle travel straight down a highway? Will it steer easily? Will the tires be subject to minimum wear? Will the steering wheel return to the straight ahead position after turning a corner? For the answer to be YES to all these questions, the vehicle must be properly aligned.

Wheel alignment is the adjustment of angles made by the front wheels in relation to 1) the vehicle's suspension (caster); 2) the road (camber); and 3) each other (toe). The alignment of one of these angles affects the other two. All three angles are adjustable on coil spring and torsion bar suspension systems.

When checking or adjusting alignment, tire pressure should be up to manufacturer specifications. Low tire pressure will affect alignment.

## CASTER

Caster is the backward or forward tilt of the wheel spindle support. On a conventional suspension system, the upper and lower ball joints form the wheel spindle support. A line drawn through the centers of the two ball joints, as seen from the side of the vehicle, illustrates the tilt of the wheel spindle support — the wheel caster.

The caster angle is measured between the center line of the wheel spindle support and a vertical line through the center of the wheel. The caster angle is positive when the center line of the spindle support intersects the road in front of the tire's point of contact with the road. Caster is negative when the spindle support center line meets the road behind the tire's point of

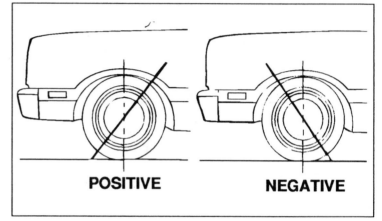

**POSITIVE**          **NEGATIVE**

contact. Zero caster occurs when the spindle support center line is vertical, meeting the road at the tire's point of contact.

Most vehicles are designed with positive caster. Positive caster provides good directional stability by tending to return the front wheels to the straight-ahead position. It also helps the front wheels maintain the straight-ahead position, which is why too much positive caster causes hard steering.

## CAMBER

Camber is the inward or outward tilt of the wheels, as seen from the front. Camber is positive when the top of the wheel tilts outward, and negative when the top of the wheel tilts inward. Camber is zero when the wheel is perfectly vertical.

The camber angle is measured between the center line of the wheel (as seen from the front) and a true vertical line, which intersects the center line at the point of tire contact with the road.

The purpose of camber is to uniformly distribute vehicle load across the tire face to minimize tire wear. Excessive positive or negative camber, however, will increase tire wear dramatically on one side of the tread—the side toward which the top of the wheel is leaning.

Incorrect camber angles can also cause steering problems. Too much positive camber, for example, will

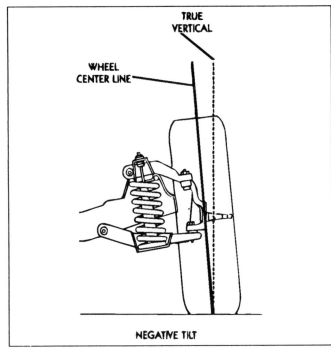

TRUE VERTICAL

WHEEL CENTER LINE

NEGATIVE TILT

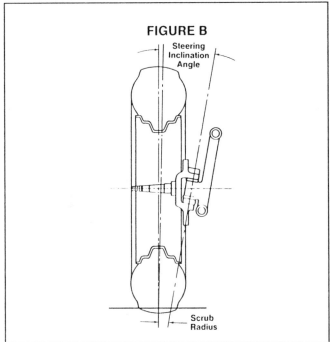

**FIGURE B**

Steering Inclination Angle

Scrub Radius

cause the vehicle to pull in the direction that the wheel is leaning. Too much negative camber will cause the vehicle to pull in the opposite direction.

## TOE

Toe is the difference in the distance between the front of the front wheels and the distance between the rear of the front wheels. If the front of the wheels are closer together than the rear of the wheels, the difference in the distance is called "toe-in." If the front of the wheels are farther apart than the rear, the distance is called "toe-out." Almost all vehicles are designed with a certain amount of "toe-in," measured in

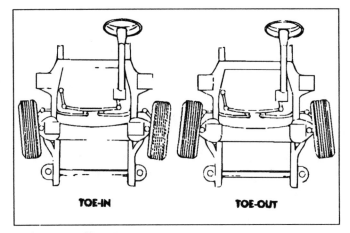

TOE-IN          TOE-OUT

inches or millimeters.

Toe is the most critical tire wearing angle. The purpose of toe is to ensure parallel rolling of the front wheels; but if either wheel has too much toe-in or toe-out, the tires will sideslip. This results in a feather-edged scuff across the face of the tire.

## STATIC AND DYNAMIC ANGLES

Alignment angles are measured and adjusted under static conditions—the vehicle is not moving and there are no passengers or load in the vehicle. When the vehicle is moving, the static angles change to dynamic angles; that is, they change as the vehicle moves.

Static angles are designed in such a way to produce the ideal dynamic angles when the vehicle is moving. With ideal angles, the front wheels are pointed straight ahead (zero toe) and they are vertical (zero camber). Although you may set the front wheels with toe-in and positive camber during an alignment, ideally, when the vehicle is driven the front wheels are pointed straight ahead and they are vertical.

It does not always happen this way, however. If, for example, the driver of the vehicle weighs 300 pounds, the dynamic angles will be incorrect, even though the static angles were set correctly. The main effect of the heavy weight on the driver's side is to increase camber toward positive on the left front wheel. This would cause wear on the outside tread of the left tire and a slight pull to the left.

In such a case, it would be best to set the static alignment angles with the driver in the vehicle. If this is not possible, add more negative camber to the left front wheel. The point is, often you must adapt your static alignment setting to dynamic driving conditions. You must do this to achieve the basic objective of a wheel alignment—to allow the vehicle to travel straight down the road, with easy steering and minimal tire wear.

## TIRES

Tires, are the most visible components of a vehicle's suspension system, and their wear patterns can be valuable clues to the condition of other suspension system components. Tire wear is a particularly good

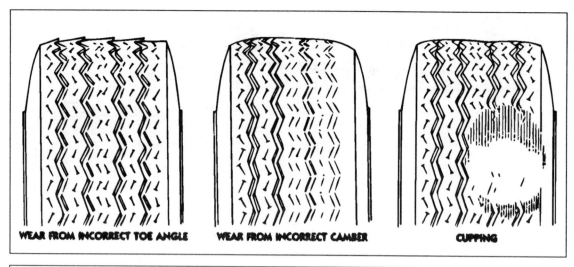

WEAR FROM INCORRECT TOE ANGLE     WEAR FROM INCORRECT CAMBER     CUPPING

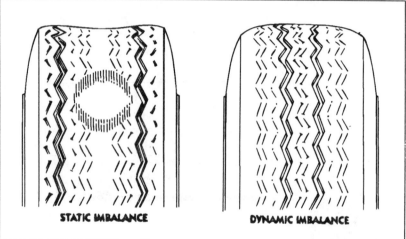

STATIC IMBALANCE     DYNAMIC IMBALANCE

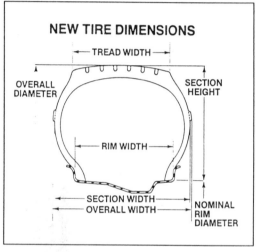

NEW TIRE DIMENSIONS

indicator of alignment problems.

For example, tire wear can tell you when a wheel has too much toe-in or toe-out. When either one of these conditions exist, the tire meets the road at an angle. This results in the tire dragging sideways as it rolls, and the tread wears unevenly, with a distinctive feather-edge pattern. With too much toe-in, the outside edge of each tread tends to wear off while the inner edge tends to become sharp and ragged. With too much toe-out, the reverse is true. Toe wear patterns can easily be felt by passing your hand across the tread.

Excessive camber angles cause tread wear on one side of the tire only. With too much positive camber, the tire will wear on the outside edge. With too much negative camber, the wear is on the inside. Again, the pattern is a distinctive one and tells you at once that an alignment is needed.

Loose or worn suspension parts can cause tire and alignment problems. Worn control arm bushings, for example, allow the tire to wobble and slip and this causes small scuff marks in the tread. Very loose connections caused by worn bushings or, more commonly, badly worn ball joints, can result in areas of such heavy wear that they actually become depressions.

Cupping is a condition caused by the tire bouncing as it rolls. Small areas of heavy wear are created. Worn shocks can be the cause of cupping, but loose suspension parts or tire imbalance are also possible causes.

Generally, a tire out of static balance will show wear toward the center of the tread. The imbalanced weight causes the wheel to lift vertically off the surface of the road. When it lands back down on the road, the tire scuffs the road surface. This action is called wheel hop or wheel tramp.

Dynamic imbalance causes the wheel to wobble from side to side (wheel shimmy). The tire scuffs the road surface from side to side as it rolls. Wear caused by dynamic imbalance usually shows near the edges of the tread.

Once you have a thorough understanding of the basic principles involved in suspension design and the various approaches to controlling these forces, the task of setting up a system for your truck should not be too difficult. However, before undertaking any major changes consult a competent source of expertise. Unlike styling changes, suspension modifications can be a matter of life and death to someone you hold very dear, yourself.

# SWAPPING A MIRADA SUBFRAME INTO A 1953 DODGE TRUCK

**PHOTOS BY GERRY CHARVAT**

Here's a great approach to building an early '50s MoPar pickup into a neat piece. This example involves a 1953 Dodge pickup that gets the full front end makeover, leaving it with a more powerful engine, smooth-riding independent front suspension and a lot of other late-model equipment.

The donor car, whence came most of the neat new stuff, was a 1980 Mirada. Parts scavenged from the Mirada include the engine, wiring harness, pedal assembly, parking brake, K member, rear springs and even some of the nuts and bolts. The rear axle came

from a big Chrysler, because the Mirada was too narrow. In the capable hands of the guys at The Hot Rod Shop (5706 Industrial Rd., Fort Wayne, Indiana 46825; 219-482-7473), this old truck was given a chance to live again.

The total project took 123.5 hours for a turn-key truck that is safe to drive home. And what a driver it turned out to be! Smooth, soft and comfortable. Not at all like the original '53 pickup — which was all truck, through and through. Of course, the trick cosmetics are due to come later.

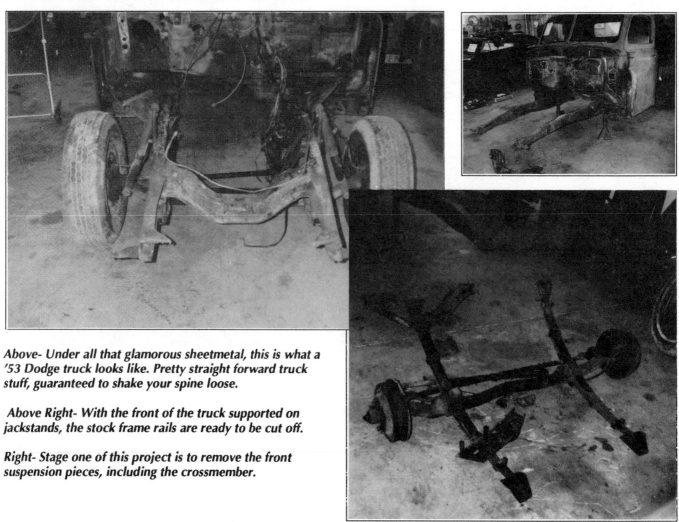

*Above- Under all that glamorous sheetmetal, this is what a '53 Dodge truck looks like. Pretty straight forward truck stuff, guaranteed to shake your spine loose.*

*Above Right- With the front of the truck supported on jackstands, the stock frame rails are ready to be cut off.*

*Right- Stage one of this project is to remove the front suspension pieces, including the crossmember.*

Measure forward eleven inches from the front body mount, and make a vertical cut through each frame rail at that point.

A trial fit of the K member from the 1980 Mirada looks good. This swap is going to give the old truck upgraded suspension, steering and brakes.

In order to mate the old Dodge frame with the new Mirada front end, 2"x4" rectangular steel tubing is used to join the two.

Overall length of the tubing is 26 inches. Measuring forward, 7 inches of the rear portion of the tube is welded to the top of the frame rail. Coming forward another 6.5 inches, we find the centerline for a 2-inch-diameter hole that must be cut through the inner side of the frame extension to permit access to a mounting bolt.

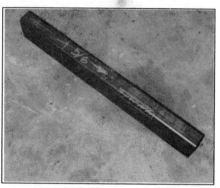

On the bottom side of the tubing, a 5/8-inch hole is drilled at the centerline of the previously-mentioned 2-inch hole. This 5/8-inch hole is for the mounting bolt to the K member. Note the marked area of the tubing to be removed for a clearance notch.

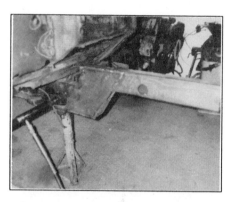

After welding the frame extension in place, reinforce it with steel plate welded to each side. Box across the end of the frame and the gusset plates for additional strength.

Use the original mounting bolts and the rubber mounting pads when fitting up the K member to the new frame extensions.

The first section of the frame extension has been completed, and the truck is ready to receive the Mirada front end for a trial fit.

The second section of frame extension is made of 2"x4" rectangular steel tubing, with clearance notch and holes drilled for access to mounting bolts.

The new extensions are installed with a 2-inch off-set to the outside. The K member now bolts to the frame extension just as if Dodge designed it that way. Neat!

Note the K member mounting bolts inside the access holes in the frame extensions. Note also how the clearance notch in the forward extension section fits over the mounting pad.

The firewall is now cut to allow clearance for the 318 V8 engine from the '80 Mirada.

After surgery to the firewall, the big engine fits with all the stock equipment still attached.

With the front sheetmetal installed, the K member torsion bars were adjusted down so the truck would sit about 2 inches above the floor. That's not practical for driving, but it demonstrates the range of suspension adjustment available with the Mirada front end.

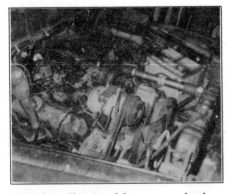

Mirada radiator, wiring, power brake unit and everything fit like it belonged in this engine compartment.

The rearend came from a big Chrysler because the Mirada was too narrow. However, the '80 Mirada leaf springs were installed, along with Monroe air shocks. Note the steel tube cross member installed for upper shock mounts. Angle iron spring mounts made this an easy bolt-on.

The steering column and pedal assembly from the 1980 Mirada fit easily into the '53 Dodge truck.

Except for the cosmetics, the truck is now ready to roll. Total shop time was 123.5 hours for a turn-key job. Ride and handling were phenomenal, and it was amazing how easily everything fit together.

The Mirada leather bucket seats fit perfectly in the truck's cab, and the driver now has the advantage of a tilt steering column and a comfortable wheel.

TOM WOJAHN

"MY NEXT PROJECT IS GETTING BETTER LIGHTING IN MY GARAGE."

# VOLARE T-BAR FRONT END

**BY TEX SMITH**

Nothing's nicer than a truck that has been slightly dumped in front, unless of course it's a truck that has also been gifted with a set of rotors/calipers to replace the drums, power steering instead of the old "armstrong" stuff, and a fully adjustable independent suspension system. Now we're talking!

So, here's the scoop on a suspension swap that does all that by using an entire Volare crossmember and making it an integral part of the original truck frame. The procedure shown is done by a couple of guys from south of the Salt Lake City, Utah area. Dennis Palombo and Steven Floyd have a place called Classic Bodies out on North Main Street in Spanish Fork, Utah, and they do just about everything that can be done, from simple fabrication to turn-key vehicles.

For this particular project, they began with a Volare/Aspen front suspension K-member, which is a junkyard piece costing between $150-$200. This is unbolted from

the MoPar at the pads, then the unnecessary edges are trimmed away. What is removed has no effect on strength, so not to worry. While at the wrecking yard, be sure to grab the steering box and a section of steering shaft. Stock manual steering will work, but the power unit interchanges nicely, is essentially the same size, and the swap works very well.

This front end swap will work on many trucks, but it is especially suitable for 1953 and later Fords, as well as 1955-'59 Chevys. Begin by removing the original front suspension, including steering gearbox. A relief needs to be cut in the frame 3 inches deep and 26 inches long. Use the original suspension centerline as the reference point for cutting. Scribe the centerline onto the frame top before removing the original front end. Position the torsion bar K-member so that the new front suspension centerline is exactly 1-1/2 inches ahead of the original centerline. This centerline is moved ahead because when the tires are stuffed up into the fenders they will

*Pausing in the construction of their latest Volare/Jag suspended truck chassis, Steven Floyd (left), wife Debbie, and Dennis Palombo of Classic Bodies smile for the camera. The completed Chevy rests on a Volare front and stock rear, and displays a pleasing stance.*

appear to be too far back unless the wheelbase is modified. A full set of installation instructions and frame cutting patterns are available from Classic Bodies for $10 (1550 N. Main, Spanish Fork, Utah 84660).

This suspension swap drops a 1955 Chevy front bumper approximately 7 inches, leaving it only about 7 inches off the ground, if the truck is running 22- to 24-inch front tires. The stock Chevy tread width is 62 inches, and the Volare assembly measures 60 inches. This means that offset wheels can be installed, and the truck will still have a fairly tight turning radius. If a small block Chevrolet engine is used, it will have to be offset 1 inch toward the passenger side to allow for power steering gearbox clearance. There will be about 3/4 inch of clearance between the oil pan and the steering centerlink.

*Compared with the stock ride height, the Volare front end drops the front bumper to within 7 inches of the ground, running 22- to 24-inch tires.*

*Unbolted from the MoPar frame, the Volare/Aspen front suspension assembly features torsion bars which mount ahead of the wheel centerline. Unit weight is about 200-250 pounds and can be bought from local junkyards for $150-$200.*

*Trucks with a beam front axle will most likely have a straight front frame section. To lower the truck, cut into the frame as indicated by this photo (pattern is available from Classic Bodies). Volare front suspension centerline will be slightly forward of the stock suspension centerline.*

*Original rubber doughnuts can be used when mounting the Volare front suspension. An alternate installation method is to weld the front crossmember to the frame at the frame lower lip. This photo shows the unit inset for even more lowering. For improved appearance, the doughnut mount area can be cut away.*

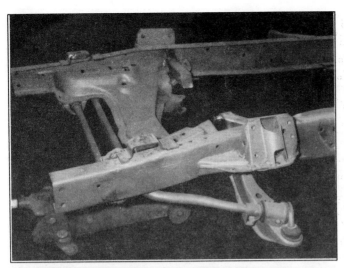

By carefully trimming and insetting the Volare unit in the frame, a factory look is achieved. Note that the crossmember top is nearly flush with the top lip of the frame.

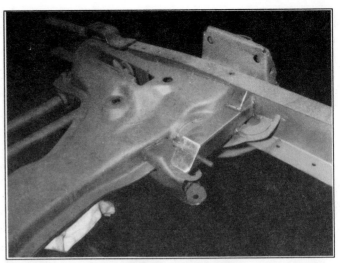

The upper suspension tower is welded flush with the outer frame rail. New motor mounts must be constructed and installed to fit whatever engine is chosen for the truck. In this example, a Chevy engine was used.

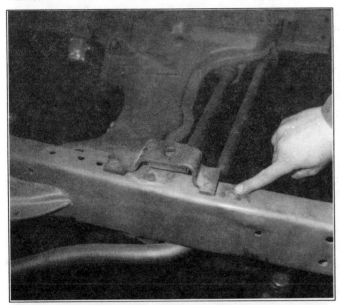

Radiator core support mounts were moved slightly to the rear for this installation.

One advantage of torsion bars is that they are fully adjustable, permitting the front end to be raised or lowered. This is particularly useful for a truck that will be driven a lot and still be displayed at shows.

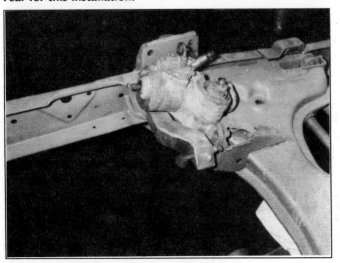

With the stock steering box installed at the crossmember, the left motor mount must be bent for adequate clearance.

Idler arm and steering linkage are stock MoPar pieces. The finished installation has a nearly factory appearance, after painting.

Because the frame hasn't been modified where the front bumper mounts, no changes are necessary to the bumper mounting hardware. Torsion bars and crossmember have plenty of room.

To provide clearance for the upper A-arms, fender splash aprons must be trimmed somewhat, but a fabric or rubber covering can then be installed to control road spray.

With the Volare/Aspen front end installation in a Chevy, there is plenty of room for both engine and steering gearbox. A steering shaft U-joint is necessary to make the connection.

# TORSION BARS FOR TRUCKS

**BY JOHN LEE**

Old pickups ride like trucks. As mentioned elsewhere in relation to swapping a late model passenger car subframe, most rodded pickups don't need the heavy duty running gear they came with. They would look, ride and feel better with a passenger car suspension.

After Packard pioneered torsion bar suspension in an American production car, Chrysler picked up the concept in 1957 and has been running with it exclusively for their frontal support ever since.

Now, Gibbon Fiberglass has a kit that makes it easy to adapt Chrysler torsion bar suspension to popular early pickups. Not only does this swap result in a smooth, soft, car-like ride, but allows you to adjust the ride height — up for highway travel, down for cool cruisin'.

Gibbon offers kits for Ford '48-'52 F-1, '53-'60 F-100, and '61-'63 Unibody pickups, as well as for '47-'53 and '55-'59 Chevy pickups. The kit consists of a front frame crossmember, rear torsion bar socket crossmember, front strut brackets and the necessary bolts and instructions.

From a donor car, you need the A-frame support plate, upper and lower A-frames, spindle, rotor and caliper assembly, torsion bars and sockets, and strut rods. The Chrysler steering box can also be utilized, and the crossmember is drilled for mounting it.

Suitable donor cars are the mid-size line from the mid-'70s: '75-'78 Cordoba, '73-'74 Plymouth Belvedere, GTX, Road Runner, Satellite or Fury, or '73-'78 Dodge Charger or Coronet. These use 15-inch wheels. If 14-inch wheels are desired, rotors, calipers and wheels from a Volare or Aspen can be adapted.

To accompany their front end kits, Gibbon also has mounting kits for installing all popular Ford and Chevy engine and transmission combinations and rear leaf spring/suspension kits for installing all common rearends.

*Gibbon kits allow installation of '70s era Chrysler, Dodge or Plymouth torsion bar suspension on early Ford and Chevy pickups. This is their setup on an F-100.*

*Chrysler A-arms, torsion bars and strut rods installed on F-100 chassis with Gibbon kit. Motor mounts for Ford or Chevy are sold separately.*

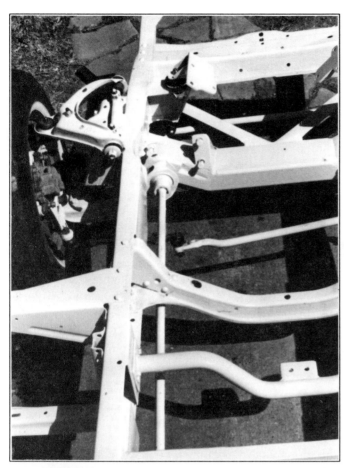

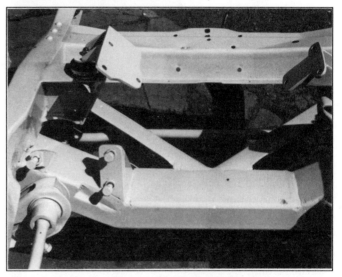

*Rear view shows how torsion bar runs under and inside frame rail.*

*Rear view shows new crossmember with torsion bars installed. Also separate motor mount kit.*

*New front crossmember fits under and around frame rails and is welded into place. Chrysler suspension components attach to it.*

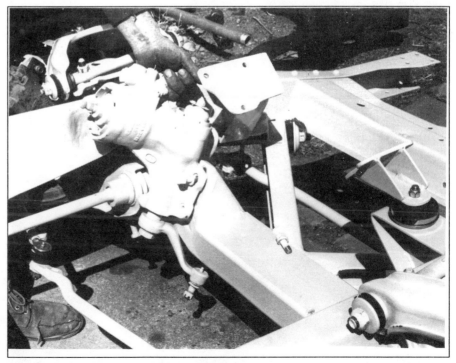

*Bracket for installing Chrysler steering gear is also available.*

*Completed installation is shown in an F-100 with body on. Note the low stance even without the weight of the engine.*

# SUBFRAMING CHEVYS

**BY JOHN LEE**

Subframing, the process of grafting a frame section from one vehicle onto another, has become a common practice in the hot rod industry. A subframe graft is appealing for several reasons: 1. You get modern suspension, brake and steering components in one process, rather than building or adapting them individually. 2. The steel frame itself may be better structurally, ie. not weakened by rust, and mounts are in place for a contemporary V8 engine. 3. You can mount the frame section in such a way to achieve lowering without modifying the suspension and possibly losing some ride quality.

But what about swapping a passenger car frame section into a pickup? In the first place, we have to assume that the most strenuous hauling a hot rodded pickup is likely to do is make an occasional run down a drag strip. It will be used more for pleasure than for toting big loads. Of course, if you're building for heavy off-road activity or monster truck bashing, stick with heavy duty components.

But for normal street duty, passenger car components will be more than satisfactory and deliver a more pleasant ride. In the examples we're about to discuss, the '74 Chevy Nova providing the front end

weighs 3330 pounds (4-door sedan with V8), while a '55 Chevy half-ton pickup receiving it weighs 3210 pounds.

We ran across two similar, yet different, approaches to subframing the popular late '50s Chevy and GMC pickups with later passenger car components. Wayne Hearne of Dixie Truck Works (9233 Sandburg Ave., Charlotte, NC 28213; 704-549-1267) set up his '55 Chevy half-ton at stock height with a '74 Chevy Nova subframe. Randy Truhlsen (Rt. 2, Blair, NE 68008; 402-426-5405) has a project underway with the same components, but he mounted the front end for an in-the-weeds stance.

Wayne pointed out that the '55 to '59 Chevy pickup frames are the same. The subframe that fits is the '73-'74 Chevy Nova. (Some sources indicate that the '75-'79 Nova series shares the same wheelbase and may have the same width, but some tape measure work would be advised.) The same frame is found under the Buick Apollo, Pontiac Ventura and Oldsmobile Omega.

Camaro and Chevelle frames (and comparable models of Buick, Olds, Pontiac) are wider than the Chevy pickup frame, so they would be more difficult to work with. Wayne, whose business deals with 1942-'72 Chevy/GMC parts, says the '77-'79 Malibu frame,

*1974 Nova subframe graft to a '55 Chevy half-ton chassis is clean and looks stock when installed at stock height, because the frame sections are the same width.*

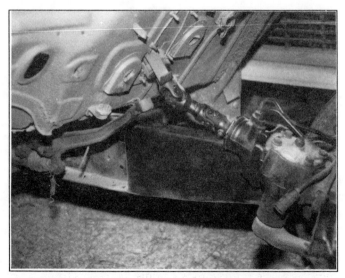

*James Dennis cut the Nova sub where it is straight, before the downward S-curve, to keep it straight like the original pickup frame. Note that the steering box behind the crossmember avoids clearance problems with fender and radiator mounting.*

*Right side view of graft shows how Dennis welded in steel plate several inches back from where the Nova sub welds on, to strengthen the graft and finish off the inside of the frame rails.*

*Wayne Hearne compares the '55-'57 Chevy inner fender panel that was trimmed to fit over the Nova A-arms with a stock '58 counterpart. A front steering setup would require more cutting, including the radiator support mount.*

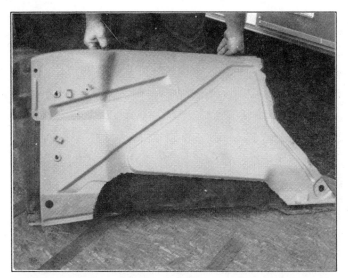

*The inner fender panel, placed over a stock panel, shows section trimmed out to fit over the Nova A-arms.*

narrower than the Nova, is right for the plentiful '47-'54 series pickups.

Hearne advises that the frame section be taken from a V8-equipped car, as the brakes, springs and suspension components are engineered stronger than for a 6-cylinder car. Also, he cautions, be sure it has the steering box mounted behind the front crossmember, which puts it out of the way of the radiator support, fender mounts and inner fender panels.

Wayne likes the setup James Dennis did on his truck because the outside of the frame lines up straight, so it appears original. The frame horns were cut off of the original frame and welded to the new clip to provide stock bumper and radiator mounting locations. If

desired, the truck can still be lowered by installing lowered spindles or cutting spring coils.

Randy, on the other hand, built about 6 inches of lowering into his truck when he installed the '74 Nova subframe. His approach was to set up the subframe for the correct (stock) wheelbase and square it up. Then cut the stock frame to follow the S-curve of the Nova sub, with the front arch rising above the pickup frame for the lowering effect. The sections are welded together with the Nova sub extending back underneath the pickup rail.

One caution Truhlsen points out: Set the bare sub frame 3/4" to 1-1/2" ahead of where measurement shows it should be, because the suspension will move back that much when you install the engine, transmission and cab, and weight the front end down to its ride height.

Once the graft is completed and welded up solidly, cut the front of the frame off to clear the front sheetmetal. The fenders will fit onto the new frame just fine, but you'll have to fabricate brackets to mount them.

Randy places the engine and transmission into position to determine the correct fore and aft location of the transmission crossmember. Drill the necessary holes and the stock Nova crossmember can then be bolted into the frame.

This combination of ride, handling, power supply and lowering for a vintage truck is tough to beat.

Truhlsen's subframe swap lowers the front about 6 inches. Frame horns, cut back to clear pickup sheetmetal, can be finished with a plate to mount bumper and sheetmetal.

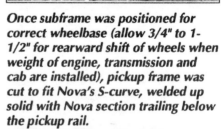

Once subframe was positioned for correct wheelbase (allow 3/4" to 1-1/2" for rearward shift of wheels when weight of engine, transmission and cab are installed), pickup frame was cut to fit Nova's S-curve, welded up solid with Nova section trailing below the pickup rail.

Setting engine/transmission unit in position will determine correct location of stock Nova transmission crossmember.

Inside view shows how frame graft is finished and welded solid.

**The Only Company Devoted Exclusively
To Manufacturing Power Window Kits For Older Vehicles**

**Specialty
Power
Windows**

(912) 994-9248 Technical Information
1-800-634-9801 Factory Sales Desk

FAX (912) 994-3124

**Route 2, Goodwyne Road, Forsyth, Georgia 31029**

Front hub, rotor and brake assembly are removed, providing access to stock spindle. Vehicle should be supported on frame stands and spring tension relieved by placing jack under lower A-arm.

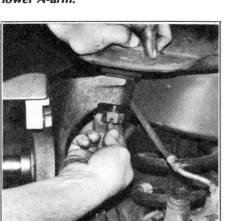

New Bell Tech spindle is installed in place of stock spindle using standard installation procedures.

The stock brake hose is repositioned by gently bending it downward, providing clearance for the rubber hose to avoid abrasion from the new spindle.

Steering link is unbolted from stock spindle by removing locknut.

Steering link attaches same way as stock unit, in elevated location parallel to raised axle spud.

Rear semi-elliptic spring attaches at the front via a bracket riveted to the frame rail. Spring rotates around this fixed point.

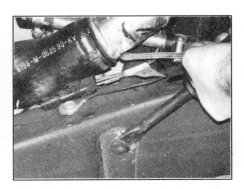

Air chisel is used to remove rivets. If chisel is not available, they can be drilled out instead.

Spindle is held in place between A-arms by ball joints. Locknuts are removed and jack lowered under lower A-arm to remove spindle.

This truck was fitted with custom wheels having more than 3-1/2 inch backspace, so a small section must be cut from the lower A-arm to allow for steering clearance. Instructions are included with spindle kit.

Left side hanger also serves as bracket to mount emergency brake cables on this model truck. They need to be cut out carefully before removal of spring mounting bracket.

Spring hanger on left is new Bell Tech unit. On right is stock hanger. Note difference in height of spring mounting point.

At left is the new longer rear shackle. It replaces original in stock spring hanger.

To unify the front end appearance, enhancing the effects of lowering, Bell Tech's bumper cap kit was added. First the bump strip is taken off the bumper.

New bracket bolts to frame rail. Bracket for emergency brake cables is supplied in kit.

New shackle bolts in place of original using stock hardware. Its added length combined with the raised front mount provides the 4-inch drop, without changing the ride.

The hand-laid fiberglass cover fits tightly over the bumper. First it is checked for fit and marked for trimming.

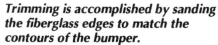

Trimming is accomplished by sanding the fiberglass edges to match the contours of the bumper.

The mask is painted and reinstalled using double-stick tape to secure the tight fitting piece.

Spring mounting pivot bolt serves double duty by also holding emergency brake cable bracket on left spring hanger.

Bell Tech's Jim Morris cut a notch in bed rear frame member to provide clearance for upper travel of longer shackles on rough roads or with heavy loads. This was done while bed was removed to accommodate our photo session.

Holes are pre-drilled in the mask to line up with those in the factory air dam.

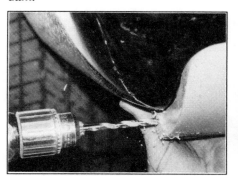

Holes are also drilled at the ends for pop-rivets to hold the panel to the stepside fender extensions.

After painting, the rolled rear pan is installed and riveted in place. Standard pop-rivets are inserted into the pre-drilled holes.

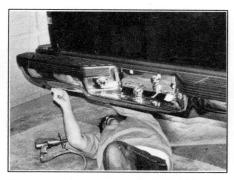

To create the same smooth fluid look at the rear, a Bell Tech rear rolled pan was installed. Begin by removing the step bumper and brackets.

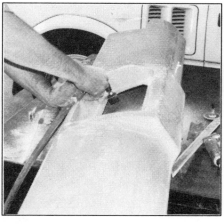

An opening is cut in the license plate recess to allow the hitch insert to project through.

The tailgate was removed and the panel trial fit to align it with the bed. Then holes are drilled for the pop-rivets to be installed later.

Bell Tech makes a receiver type hitch that mounts to the frame and has the receiver located high enough to exit through the center of the rolled pan.

The rolled pan provides the same smooth fluid look at the rear as the bumper cap and air dam did up front. Hitch receiver can be seen in license plate opening.

**BY TEX SMITH**

S ome years ago, I had a 1954 Chevrolet half-ton pickup with a big-inch Olds engine and trans. I wanted to drop the front end, and wanted to get rid of the Chevy 6-lug wheels in front. It was all a fairly straight forward bit of swapping, so when we scheduled this book, I asked around if the same things held true for the swap. Answer: Yep.

So, rather than reinvent the wheel, herewith is how I accomplished that particular swap. The result was a beam axle front end (just in case you want to keep one, rather than go with a subframe swap, which is really common now). That got the truck down, and the brakes were much better.

# DROPPED BEAMS
## BETTER BRAKES

*Although there is a minor amount of machine work necessary with this dropped axle/spindle swap, it is a job that the average person can do at home with minimal tools. Plan a weekend for time.*

*Since the idea is to get the truck in the weeds, aftermarket helper springs may not be wanted or needed. If the stock springs are in bad condition, the local spring shop can make replacements. Fully loaded, there should be at least 4 inches of operating room between the top of the axle and the frame. A 1-inch clearance notch can be cut in the frame. If so, the frame area should be boxed on the inside.*

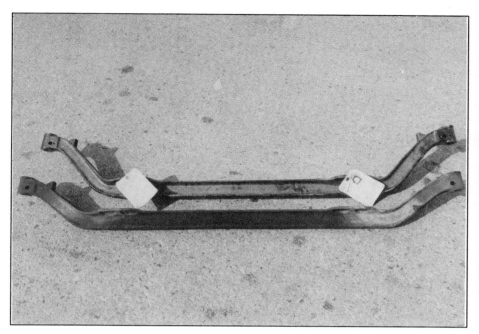

You can get dropped axles for Chevy products from several sources, including tubing units from SuperBell and Butch's Rod Shop. This beam unit comes from Mor-Drop, 600 29th Ave., Oakland, CA 94601, and has an effective drop of 2-1/2 inches.

No matter what axle is used, always carefully check fit of the desired spindle to the axle boss. Do this checking with a new kingpin kit, so that you have spindle-to-boss bearing and shims on hand. In this case, the axle boss had to be cut down slightly. To use Olds/Pontiac brake drums and wheels, use 1941-'52 Oldsmobile or 1941-'54 Pontiac backing plates and drums with the stock pickup spindles. The '52 and later Chevy truck will accept just the '50-'54 Chevy passenger car drums as a way to get the 5-bolt wheel pattern. Mounting the Olds/Pontiac backing plates is done the same way that we show here.

Bearings on the passenger car for Chevy/Olds/Pontiac should check out the same, but if you run into a problem, use the new spindle bearing spacer and your local bearing supplier can find an inner bearing that has the correct inner/outer diameters.

Hold the passenger car backing plate to the spindle. The two upper mounting holes will align, but the two lower holes will be off. Mark the backing plate (backside, through the spindle mount) and drill new lower mounting holes.

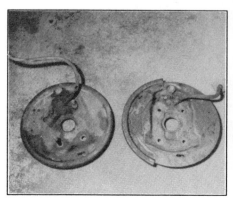

The stock Chevy truck backing plate at left, compared to the passenger car unit at right. Note the offset on the car backing plate. Brake hoses all interchange.

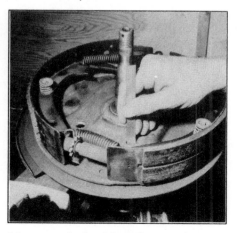

Now, set the backing plate on the spindle. The center register hole is the same for Chevy/Olds/Pontiac. Measure through the backing plate mounting hole to the spindle mount. This is the length of the new spacers.

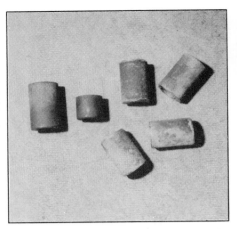

*Spacers are made from 1/2" pipe. Be sure the ends are perfectly square to the length.*

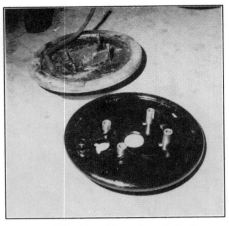

*The modified backing plate is in front, with spacers in place. Note the lower holes, with spacers in position for Chevy truck spindle.*

*Use donor car backing plate bolts, or get new ones that are at least grade 8.*

*Spindle in place, note that the kingpin bearing goes between the bottom of the axle boss and the spindle.*

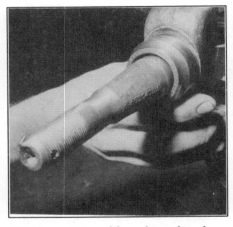

*If you come up with an inner bearing race that does not fit the spindle snugly (as shown here), use the stock inner race and get bearings to fit race/hub inner bearing.*

*Rebuild or get new wheel master cylinders. Brake hoses will fit.*

*If the stock steering arms are to be used, check the shape of the arm ball. If it is out of round, get another arm. Usually, the arms do not need to be bent for tie rod-to-spring clearance.*

*It is essential to take the finished conversion straight to the front end alignment shop, especially if a dropped axle is used. In the case of a beam axle, bending it to fit factory specs is no big deal. We haven't confirmed the rumor that 1957 and later Corvette drum brakes will fit 3/4-ton Chevy truck spindles. Worth looking into perhaps.*

# Small Block Chevy
# Big Block Chevy
# Angle Plug Heads
# Small Block Ford
# Big Block Ford
# Ford Cleveland
# Ford Y-Block V-8
# Flathead Ford
# Buick V-6
# Chevy 90 V-6
# Small Block Dodge
# Big Block Dodge
# Inside Chassis
# Outside Chassis

# BRAKES

**BY WARREN GILLILAND**

**W**hether you're a Chevy lover, Dodge diehard or Ford fan, customizer or restorer, drag racer or off roader, the one area that is likely to present problems is the brake system. Don't blame yourself that the front brakes wear out 4 times as often as the rears, sometimes in as little as 6000 to 7000 miles. Or that you did a beautiful, though unintentional, 360 when you had to slam on the brakes at 60 mph. It's difficult for the enthusiat to build a perfect brake system for a truck when these same systems have kept the "Big Three" pulling their collective hair out for the past 80 years.

Pickups, by the very nature of their design, put a large percentage of the weight on the front wheels so as to allow a largely varying amount of weight to be put on the rear. The reason some folks chose to make a pickup their personal transportation suggests that on some occasions they may need to move heavy or bulky objects that probably won't fit in the family sedan.

Others, however, have always admired the clean lines and good looks of the ruggedly handsome pickup. But whatever the reason for making a pickup your project vehicle, the first thing you must analyze in order to do a good job on the brakes is how you're going to use them.

Most brake systems are subjected to little more work under normal circumstances than stopping the weight of the vehicle and a couple of passengers. The pickup truck, however, is a breed of its own. The possibilities of how a prospective purchaser of a truck will use that vehicle are almost endless, varying from mild to wild. Pity the poor designer, who doesn't really know what application to design the brake system to handle. Since he must try to design a vehicle suitable for all possible applications, the only real answer is to design the system for the average load and hope it will work halfway decently for everyone.

This is really the way a brake system is designed on all passenger vehicles, but the differences are far more noticeable on pickups because of the variety of uses. The average passenger car is not commonly as abused as the average truck. When a vehicle is loaded to the recommended capacity and beyond, the brake system and suspension suffer. If we know we are going to carry additional weight that will always be present, we can make modifications to allow the vehicle to meet our individual needs. If we know we will never be using the truck to carry Aunt Edna's topsoil for her garden, we can make some modifications that will improve stopping on the lighter vehicle as well.

The more radical the creation, the more you will have to consider its end use in order to develop a safe brake system. The restorer has probably the easiest job, since his concerns should be confined to safety and maintenance. The other end of the spectrum will find the fully tubbed, pro street pickup trying to find a way to stop monster slicks. Both builders, and other variations in between, need sound solutions.

Since this chapter is to help you deal with your own personal choices, we will first give some insight into what each brake system component does, then offer guidelines about how this applies to specific situations. Obviously, if you're restoring a pre-'40s truck with mechanical brakes, the master cylinder information will not apply, but everything else will.

Under no circumstances should you take a modified vehicle onto the street without properly testing and evaluating the brake system under all driving conditions. We can help you build a balanced, safe system, but mistakes can still happen. It doesn't take very long to test drive a vehicle under controlled conditions, and have someone else double check your work. Safety is something worth double checking.

## BRAKE PEDAL & MASTER CYLINDER

The brake pedal and master cylinder work together to create the system operating pressure, so we will discuss them as a unit. The master cylinder must be large enough to supply a sufficient amount of fluid to actuate all the calipers and wheel cylinders that will be feeding from it in approximately half of its available stroke, but not any more than 2/3. The second, and most often overlooked requirement of the master cylinder, is that it must have a reservoir large enough to hold reserve fluid in a sufficient amount to accommodate the displacement required when the pads wear down and the pistons move. When the linings and pads are in a totally worn state, the reservoir should still have approximately 25% of its total reserve in the tank, for a safety factor. Failure to make sure that your system meets this requirement could result in a partial or full system failure.

The brake pedal is designed for the purpose of being in a comfortable position for use, but more important, since it is a lever it must be of a proper ratio to give the best result. The pedal ratio is the reference to a comparison of the measurement from the pivot point to the master cylinder pushrod point, when compared to the measurement from the pivot point to the center of the pedal (see figure 1). If the first measurement "A" is divided into the second measurement "B", the result is the ratio. For example, in this case "A" is 3 inches and "B" is 12 inches, so the ratio calculation is 12÷3=4, which is a ratio of 4:1. If you wish to increase the leverage, it can be done by either enlarging the "B" dimension or decreasing the "A" dimension. If you decrease the "A" dimension to 2 inches by drilling a new hole for the pushrod, the formula would now be (12" ÷ 2" = 6"). If you used the same amount of pushing effort from your foot, you will have increased the brake pressure by 50% in the second equation. The problem is that the pushrod will be pushing into the bore on an angle. It will be necessary to relocate the master cylinder closer to the pivot point or premature wear to the master cylinder bore will result. This will also increase pedal travel by 50%, creating an uncomfortable and slow reacting pedal. Small changes make a large difference. Be careful to consider all factors before making any modifications in this area.

There is a formula that clearly shows the relationship of the master cylinder bore size and the pedal ratio. If you use it and plug in different values, you will be able to determine what the system is doing and whether it is in a proper proportion. This will also allow you to explore the best way of making system modifications that achieve all your goals. The formula is: input pressure x pedal ratio ÷ surface area of master cylinder = line pressure in psi.

Let's try the formula. Input pressure refers to the force from your foot on the pedal. Most people can develop 150 pounds with effort under a maximum braking situation. We don't want the brakes too touchy, or they will lock easily, which increases stopping distance. The ideal pedal ratio for a _manual_ brake system is about 6:1. The surface area of the master cylinder refers to the surface area of the bore size. 7/8" diameter = .60 square inches. 1" diameter = .79 square inches. 1-1/8" diameter = 1.01 square inches.

Using the formula, 150 (input pressure) x 6 (pedal ratio) ÷ 1.01 (surface area of the 1-1/8" master cylinder) = 891 psi line pressure.

About 900 psi line pressure, when used to supply adequate calipers and drum brakes, will result in a proper operating effort for most vehicles. On heavier trucks, we may want the system pressure a little higher, and on lighter trucks we may want it a little lower. But the example supplied here helps us understand the relationship of the numbers. Never exceed the maximum suggested operating pressure of the system. This is usually 1200 psi, but always check with the manufacturer of the components first.

If input pressure or pedal ratio is increased, the psi increases. If the master cylinder bore size increases, the psi drops. System pressure can be increased by decreasing the bore size of the master cylinder, but don't forget its other primary duties mentioned earlier. This is only an option if the other criteria can be met.

If a system has a problem of simply too high an

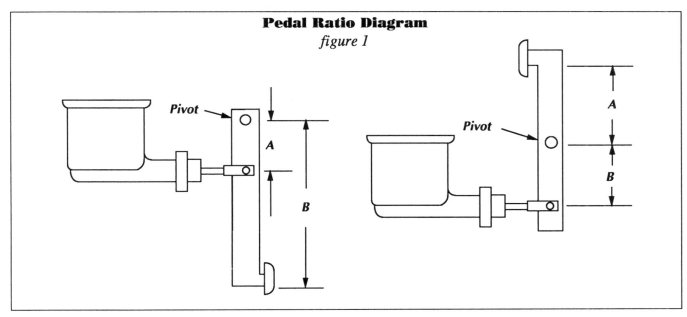

**Pedal Ratio Diagram**
_figure 1_

effort required to make the brakes work, the entire problem may lie with developing line pressure. It doesn't make any difference how big the calipers or drum brakes are, if they don't receive sufficient pressure they will not do what they are capable of doing.

It is not only important that the master cylinder create pressure, it is also important that it relieve the pressure when the foot is taken off the brake pedal. If the master cylinder has an internal residual valve (made to operate with drum brakes), it will not release the pressure sufficiently for disc brake calipers, and a serious drag will result, causing extreme wear and overheating of the brake system. This also causes an unnecessarily high load on the drivetrain. If the brake pedal is not allowed to return all the way, it is possible that the piston inside the master will not return far enough to open the pressure compensating port (see figure 2). This would also result in serious brake drag.

Historically, from the time of the first hydraulic brakes until the early '50s, the master cylinder was located under the floorboard. It wasn't until a few years later that trucks came out with the master cylinder moved up to the firewall. As insignificant as this may seem, it constituted a major improvement in brake safety for a couple of reasons. First, under the floorboard, bolted to the frame, the master cylinder is exposed to all elements of the weather. Since the master cylinder is made of cast iron, it is vulnerable to moisture which causes rust. Once the bore of a master cylinder begins to rust, it also begins to leak. Loss of brake fluid results in total loss of brakes. Since the master was out of sight under the floorboards, it was frequently overlooked during maintenance checks, increasing the likelihood of eventual brake loss.

In the early '50s, the master cylinder was moved to the firewall. The entire pedal assembly was now inside the passenger compartment, and the master cylinder was up underneath the hood in a more protected location. Since the master cylinder was now easier to get to, and could be seen during normal inspections of the oil and water level, it was more commonplace to check the brake fluid level as well. If the master did begin to leak, it would do so down the firewall, making it easier for an alert mechanic to catch before total brake failure resulted. This was a major help in reducing brake failures.

The under floorboard location places the master cylinder below the height of the calipers and drum brake pistons. This low mounting causes the fluid to attempt to drain back to the master cylinder. Since many modern master cylinders do not have an internal residual valve, this could result in a condition where the next stroke of the brake pedal will not be able to supply enough fluid to actuate the pistons, causing a temporary brake failure. This condition would only be a potential problem if you are going to adapt disc brakes somewhere in the system, or if you intend to upgrade your stock master with one from a newer vehicle. If your truck has drum brakes all around and a drum brake master cylinder with an internal residual valve, you will not have this problem. If you don't have an internal residual valve, install a 2-pound external inline residual valve for disc brake calipers and a 10-pound inline residual valve for drum brakes. Since the drum brakes have large return springs, they are more than capable of pulling the shoes back in spite of the valve. Disc brake

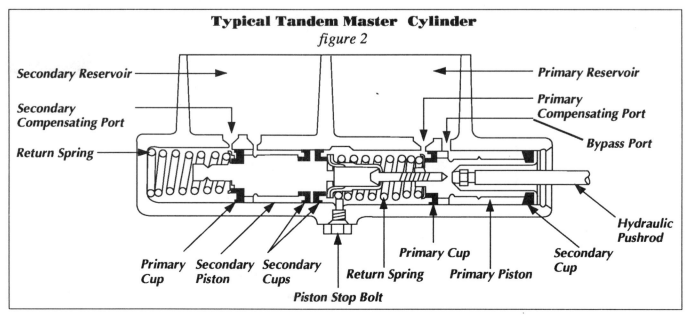

**Typical Tandem Master Cylinder**
*figure 2*

Secondary Reservoir

Secondary Compensating Port

Return Spring

Primary Reservoir

Primary Compensating Port

Bypass Port

Hydraulic Pushrod

Primary Cup  Secondary Piston  Secondary Cups

Return Spring  Primary Cup  Primary Piston

Secondary Cup

Piston Stop Bolt

calipers, however, have nothing pulling the pistons back after application, and any pressure present will cause the pistons to remain applied. The 2-pound valve creates so little force, no drag problem will be created.

One final note of caution, if your master cylinder is mounted under the floor, keep the exhaust system at least a foot away from it. Failure to do so will result in heat transfer to the fluid, causing the fluid to boil, resulting in possible brake failure. If it is necessary to run the exhaust near the master cylinder, use a deflection shield or insulation material to prevent heat transfer.

An abundance of speed shops sell the old 1-1/8" bore fruit jar master cylinder that was commonly found on Fords of the early '60s. This master cylinder, although it has sufficient volume for many disc and drum combinations, is not a good choice because it is only a single bore unit. In the late '60s, the tandem master was developed, which is simply two masters in one. On the old fruit jar unit, if there was an internal failure, the brake pedal went to the floor and you had no brakes. On the later tandem cylinders, if a seal goes bad it will probably only result in a loss of half of the system, allowing the car to be stopped with the other two wheels. It's a good rule of thumb that whenever possible, use the stock pedal and master cylinder that came on the truck if it is capable of meeting the pressure requirements stated in this section. If you need smaller components because of a space limitation, try to make the mounting match what you are removing so that new mounting holes will not be necessary. The less you modify here, the better off the system will be.

## CALIPERS AND WHEEL CYLINDERS IN DRUM BRAKES

The wheel cylinder or caliper (they both perform the same function) take the pressure present in the system and turn it into force. The force is the push on the shoes or linings, and is determined by the size of the piston. The larger the piston, the greater the force. On pickups since 1950, the drum brakes that came on them work reasonably well, unless you are considering increasing weight or installing a modern motor. The best choice to easily improve the brake system if installing a modern motor is to also install the entire front clip from a '70s mid-size car such as a Camaro or Mustang. Choose a mid-size from the same family of cars that match your truck, because common bolt sizes and mounting patterns are often found. Other modification will be kept to a minimum, using this method.

Front brake components handle the biggest portion of the braking requirement, and they need to be

adequate to handle the worst situation. If you intend to carry heavy loads, the brake system design needs to be sufficient for the highest load. If you intend to drive the vehicle at a high rate of speed and want to attain high deceleration rates, the system must be prepared to handle the weight that will transfer to the front wheels from the rear during deceleration.

A simple method of improving drum brakes is to adapt a larger wheel cylinder. If the stock unit was 1-1/8", going to 1-3/16" will result in more force. The amount of additional force increases proportionately with the surface area of the master.

If you upgrade to front disc brakes, it is necessary to prepare the master cylinder as mentioned in that section. Don't even think about disc brake adaptation until that portion of the job is handled first. Remember that disc brakes require more wheel clearance, which may mean a new wheel selection. If you intend to run stock wheels, be prepared to make major modifications to the new brake components or their mounting location in order to make them fit. If the brake system will see hard use, keep in mind that the later disc brake vehicles use larger spindles with bigger bearings to deal with the increased loads. The system is only as strong as the weakest component, so be sure to compare stock bearing diameters with those of the new components to make sure a weak link isn't being created.

After selecting front brake components, it's time to choose the rear. Remember that the choices for the front depended on the worst possible weight loading and speed. For the rear, we use this same information, almost in reverse. During high rates of deceleration, the weight that was on the rear wheels moves forward, unloading the rear. The lack of downforce presents a problem in that the wheels will lock up much easier. If you refer to the brake output charts, you can see that a truck has a unique situation because the high loads transferring forward during braking are unloading the rear axle, and at the same time hard deceleration is resulting in high line pressures that cause drum brakes to achieve a tremendous amount of torque that is not needed. This results in rear brake lockup, which will cause a truck to want to spin. It is imperative to limit some of this high end brake torque, and one of the best ways is with a proportioning valve. We'll cover this in the section on valving.

When it comes to street brake system modifications, I've never placed much importance on installing rear disc brakes. Pickup trucks, however, are a major exception. This type of vehicle is much better served throughout the range of driving speeds and types of loads by having disc brakes all around. This limits the high end spiking or brake torque that

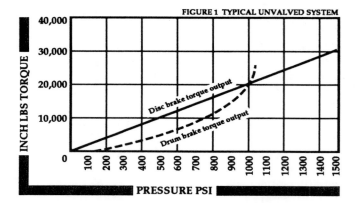

FIGURE 1 TYPICAL UNVALVED SYSTEM

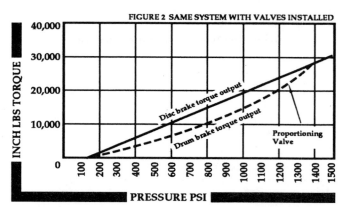

FIGURE 2 SAME SYSTEM WITH VALVES INSTALLED

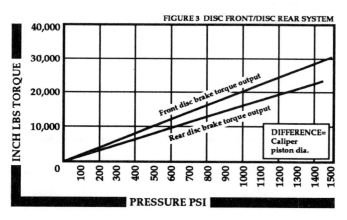

FIGURE 3 DISC FRONT/DISC REAR SYSTEM

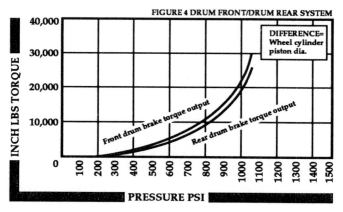

FIGURE 4 DRUM FRONT/DRUM REAR SYSTEM

figure 3

occurs in drum brakes. Installing rear disc brakes and a proportioning valve are the best ways to achieve good balance under all conditions.

Front and rear tire size plays a key role in how well the front and rear brakes will be balanced. If you intend to use larger diameter tires on the rear, compare the rolling radius (distance from the center of the wheel to the ground) of the front tire to the rolling radius of the rear tire. If you install a larger rear tire, the torque required to stop the wheel from rotating increases as well. For example, if you have a front tire rolling radius of 13 inches and a rear tire tolling radius of 14.5 inches, the need for more rear brake is increased by approximately 10%. Increasing the width of the tire doesn't alter the brake torque requirement, but rather improves the coefficient of friction between the tire and road so that higher deceleration rates may be achieved.

## GENERAL DRUM BRAKE INFORMATION

The evolution of the drum brake has seen it go from a cable operated mechanical system to a variety of designs of hydraulic application. Earlier vehicles had a fixed pin brake system, which means that the brake shoes were actuated by the wheel cylinder pushing out on the top of the shoe, the front shoe moving forward and the rear shoe moving backward, independently of each other. There was fixed pin at the bottom that held the bottom of the shoe firmly in place. With this type of brake system, the shoes expand out against the drum to create the friction necessary to slow wheel rotation. In order to achieve optimum effectiveness with this type of system, it is extremely important to keep the brakes properly adjusted. Since self adjusters were not available during those years, this meant having the brakes adjusted manually every few thousand miles.

In the late '40s, this was changed to the floating shoe style of brake. With this system, a wheel cylinder still pushes out on both shoes, but the bottom of the shoes are allowed to float freely. As the front shoe moves out to contact the drum, the bottom of the front shoe moves to the rear. Since the front and rear shoes are now moving together, this forces the rear shoe into the drum from both the bottom and top. Rotation of the brake drum causes the shoe to be pulled into the drum and creates a more rapid increase in brake torque, making the brake feel self energized.

This basically means you get more braking effect than you would have gotten with the same pedal force with the old system. Effort required to stop the car is reduced, and the feeling is more like a power brake. This feature of self energized brakes is why the brake system on an older vehicle is so unreliable in wet weather. When rain enters the brake drum, it reduces friction between the shoe and drum, requiring more pedal effort to get the same stopping ability as in dry weather. Late model vehicles with disc brakes don't loose any significant amount of stopping ability in wet weather, because the system doesn't rely on being self energized to create the friction necessary to stop the vehicle.

Over the years, subtle improvements were continually being made, such as increasing the width of the front shoes. Wider shoes not only help stop the vehicle better in repetitive stops, but also increase the life of the lining. As speeds increase, more frontal weight transfer takes place during stops, which increase the loads on front shoes. Increased surface area of wider shoe takes care of the problem of extra heat. Other design improvements include adding self adjusters to the brake so frequent adjustments can be avoided. This was especially a problem on pickups because there was usually a dramatic difference in the rate of wear between the front and rear brakes, causing a low pedal, and front brakes that react slowly due to the extra travel required to actuate them.

## BRAKE SHOES AND LININGS.

Many people have the mistaken impression that the size of the pad or shoe also determines the amount of brake you get. In the case of a drum brake shoe, the surface area of the shoe is not the factor, but rather the size of the drum that is being used. The surface area of both the pad and shoe determines two things. First, it determines the life of the lining. The larger the surface area, the greater the life. Second, the larger the surface area, the lower the resultant temperature during the same amount of braking. In other words, if you install larger pads, the heat at the pad is absorbed by a larger surface and the temperature stays lower. In the case of brake lining materials, they have a temperature point at which they lose their coefficient of friction, or ability to grab another material. You also experience this condition when brakes get wet. There is a noticeable change in braking effectiveness when the coefficient of friction goes down. Once the friction material cools (or dries), it regains its ability to grab effectively again. This is known as fade recovery.

In rare cases of overheating, permanent damage to the material may be done. Because using brakes creates heat, you are constantly heat treating the brake material. Overheating it severely can cause permanent damage and require replacement, even though the material is not worn thin. Not only is this heat seen by the brake material, it is also seen by the brake drum or rotor. These components can develop hard spots that will not allow them to be turned flat

again, and can cause excessive noise like a grinding sound, even though no metal-to-metal contact has taken place. When resurfacing drums or rotors, hard spots will be apparent as discoloration in the turned surfaces. There really is no serious safety problem. The noise, however, can be terribly annoying.

## DRUMS AND ROTORS

The purpose of both the drum and rotor is to remove heat that develops during braking. This is done by supplying a suitable friction contact surface and a heat sink to remove it from the friction material. Unfortunately, when customizing a brake system, this component is usually too small for the job. One of the major reason for component failures on vehicles imported from the Orient is that they do not comprehend the harder use of the brake system by American drivers, and consequently every major Oriental import has had brake problems that are most often caused by inadequate rotor size and design. The problem is comparable to running kitchen faucets full blast and having a drain that is inadequate to get rid of the water filling the sink. Sooner or later, the sink begins to overflow. In the case of a brake system, the result is severe warpage to components, which causes pedal pulsation or fast friction material wear. If you have ever driven a car that, when decelerated from a high rate of speed, begins the stopping sequence with good stopping power but then seems to fade, you are experiencing lining that is going beyond its thermal ability, probably because the drum or rotor is not removing the heat fast enough.

## POWER BOOSTERS

One of the most misunderstood components on the entire car is the power booster. First, since the pre-'50s trucks mount the master under the floor, it is difficult to fit a stock power unit in that location. To get around this problem, some folks opt for a small aftermarket booster. This smaller booster offers a great deal less boost than a stock unit, defeating the whole purpose of installing a booster in the first place. Actually, the real question is, "Do I need a power booster for what I'm trying to accomplish?" The answer, in most cases, is no. Most power boosters would not be necessary if more consideration was given to choosing the proper pedal ratio and master cylinder bore size. Since power boosters typically run off of vacuum, they rob engine performance and are subject to not working if the engine dies. If components are chosen wisely, this is one of the first items that can be left out. Of course, if you are dropping a fire-breathing 428SCJ under the hood of a fully tubbed '58 F-100, you'll probably want to include a booster in the project, only because of the potential speeds that will be driven. If you decide to install a power booster, choose a factory unit that will do some good. Tank size determines the amount of boost, and small tanks often provide very little assist. In the case of heavy post-'60s pickups, a power booster is a good idea, given the type of driving and comfort that will probably be desired.

The power booster represented the last significant brake improvement until the advent of the disc brake. It was mounted on the left fenderwell under the hood, or on the left firewall immediately in front of the driver, depending on manufacturer. Engine vacuum is supplied to a large diaphragm. When the brake pedal is depressed, line pressure is magnified by the power booster, resulting in the same stopping ability with less effort. These improvements make it easier for people who lack physical strength to drive comfortably. It also increases stopping ability in emergency situations. This system was so effective that it was used for many years virtually unchanged.

## PLUMBING

To successfully carry fluid from the master cylinder to each of the wheels is the job of brake lines. Most cars are plumbed with a combination of solid line and flex line. Never use more flex line than is absolutely necessary, because it "grows" under pressure, requiring more fluid movement, making the pedal feel mushy. Avoid the use of large loops in the brake lines, such as over the rear axle. In order for the bleeding operation to be successful, the lines must be routed so there are no potential places for the air to be captured. It's a good rule of thumb that once the fluid leaves the master and moves downhill to a point below the wheel cylinder or caliper, the line should not be higher than the outlet port at the cylinder, and certainly not in a sharp arc. If it is, air will not move easily to the bleed screw and a power bleeder will be necessary to clear the system.

Use quality steel line, recommended for use as a brake line, and use a double flare to ensure quality connections. Never use nylon line, as is seen on go-karts, because this type of line will fatigue over time and is much more vulnerable to damage. When routing brake lines, stay away from heat sources or areas that may be subject to damage, and always run the lines where they are least prone to being hit by rocks or other debris. If you intend to drive off road, route the lines along paths where branches and rocks hitting the underside of the vehicle will not pull or crush the brake line. Make sure the lines are tied firmly in place at least every few feet so they will not move or vibrate, which can cause wear and fatigue failure. If unsure how to route lines, look at other trucks or check with professionals to ensure all safety conditions are met.

## BRAKE SYSTEM VALVING

Even with perfect choices of components to achieve a well balanced system, it will still be necessary to do some fine tuning to really make the system effective under all stopping conditions. The three main valves used in the brake system balancing act are: 1. residual valve, 2. metering valve, and 3. proportioning valve.

The residual valve maintains pressure in the brake line even when the brakes are not being used. This valve should always be used with drum brakes. The system requires less pedal travel when residual pressure is present, making the entire system feel firmer and react quicker to the driver. Never use a residual valve with disc brakes, except when the master is lower than the caliper, then use only a 2-pound valve.

The metering valve is the most overlooked valve for vehicles that have been upgraded to disc brakes on the front, as is often done on post-'60s customized trucks. Its purpose is to delay initial pressure from reaching the front calipers until pressure is high enough to overcome the return springs on rear drum brakes (usually around 50 to 100 PSI). When this valve is absent from a disc/drum combination system, the disc brakes do all the work in stopping the vehicle at low speeds. This results in extremely premature wear to the pads. The accompanying graphs indicate that brake pressure from a drum brake does not begin until the system pressure has risen substantially. As soon as the brake pedal is touched, however, disc brakes begin to apply.

If you have converted the front brakes to disc on any of the trucks covered by this book, then another necessary valve is the proportioning valve. Its function is to restrict high brake pressure from reaching the brakes it protects. The main purpose for installing this valve is to stop high speed rear brake lock-up. (See Testing The System). Once again refer to the graphs, and notice that the rear drum brake puts out torque on a curve. Even though it takes significant pressure to get a drum brake started, once it starts climbing it climbs rapidly, eventually crossing the disc brake torque output, if left unrestricted. By installing the valve, the rate of increase will not be as rapid and will help stop excessive rear brake torque. When installing this valve on a truck, always choose an adjustable valve. Kelsey Hayes manufactures an adjustable valve that is perfect for this application. The most important reason to choose this valve is that if you decide to carry heavy loads when you originally did not intend to do so, you may now open up the proportioning valve and let the pressure reach the rear wheels where it can now assist in dealing with the higher rear loads.

## BRAKE FLUID

A hydraulic brake system will not operate without brake fluid. To a large degree, the level at which it does operate is dependent on the choice of fluid. Among other things, the more important characteristics of brake fluid are high boiling point, consistent viscosity, and good lubricating ability. All brake fluids commonly used in automobiles in the United States are regulated by the Department of Transportation (DOT). The fluid container will have a number such as DOT 3, which refers to the test designation that the fluid meets. DOT 3 and DOT 4 fluids are polyglycol base products and are hygroscopic, which means that they absorb moisture. As the amount of moisture absorbed increases, the boiling point decreases. In a well sealed brake system, these fluids require changing approximately every 1 or 2 years, depending upon the severity of use. Early master cylinders, such as those found on the '49-'54 Fords, will not have a suitable diaphragm capable of expanding to fill the void created by the brake fluid being used in the system to compensate for lining wear, and as a result air becomes present in the reservoir. The air contains moisture and contaminates the fluid. Use of this type of cylinder automatically means that you should change your fluid much more frequently.

| DOT Minimum Boiling Points | |
| --- | --- |
| *Dry Boiling Point* | *Wet Boiling Point* |
| Dot 3 401 F | 284 F |
| Dot 4 446 F | 311 F |
| Dot 5 500 F | 356 F |

This is also why you should never buy brake fluid by the gallon. A half used gallon of brake fluid will result in the other half of the gallon container being occupied by air. This amount of air is sufficient to cause the remaining fluid to become contaminated with an excessive amount of moisture before it is even put in the vehicle. When bleeding the brake system, never reuse any fluid recovered from the system.

Be very careful never to install anything but brake fluid in the system. The seals are made from ethylene propylene rubber, which is not compatible with transmission fluid or motor oil. If either of these fluids is inadvertently placed in the system, it will be necessary to replace all of the seals in the entire system.

There is one area of caution that needs to be noted concerning DOT 3 and DOT 4 fluids. They attack paint, especially if allowed to be in contact for some time. If fluid is spilled on a painted surface, flush with water and wipe dry immediately.

DOT 5 brake fluid is more commonly known as silicone fluid. This is because it is primarily a silicone based product. It does not attack paint, and it does not absorb moisture. However, it has some characteristics that, in my opinion, make it unacceptable for use in street driven automobiles. First, the compressibility of silicone fluid is very unstable and changes with temperature. Since the temperature of the fluid in a brake system changes under normal driving conditions, the pedal feel is affected, sometimes radically so. It is also affected by changes in atmospheric pressure (altitude). If you live in high country, don't even consider silicone brake fluid. In the racing industry, where brake systems are subjected to extreme use and temperature, it was discovered long ago to be an unacceptable fluid. The expansion characteristics of the fluid under these conditions would be so severe as to lock up the brakes and not allow movement until sufficient time passed for the fluid temperature to come down. If you experience extreme changes in pedal travel or feel, it is possible that you may have silicone fluid in your system.

## TESTING THE SYSTEM

The job of building a safe brake system cannot be considered complete until it has been tested and proven to perform under conditions similar to those it will experience when actually driven. Go to a safe area to perform deceleration tests, subjecting the truck to varying types of stops to check for feel, safety, and balanced braking under a variety of conditions, including both easy and hard deceleration. Begin with easy stops from low speeds, to check pedal height and to be sure no side-to-side pulling is present. Once satisfied that there are no major errors, make several stops from about 30 mph in rapid succession, to check for brake fade. You should be able to make at least 3 stops from 30 mph with no noticeable change in braking characteristics. Now from the same speed, attempt to make a hard deceleration and see if there is either front or rear wheel lockup. If so, the system is not yet properly balanced and needs more fine tuning (see the section on Brake System Valving). This should be checked up to full highway speed, prior to actually driving on the public streets. Never drive any highly modified vehicle until it has been thoroughly tested for handling characteristics.

The very characteristics of a pickup truck will guarantee that the most likely out of balance condition will be rear wheel lockup. As driving speed increases and the demand for deceleration increases, weight shifts to the front wheels, unloading the rear wheels. As weight on the rear wheels decreases, the ability of the wheels to lock up gets easier. In order to test for all variations that may be encountered with a pickup, start with an empty cargo bed and perform all tests stated above. Then fill the back of the truck to simulate loads you will likely carry. Since a loaded truck should always be driven with more care, it is not necessary to see if you can perform racing style maneuvers. Make sure safe stops can be performed from freeway speeds in reasonable stopping distances.

Premature front wheel lockup is possible if a truck is modified by installing oversize rear tires (referring to height, not width). The taller the tires, the longer the lever arm, and the more torque required to lock the wheels. In the case of a pickup, rear tires have to be quite a bit larger than the fronts to create serious problems with the front brakes. A proportioning valve may be used to correct an out of balance condition, but it is wise to do as much as possible with the basic choice of modified components first. If extremely large rear tires are the choice, it's a good idea to opt for a rear disc brake conversion. The reason is that the disc brakes will be much more effective in assisting the fronts in lower speed, normal stop situations. They also help increase front lining life.

Don't forget to check the vehicle for hard deceleration from higher speeds. As shown in the graphs, rear drum brake torque output increases rapidly. If the rear brakes lock up before the fronts, the rear of the truck will be attempting to travel faster than the front, and the vehicle will spin out. Do not drive a truck that has this condition, because it can be extremely dangerous.

## NOTES FOR THE RESTORER OF TRUCKS WITH MECHANICAL BRAKES

1. Most trucks prior to about 1936 are equipped with mechanical brakes. The two most common are cable and rod types. In the case of cable actuated brakes, the cables rust and fray on the inside where it cannot be seen. Cable repair and/or replacement is highly recommended, because these brakes were marginal even when they were new. The rod brakes need to be checked for rust at the joints, and properly lubricated in order to function at their best. If you intend to use a vintage truck on a daily basis, or to really perform hauling work, it is suggested that you retrofit the vehicle with an improved hydraulic brake system.

2. Adjust mechanical brakes correctly and often. The key to getting the best brake performance from a mechanical system is to make sure the adjustment is maintained. Adjustments should be made

approximately every 2000 miles or less. Don't drive when excessive pedal travel is present.

3. Regardless of how well the brake system has been restored, vintage vehicles were not designed for modern driving conditions. Always allow more room for stopping than you would in a modern vehicle.

## NOTES FOR THE RESTORER OF TRUCKS WITH HYDRAULIC BRAKES

If you're only interested in restoring your vintage truck, here are a few special items to watch out for.

1. Watch for signs of leakage from master cylinder and wheel cylinders. Because these components are frequently overlooked during maintenance, the possibility is high that brake fluid is old, contains a great deal of moisture, and has probably pitted the bores from rust. Once leakage starts, it gets bad fast. Replace or overhaul immediately. If overhauling, do not hone the cylinder excessively, or the new cups may fail to seal. The manufacturer should be able to provide guidelines in this area.

2. If the system appears to be operating well and you add fresh fluid, be aware that this is when a borderline bad master cylinder or wheel cylinder will be first noticed. The reason is that the old fluid in the system has thickened with age, making it easier to seal. Fresh fluid is thinner and harder to seal. It's not uncommon to discover the need to replace a hydraulic component after new brake linings have been installed.

3. Check the emergency brake cable for rust and deterioration. For safe operation, you may need to make repairs in this area.

4. On models with the brake pedal under the floor, check the bolts holding the pedal to the master, and replace if necessary. Most likely, weather has taken its toll here. If a rusted bolt breaks during use, the brakes could fail.

5. When performing a brake job, don't forget to change the return springs. Return springs are tempered from heat during braking and lose their ability to return the shoes from the drums. Premature brake wear could result, if old springs are used.

## NOTES FOR THE MODIFIED STREET BUILDER

When building a mild modified street machine, here are a few ways to make simple upgrades to the brakes to help deal with the added performance.

1. Often, wider shoes and drums from late model trucks can be installed to deal with higher loads and resulting faster wear. Wider shoes do not produce more torque, only longer life.

2. On trucks not equipped with power brakes, add the stock power unit if one was available as an

option. Remember to put an inline check valve in the source line from the motor. This will keep sufficient vacuum in the system for one more brake actuation if the motor should die.

3. If installing a non-stock motor in any truck with a master under the floor, make provisions to shield exhaust heat from the brake lines. Boiling brake fluid will definitely cause brake failure.

4. See if there is a larger wheel cylinder available. For example, if you have an 11-inch drum brake from a Ford, see if a larger wheel cylinder was used with that 11-inch brake for a different application, in this case possibly a Lincoln. Often, the factory had several variations of the same package available, such as what is offered in the "towing package."

5. Check all items mentioned under Notes For The Restorer.

## NOTES FOR THE HIGH PERFORMANCE BUILDER

When building a high performance truck that will substantially increase the deceleration and acceleration loads, make sure all of the following items have been considered.

1. Upgrade any existing stock components as mentioned in the two previous Note sections.

2. If adapting a subframe from a newer vehicle, make sure the components come from a vehicle with equal or greater weight than what you are building. If you don't know exactly what you will end up with, play it safe and use the larger brake components. If adapting later disc brakes to truck's existing spindles, check the donor vehicle to determine what the manufacturer used for spindles and bearings. If stock components don't match favorably, you may be creating a potential stress problem. Since pickup trucks have been designed to perform utility functions with weight loads greater than that of automobiles, the car's frame and suspension systems are not stressed to deal with the loads of acceleration and deceleration that may be present in a loaded truck. Check with

experts to ensure safety.

3. If tire size on the rear axle will be radically increased (more than one size different than the front), remember that the brake torque requirements to stop the wheel is being altered and the brake output will have to be increased. Larger brake shoes and larger wheel cylinders are two possibilities. Since the design of the pickup bed does not allow the wheel to be moved out very much, any increase in tire width will have to be done inboard. This requires special positive offset wheels in order to keep the tires tucked neatly inside the wheel openings. (Refer to Hot Rod Mechanix, July/Aug 1989, page 58, for a detailed article about wheel specifications). Take careful measurements and find wheel components that can be used, because this is an area of potential problem.

One final note. Since speeds and weights of trucks have increased over the years, most of the systems that are truly incapable of performing adequately on modern roads will be the pre-'40s vehicles. Later trucks were designed for the speeds and weights more common today. Repairs and maintenance on stock late model equipment will normally be adequate for everyday driving. Obviously, if performance is your goal, system updating will be necessary. If you intend to make modifications to improve the performance, however, don't be content with the brake system as it is. The brake system may only be important to you one time, but make sure it is there for you when that time comes.

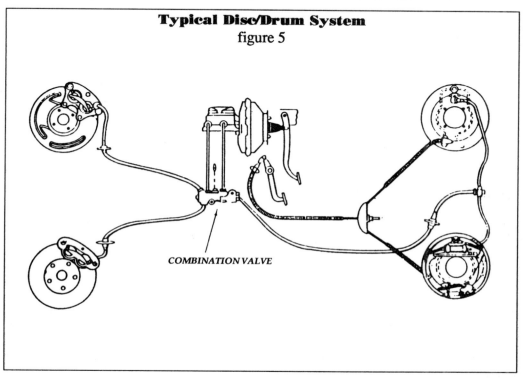

**Typical Disc/Drum System**
figure 5

*COMBINATION VALVE*

# Dakota Digital

## VACUUM FLUORESCENT DIGITAL INSTRUMENTATION

*NSRA 1991 NEW PRODUCT OF THE YEAR AWARD*

Bright displays that are easy to read, even in bright sunlight. Systems are available from universal panels and year specific packages to full customs. All systems come with a **LIFETIME WARRANTY**.

### Features:
* Automatic Night Dimming
* Adjustable Speedometer
* Odometer/Tripometer
* Quick Response Tachometer
* Turn Signal Indicators
* High Beam Indicator
* Gear Shift Indicator
  (with optional sender)

Available in blue, green, red, amber, and other custom colors.

### Complete Kit Includes:
* Aluminum Panel
* Display system
* Operation Manual
* Control Unit
* Speedometer, Oil, and Temp Sending Units

**CALL FOR PRICE & AVAILABILITY**

---

**DON'T WIRE 'EM . . . . SHOOT 'EM**

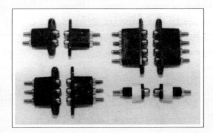

Patent pending contacts shoot electricity through door jambs, eliminating the need for wires.

**Use for:**
* Power windows
* Remote systems
* Alarm systems
* Power locks
* Stereos
* many more...

**Eliminate wires in:**
* Door jambs
* Tailgates
* Trailer ramps
* Trunks
* Tops
* more...

Order one set for each door

| | | |
|---|---|---|
| 1 shot (function) | **$7.95** |
| 2 shot (function) | **$10.95** |
| 3 shot (function) | **$14.95** |
| 4 shot (function) | **$19.95** |

---

## REMOTE CONTROL VEHICLE ENTRY SYSTEMS

All Dakota Digital's remote entry systems come complete with two hand held transmitters, receiver, door motors (REM-3 & REM-4), wiring diagram, mounting hardware, and a **LIFETIME WARRANTY**.

**REMOTE WINDOW CONTROL**

**REM-2** Raises and lowers single power window. Works with all power windows. **$165.00**

**REM-5** Raises and lowers both driver's and passenger's window independently. **NEW!** **$245.00**

**REMOTE DOOR RELEASE**

**REM-3** Two channel system remotely release driver's and passenger's door. **$195.00**

**REM-4** Three channel system releases driver's door, passenger's door, and trunk. **$275.00**

---

## ELECTRIC SERVO CRUISE CONTROL
### The one that really works.

 VACUUM

The most accurate, advanced, and reliable cruise control on the market today. Works with blown and radically camed motors. Electric servo needs no vacuum.

**CRS-2** **$159.95**

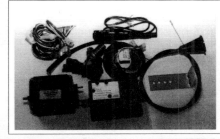

Choose from: universal cutoff, dashmount, original GM or many others.

---

## ORDER TOLL FREE 1-800-852-3228

 1993 SUPER PRIZE PROGRAM SPONSOR

 VISA   MasterCard   DISCOVER

Tech line: (605) 332-6513
Fax line: (605) 339-4106

## Dakota Digital
**3412 Hovland Drive**
**Sioux Falls, SD 57107**

# POWER STEERING SWAP

**BY JIM CLARK**

**W**hen building an older truck, it's nice to get rid of the old "Armstrong" steering system and install a power unit that allows the driver to control the steering wheel with greater ease. What we show on these pages is the installation of a Saginaw power steering unit, and the application in this case is '55 to '59 Chevy pickups.

SoCal Pickups, Inc. at 6321 Manchester Blvd., Buena Park, CA 90621; (714) 994-1400 or (213) 941-4693 has been a supplier of the power steering swap kit shown in these photos, and would be a good resource if this kind of modification is on your list. The kit consists of 2 plates for mounting the steering box, 1 tie rod, 2 tie rod ends (one with a drag link mounting hole), 1 drag link, 2 drag link tie rod ends, 2 engine relocation mounting plates, as well as all the necessary hardware for installation.

The owner/builder needs to supply a steering box, power steering pump and mounting brackets, necessary pulleys and belts, hoses and adapter fittings, and a steering column coupler or a new column. The steering box that should be used with this kit is an early GM Saginaw steering assembly that was used in Cadillacs, Oldsmobiles, and Pontiacs. It should rotate at least 4 times lock-to-lock at the steering column input side, with the most desirable units making up to 5 turns. Anything less than this provides steering that is too quick for this application.

Follow along with the photos and captions to see how easy it is to upgrade a mid-'50s Chevy pickup to Saginaw power. After the installation is complete, it'll be time for an alignment job. Keep in mind that a power steering assembly may give a more pronounced indication of worn front end components, so put the entire front end in top shape before having the alignment done.

*Here are the items included in the basic power steering swap kit. To complete the job, the owner needs to supply a steering box, power steering pump and mounting brackets, pulleys and belts, hoses and adapter fittings, and a steering column coupler or a new column.*

*Check the engine location by measuring the distance from the top of the front crossmember to the center of the fan pulley. This dimension should be 15 inches. If it is less than 13 inches, it may be necessary to raise the engine in the engine compartment so that sufficient clearance will be provided between the drag link and the oil pan. This clearance should be a minimum of 3 inches. For the small block Chevy application, a pair of engine mounting plates are supplied in the basic kit to raise the engine when used with a tube crossmember.*

Cut or grind off the rivets holding the emergency brake bracket to the left frame rail on the '55-'59 Chevy pickup. It must be moved forward about 3 to 5 inches and bolted to the frame again, after drilling new mounting holes. This is necessary to provide space for the new steering box. An extension must be added to the linkage rod extending through the firewall and to the lower end of the arm where it connects to the cable. Another alternative to these modifications would be installation of a later model pedal-operated emergency brake mechanism to replace the stock pull handle.

Remove the old tie-rod, drag link, steering box and spindle arms. Chevy '55-'59 spindle arms must be modified by cutting off the pivot ball and drilling a hole in the end of the arm. The hole must be reamed to create a tapered hole that will accept the tie rod end. A machine shop should be able to do the job. Then bolt the outer mounting plate to the frame rail using the hole indicated in the photo. Align the lower edge of the plate with the bottom of the frame rail.

Drill new mounting holes in the frame rail, using pre-drilled holes in the plate as a guide.

Install the steering box against the inner mounting plate. The bolts extend into the steering box from outside through both plates and the frame rail. Some minor trimming or bending of the flanges on the frame rail may be necessary to achieve the desired alignment. Both plates may be welded in place at this time, or all of the mounting bolts tightened and the plates welded later. We recommend that the welding be performed as soon as possible to provide the maximum margin of safety.

Install the modified spindle arms onto the backing plates, the same as a stock installation.

Install the tie rod between the modified spindle arms. Be sure the special tie rod end is on the right-hand side of the truck.

Install the drag link between the pitman arm on the steering box and the special tie-rod end at the right spindle arm.

Shorten the stock column and add a coupler between the steering box and column or replace the column with one from an early '70s Camaro, Grand Prix, or Chevelle. It may be necessary to shorten one of these columns, so measure the distance from the steering box to the proposed steering wheel location before going to a wrecking yard for a new column.

Install the power steering pump. Be sure to get the necessary pulleys, belts, hoses and mounting hardware to go with the pump. Adapters that will connect the stock hoses between the pump and the steering box are available at any good parts supplier. Take hoses and fittings along and have the parts house match them up.

# REBUILDING F-100 STEERING

**BY RON CERIDONO**

If you have to herd your F-100 down the road as opposed to driving it, help from your passengers is required to turn corners, and parallel parking is completely out of the question, chances are the steering box is due to be rebuilt. But don't despair, all the parts required for a rebuild are available from Ford, or any number of suppliers, and the job itself is a snap.

The first step is to remove the steering from the truck. An F-100's steering gear is taken out through the floorboards. After removing the steering column/pedal seal plate, disconnecting the drag link and removing the steering wheel (shift linkage too, if it's on the column), unbolt the gear box from the frame and remove it through the cab.

Once the gear is out, remove the mastjacket, along with its upper bearing and lower felt seal (in the top of the box where the shaft comes out). Remove the sector shaft cover (that's the big one with the adjusting screw in the middle), then the sector roller assembly will slide out. Remove the end plate and tube assembly (the tube is what the horn wire runs through), and the shim gaskets. The steering worm and shaft, along with the upper and lower bearings will now come out.

The hardest part of the whole process is removing the upper bearing race. A short bead run on the race with an arc welder will shrink the race and it will fall right out. (Use that trick on any race you have trouble with). Remove the sector shaft bushings from the gear box, then clean the housing thoroughly.

Reassembly begins with pressing new sector shaft bushings into the housing. I use two pieces of pipe, one that fits through the inside diameter of the bushing, and one that fits the outside diameter, and tap the bushings in. After installation, the bushing nearest the oil seal should be flush

with the inside surface of the case. The secret to long life from these boxes is to have the bushings fit to the sector shaft with a piston pin hone. Any good automotive machine shop should be able to do the job for you. Once the bushings are taken care of, tap in a new grease seal, with the lips of the seal facing in.

Next, install the upper bearing race, upper bearing, shaft and worm assembly, and lower bearing and race. Now it's time for the first adjustment. With the steering wheel on the shaft, install the end plate and tube assembly with gaskets that are the same thickness as the originals. It should take from 1/4 to 3/4 pounds to turn the worm assembly, measuring at the outside of the wheel. I use a fish scale, hooked to the spoke of the steering wheel, to check the effort necessary. Add shims to increase the preload, remove them to decrease.

Lubricate the sector shaft, then slide it into the housing. Install the gasket, cover, and adjusting screw (make sure the adjusting screw fits into the slot in the end of the sector shaft).

Now for the second adjustment. Turn the wheel from lock to lock and find the center position (count the turns it takes from one extreme to the other, and come back halfway). Turn the adjusting screw in until all end play is removed from the sector shaft. Now adjust the screw until it takes 1 to 2 pounds of pull on the wheel to turn through the center point. That's it. Put a new felt on the steering shaft, reinstall the mastjacket, and put the gear back in.

By the way, on a '53, '54 or '55, a chopped column can be had by using a '56 worm gear and shaft assembly. The '56 shaft is about 1-3/4 inches shorter, so if you shorten the mastjacket tube, you've got a custom "chopped" column.

Once the steering gear is rebuilt and reinstalled, it's time to turn attention to the drag link. The most

## F-100 STEERING GEAR PART NUMBERS

B6C 3524-A  worm gear

B 3552  race

8A 3553  race

68 3571 A  bearing (2 required)

B6C 3575 A  sector

81T 3576 A  sector bushing (2 required)

7RC 3581 A  gasket

B6A 3591 A  seal

B 3593 A  shims

*The Ford F-100 steering is a through-frame unit, very similar to 1934 and earlier Ford units, but it is far superior. The boxes of the mid '50s place the big part of the box above the sector. But for more engine clearance, the earlier F-100 boxes have the big part of the housing below the sector.*

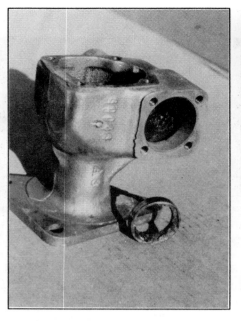

The gearbox comes apart very easily, using ordinary tools. Sector roller, adjusting screw, and cover are at the top of photo. Steering shaft and worm gear are to the left.

Bearing races should be removed prior to cleaning the housing. A short weld bead will shrink the race enough to fall out.

Worn sector shaft bushings will make the box difficult if not impossible to adjust, as well as causing rapid wear of the worm and roller. Always replace these bushings during a rebuild.

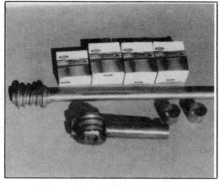

All the parts needed for a rebuild are still available from Ford or aftermarket suppliers.

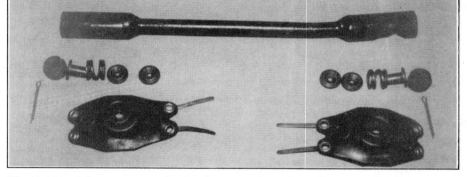

The F-100 pickup uses a spring/socket type tie rod, similar to earlier Fords. Broken springs and worn ball seats are commonly found in these.

common problems with the drag link are worn ball seats (the parts that go around the balls on the sector shaft arm and spindle arm), and broken cushion springs.

At each end of the drag link are plugs retained by cotter pins. Remove the rear plug first, take off the dust shield, turn the steering wheel to the right, remove the outer ball seat, and the drag link will come off the steering gear arm. Now remove the inner ball seat, spring, and the spring seat.

Remove the front plug. Notice the spring, spring seat, and ball seat come out first on the front. Remember that when it's time to go back together. Clean up the drag link, and get rid of years of old grease and grime.

When the rebuild kit for the drag link arrived, I found the new cushion springs furnished were shorter than the originals. My kit came from an after-market supplier, and when I called them and explained the situation they said that was a problem with the kits they had available. My local Ford dealer came through and

got me the right springs. In any case, check the spring length to make sure it's correct.

To reinstall the draglink, put new dust shields on the balls of the steering gear and spindle arms. Put a new ball seat in the spindle arm end of the drag link (just in case you lost track of which end is which, the spindle arm end has the hole farther from the end than the steering gear end), and install it on the spindle arm ball. Install the outer ball seat, spring, and the spring seat. Install the plug, but don't tighten.

Now for the other end. Install the spring seat (the spring seat is in right when the skinny part sticks into the spring), spring, and inner ball seat. Then put the drag link on the sector shaft arm. Install the outer ball seat and the plug.

To adjust the drag link, tighten the plugs down all the way, then back off to the first cotter pin hole. Install a cotter pin, and you're done. Following these easy steps will make your F-100 steering smoother than a baby's bottom.

"THAT'S THE SELLING PRICE, THE ACTUAL MILAGE AND THE APPROXIMATE NUMBER OF DAYS IT WILL TAKE YOU TO PAY FOR IT."

# SELECTING TIRES . . .

**BY JIM CLARK**

T ires and wheels are the link between the vehicle and the road. Four small patches of rubber that support everything. Without them you have little more than an enclosed porch where you can sit and watch the world go by.

That makes their selection critical. However, many hot rod and custom truck builders tend to make this choice based on appearance instead of sound engineering principles. An extremely dangerous practice, considering what is at stake.

A decision this important deserves much more attention than that. An understanding of how tires and wheels are sized and the processes behind selecting them is imperative to successfully building a hot rod truck. The folks at BFGoodrich, makers of T/A radials, provided us with much of the technical assistance needed to write this section, and illustrations to show the points in greater detail. Their dealers have been leaders in providing fitment information to the automotive enthusiast, and are a prime source of both information and products to complete this task.

## READING A SIDEWALL

The sidewall of a tire is, in effect, an owner's manual. The designations and classifications that appear on it identify everything from common dimensions to standard test identification numbers.

Being able to read sidewall branding will help you better understand the performance standards of each tire. It will also provide a guide when mounting and servicing the tire.

### Aspect Ratio

As the aspect ratio of a tire is part of most sizing systems, it is important to know what it is and what it means to a performance enthusiast before you read on. A tire's aspect ratio is the dimensional relationship of the tire's section height to section width. The lower the aspect ratio, the shorter the sidewall, and the quicker the steering response. When the aspect ratio appears in the sizing of a tire, it precedes the tire construction designation, except in the Alpha-Numeric system.

## PASSENGER VEHICLE TIRE SIZING

Three sizing systems exist for passenger tires today: P-Metric, European Metric, and Alpha-Numeric. Each of these systems evolved from the first tire sizing system,

the Numeric Sizing System, which is now obsolete. It was developed when all tires had the same aspect ratio, and it provided only the nominal crosssection width of the tire and the rim diameter in inches. Here are examples that identify the three sizing systems that are commonly seen today.

### P-Metric

Today, most U.S. tire manufacturers build tires that conform to this system. It evolved in the 1970's to accommodate the small tires used on economy cars and is based on the metric system.

| | | P215/65R15 | | |
|---|---|---|---|---|
| Passenger Car Tire | Section Width In Millimeters | Aspect Ratio | Type Of Construction | Rim Diameter In Inches |

**P**—Passenger Car Tire
**215**—Section Width in Millimeters
**65**—Aspect Ratio
**R**—Radial Construction
**15**—Rim Diameter in Inches

### European Metric

Essentially, this system was a conversion of the Numeric System from inches to millimeters. Aspect ratio appears in the size designation in most cases where it is other than 82.

| | | 155SR13 | | |
|---|---|---|---|---|
| Cross Section Width In Millimeters | Aspect Ratio Assumed 82 | Speed Rating | Type Of Construction | Rim Diameter In Inches |

**155**—Cross Section Width in Millimeters
Aspect Ratio Assumed 82
**S**—S Speed Rating
**R**—Radial Construction
**13**—Rim Diameter in Inches

### 185/70SR14

| 185/70SR14 | | | | |
|---|---|---|---|---|
| Cross Section Width In Millimeters | Aspect Ratio | Speed Rating | Type Of Construction | Rim Diameter In Inches |

**185**—Cross Section Width in Millimeters
**70**—Aspect Ratio
**S**—Speed Rating
**R**—Radial Construction
**14**—Rim Diameter in Inches

### Alpha-Numeric

In the late Sixties, this load-based system evolved. The first letter of the designation identifies the load/size relationship of the tire. The letter can range from "A" to "N." The lower the letter, the smaller the size and load carrying capacity at a given inflation pressure.

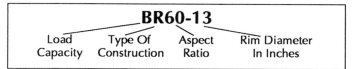

| BR60-13 | | | |
|---|---|---|---|
| Load Capacity | Type Of Construction | Aspect Ratio | Rim Diameter In Inches |

**B**—Load Capacity
**R**—Radial Construction
**60**—Aspect Ratio
**13**—Rim Diameter in Inches

## LIGHT TRUCK TIRE SIZING

Sizing for light truck tires takes the performance requirements of the vehicle, and also the tires, into account. Light truck tires have evolved along with the expanded applications of trucks. Originally, light trucks were used solely for commercial hauling. Today, they have grown to be multi-purpose vehicles that encompass services from work to play to passenger vehicle. There are three different light truck tire sizing systems: Light Truck Metric, Light Truck High Flotation, and Light Truck Numeric.

### Light Truck Metric

This sizing system mirrors the P-Metric system for passenger tires and will probably expand in the future to appear on all light truck tires.

| LT235/75R15/ C | | | | | |
|---|---|---|---|---|---|
| Light Truck Designation | Section Width In Millimeters | Aspect Ratio | Type Of Construction | Rim Dia. In Inches | Load Carrying Capacity |

**LT**—Light Truck Designation
**235**—Section Width in Millimeters
**75**—Aspect Ratio
**R**—Radial Construction
**15**—Rim Diameter in Inches
**C**—Load Carrying Capacity

### Light Truck High Flotation

Light truck high flotation tires evolved in the mid-Seventies as lower aspect ratio tires became more popular on light trucks. The combination of lower aspect ratios and high flotation yielded better traction on sand and soft soil found in watery off-road situations.

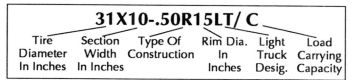

| 31X10-.50R15LT/ C | | | | | |
|---|---|---|---|---|---|
| Tire Diameter In Inches | Section Width In Inches | Type Of Construction | Rim Dia. In Inches | Light Truck Desig. | Load Carrying Capacity |

**31**—Tire Diameter in Inches
**10.50**—Section Width in Inches
**R**—Radial Construction
**15**—Rim Diameter in Inches
**LT**—Light Truck Designation
**C**—Load Carrying Capacity

### Light Truck Numeric

This older system is still widely used, mostly on commercial vehicles.

| 7.50R16LT/ D | | | | |
|---|---|---|---|---|
| Section Width In Inches | Type Of Construction | Rim Diameter In Inches | Light Truck Desig. | Load Carrying Capacity |

**7.50**—Section Width in Inches
**R**—Radial Construction
**16**—Rim Diameter in Inches
**LT**—Light Truck Designation
**D**—Load Carrying Capacity

## SPEED-RATING SYSTEM

The speed rating of a tire indicates the speed category (or range of speeds) at which the tire can carry a load under specified service conditions. The speed-rating system used today was developed in Europe in response to the need to control the safe performance of tires at standardized speeds. A letter from A to Z symbolizes a tire's certified speed rating, ranging from 5 km/h (3 mph) to over 240 km/h (149 mph). This rating system, listed below, describes the top speed for which a tire is certified. It does not indicate the total performance capability of a tire.

When this speed-rating system was originally developed, the Unlimited V category of over 210 km/h (130 mph) was the top speed rating a tire could achieve. As manufacturers made more tires that fit into this category, it was necessary to better regulate performance at standardized speeds to ensure safety. The Limited V category of 240 km/h (149) was then created, and the Z speed rating was added as the top speed rating that a tire could achieve.

Always consult the manufacturer for the maximum

speed of Unlimited V and Z tires.

Speed rating is identified as a part of the tire's sizing or service description. For example, as part of the tire's sizing it appears as follows:

### Old System

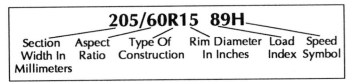

| 205/60HR15 | | | | |
|---|---|---|---|---|
| Section Width In Millimeters | Aspect Ratio | Speed Rating | Type Of Construction | Rim Diameter In Inches |

**205**—Section Width in Millimeters
**60**—Aspect Ratio
**H**—Speed Rating
**R**—Radial Construction
**15**—Rim Diameter in Inches

## Speed Symbol

| SPEED SYMBOL | SPEED (km/h) | SPEED (km/h) |
|---|---|---|
| A1 | 5 | 3 |
| A2 | 10 | 6 |
| A3 | 15 | 9 |
| A4 | 20 | 12 |
| A5 | 25 | 16 |
| A6 | 30 | 19 |
| A7 | 35 | 22 |
| A8 | 40 | 25 |
| B | 50 | 31 |
| C | 60 | 37 |
| D | 65 | 40 |
| E | 70 | 43 |
| F | 80 | 50 |
| G | 90 | 56 |
| J | 100 | 62 |
| K | 110 | 68 |
| L | 120 | 75 |
| M | 130 | 81 |
| N | 140 | 87 |
| P | 150 | 94 |
| Q | 160 | 100 |
| R | 170 | 106 |
| S | 180 | 112 |
| T | 190 | 118 |
| U | 200 | 124 |
| H | 210 | 130 |
| V | 240 | 149 |
| V | Over 200 | Over 130 |
| Z | Over 200 | Over 149 |

## SERVICE DESCRIPTION

In another attempt to standardize tire designations, S,T,H and Limited V tires incorporate the speed symbol and load index as the tire's service description. For example:

### New System

| 205/60R15  89H | | | | | |
|---|---|---|---|---|---|
| Section Width In Millimeters | Aspect Ratio | Type Of Construction | Rim Diameter In Inches | Load Index | Speed Symbol |

**205**—Section Width in Millimeters
**60**—Aspect Ratio
**R**—Radial Construction
**15**—Rim Diameter in Inches
**89**—Load Index
**H**—Speed Symbol

The load index is an assigned number ranging from 0 to 279 that corresponds with the load carrying capacity of a tire. Most passenger car tire load indexes range from 75 to 100, although some T/A passenger tires carry more.

In the above example, the load index of 89 corresponds to a load carrying capacity of 580 kg (1279 lbs) at maximum inflation. The speed symbol of the tire is the second part of the service description. (See the previous section for speed categories). The service description system is used only with tires that have assigned limited speed ratings—S,T,H and V. For Unlimited V and Z rated tires, consult the manufacturer for maximum speed.

Note: For the time being, the speed symbol may appear in two places as the transition from the old to the new system occurs. The speed symbol may be located in the tire size between the aspect ratio and construction symbol as shown in the above "Speed-Rating System" section and/or as part of the service description as shown.

## UNIFORM TIRE QUALITY GRADE LABELING

The Uniform Tire Quality Grading System (UTQGS) is a government directed program that provides buyers with information on three categories: treadwear, traction, and temperature. Each tire manufacturer performs its own tests in these areas, following the government prescribed test procedures. Each manufacturer then assigns grades that appear as labels on the tire. This is known as Uniform Tire Quality Grade Labeling (UTQGL).

### Treadwear

Treadwear grades typically range from 50 to 400, in ten point increments. It's important to remember that the actual life of any tire is determined by the road surface quality, driving habits, inflation, wheel alignment and rotation it experiences. To receive a treadwear grade, a tire is tested under controlled conditions on a government prescribed test course which does not necessarily simulate the actual application for which a given tire is designed to perform. As a result of these test parameters, there is no reliable way to assign miles of wear to treadwear grade points.

### Traction

Traction grades indicate the measurement of a tire's ability to stop a car in straight ahead motion on a wet test surface pavement. It's important to remember that traction rating tests are performed only for straight ahead sliding on concrete or asphalt surfaces that have a specified degree of wetting which simulates most road surfaces in a rainstorm. The ratings that result from these tests may not apply to cornering traction or peak values of straight ahead braking force like those experienced in non-skid braking tests. Traction grades range from A to C, A being the highest attainable grade.

### Temperature

Temperature grades also range from A to C, with A being the highest. Temperature grades represent a properly maintained tire's ability to dissipate heat under controlled indoor test conditions. All tires must meet the 85 mph minimum speed requirement of the Federal Motor Vehicle Safety Standard 109.

Temperature ratings are determined by running tires that are being tested on an indoor drum under specified conditions. Successive 30-minute runs are made in 5-mph increments between 75 and 115 mph, or until the tire fails. A tire is graded "C" if it fails between 85 and 100 mph; "B" if it fails between 100 and 115 mph; "A" if it exceeds 115 mph.

### Max. Load and Max. Inflation

This branding indicates the maximum load that can be carried at the maximum pressure. In the example shown on this page, the maximum load at maximum pressure is as follows:

What holds the air in the tire? The reinforcements (belts, beads, carcass, innerliner, etc.) in a tire's body form the vessel that contains the air pressure. The stronger the reinforcements, the more air a tire can hold.

The Alpha-Numeric tire sizing system shows specific load range symbols on the sidewall that indicate how much load the tire is designed to carry at a defined pressure. Most Alpha-Numeric sized tires are Load Range B, meaning they are restricted to the load that can be carried with a maximum inflation pressure of 32 psi. For greater load carrying capacity, C, D or E tires can be used. (Note: most load range C, D and E tires are for light truck applications). These load carrying capacity designations will appear directly after the size of the tire as follows: LT235/75R15/C.

The load carrying capacity of P-Metric tires is rated either Standard Load or Extra Load. Standard Load tires are limited by the load that can be carried with a maximum inflation pressure of 35 psi. Extra Load tires are limited by the load that can be carried with a maximum inflation pressure of 41 psi. An Extra Load Tire will be branded with "XL." A Standard Load tire does not bear any special designations.

Note: A tire with a normal inflation pressure of 35 psi may also be branded with a maximum inflation of 44 psi, indicating the tire's ability to meet special performance requirements. It does NOT increase the tire's load capacity.

## SELECTING REPLACEMENT TIRES

The following methods of tire replacement selection help determine the correct fitment for your needs. No matter which method is used, always verify that the load carrying capacity of the replacement tire is equal to or greater than that of the original equipment (OE) tire.

### Tire Manufacturers Fitment Guide

The Tire Manufacturers Fitment Guide is a complete source for selecting fitments on standard models in the United States. It provides the optimum tire size with recommended air pressure for a standard rim diameter, Plus 1 and Plus 2 fitments. If your vehicle has been modified, refer to the other methods of substitution and inflation outlined herein. Your local dealer will have a fitment guide and can assist you in selecting the proper tire and wheel combination.

### GAWR Method

This method will help determine the tire that will carry the vehicle's axle weight. It provides an alternate guide to fitments when the Tire Manufacturers Fitment Guide cannot yield a satisfactory substitute tire size. Use this procedure only when the other method is inappropriate. The following steps will ensure that the load carrying capacity of the substitute tire size will support the weight of the vehicle.

1. Refer to the vehicle's GAWR placard (located on the door edge, door post, inside the glove box or inside the trunk) for the GAWR for both the front and rear axles.

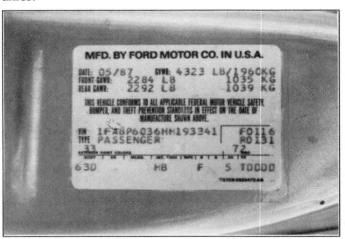

2. In the Tire Size and Max. GAWR tables, find a GAWR that is equal to or greater than either the front or rear axle, whichever is larger. Note: If a larger rear tire size is desired, the front and rear tire sizes can be selected independently.

*P-Metric Sizes. When passenger car tires are used on light trucks, the rated load carrying capacity of the tire is reduced because of the severe service often encountered by light trucks. Note: These tables are based on maximum tire load capacity times 2 (two tires per axle), less 10% (for a reserve load safety factor). Tires selected using this method are the smallest suitable for the weight of the vehicle and must be inflated to their maximum inflation pressure.*

*3. The tire size listed to the right of the GAWR is the smallest size that will carry the vehicle load. If it is not the size you want, read up the table until you find the desired size for the vehicle in terms of rim diameter, aspect ratio, etc.*

*4. Inflate the tires to their maximum inflation pressure. This is important, as the tires that are selected using this method are the smallest suitable for the weight of the vehicle.*

| Max. Vehicle GAWR | Flotation Series | 85 Series | 75 Series |
|---|---|---|---|
| 6093 | 35x12.50R16.5LT,D | | |
| 5949 | | | LT285/75R16,D |
| 5476 | | LT235/85R16,E | LT245/75R16,E |
| 5476 | | | LT265/75R16,D |
| 5400 | | LT255/85R16,D | |
| 5274 | 33x12.50R16.5LT,D | | |
| 4941 | 31x10.50R16.5LT,D | | |
| 4716 | 33x10.50R15LT,C | | |
| 4599 | 35x12.50R15LT,C | | |
| 4554 | 32x11.50R15LT,C | | |
| 4491 | 33x9.50R15LT,C | | |
| 4203 | | | LT225/75R16,D |
| 4050 | 31x10.50R15LT,C | | |
| 4005 | 33x12.50R15LT,C | | |
| 3582 | 30x9.50R15LT,C | | |
| 3573 | | | P235/75R15,XL* |
| 3573 | | | LT235/75R15,C |
| 3177 | | | LT215/75R15,C |
| 2727 | 27x8.50R14LT,C | | |
| 2615 | | | P205/75R15,SL* |
| 2507 | | | P205/75R14,SL* |

Table title: **Tire Size and Max. GAWR for Light Truck Applications**

### Passenger Tires on LT'S and MPV'S

When a passenger car tire is fitted to a light truck (LT) or multi-purpose vehicle (MPV), the rated load carrying capacity of the tire must be reduced as these vehicles often experience more severe service situations. If you examine the vehicle's tire placard and determine that passenger car tires were original equipment on the vehicle, the vehicle manufacturer has already reduced the tire load to what appears on the placard.

On the other hand, if the vehicle's tire placard indicates that the vehicle's original equipment fitment was a light truck tire, and you want to use a passenger tire as replacement, you must reduce the rated load shown on the tire sidewall.

The amount of the reduction is:

## Tire Size and Maximum GAWR for Passenger Car Applications

| Max. Vehicle GAWR | 75/70 Series | 65/60 Series | 55/50/45/40/35 Series | Max. Vehicle GAWR | 75/70 Series | 65/60 Series | 55/50/45/40/35 Series |
|---|---|---|---|---|---|---|---|
| 4950 | P285/70R16 | | | 2619 | | P225/60R14 | |
| 4822 | P285/70R15 | | | 2610 | | 225/60R14 | |
| 4650 | P265/75R16 | | | 2579 | P205/70R14 | | P275/40R17 |
| 4400 | P265/75R15 | | | 2579 | | | P315/35R17 |
| 4070 | P245/75R16 | | | 2579 | | | P245/50R14 |
| 3929 | P255/70R15 | | | 2538 | | 215/60R15 | |
| 3868 | | P275/60R15 | | 2520 | | P205/65R15 | |
| 3710 | | | P295/50R15 | 2500 | | | 225/50R16 |
| 3600 | P245/70R15 | | | 2500 | | | P255/45R17 |
| 3492 | P225/75R16 | | | 2457 | | 205/60R15 | |
| 3413 | P235/70R15 | | | 2457 | | 215/60R14 | |
| 3402 | | 255/60R15 | | 2441 | P205/70R13 | 195/65R15 | |
| 3393 | | P255/60R15 | | 2421 | | P215/60R14 | |
| 3344 | | P245/65R15 | | 2412 | 195/70R14 | | |
| 3294 | | | P275/50R15 | 2381 | | | 225/50R15 |
| 3254 | P235/70R14 | P235/65R16 | | 2381 | | | P255/45R16 |
| 3175 | | P235/65R15 | | 2362 | P195/70R14 | | |
| 3155 | P225/70R15 | P245/60R15 | | 2302 | | P215/60R13 | P245/45R17 |
| 3114 | 225/70R15 | | | 2282 | | | P235/50R13 |
| 3096 | | | P265/50R15 | 2277 | 185/70R15 | | |
| 3076 | | | P315/40R16 | 2250 | | 195/60R15 | |
| 3067 | | | | 2243 | P195/70R13 | | |
| 3037 | | | P255/50R16 | 2223 | | | 205/55R16 |
| 3015 | P225/70R14 | P245/60R14 | | 2223 | | | P285/35R17 |
| 2975 | | P225/65R15 | | 2178 | 185/70R14 | 195/60R14 | |
| 2956 | | P235/60R15 | P265/50R14 | 2162 | P185/70R14 | 185/65R15 | 205/55R15 |
| 2934 | | 235/60R15 | | 2122 | | P205/60R13 | |
| 2916 | P215/70R15 | | | 2088 | | 205/60R13 | P245/40R17 |
| 2890 | | P225/60R16 | P335/35R17 | 2052 | 185/70R13 | | |
| 2844 | | 235/60R14 | | 2043 | P185/70R13 | P195/60R14 | 205/50R15 |
| 2837 | | | P245/50R16 | 2016 | | 185/60R14 | |
| 2817 | | P235/60R14 | | 1964 | | | P215/50R13 |
| 2797 | P215/70R14 | | | 1944 | | P195/60R13 | |
| 2718 | | P215/65R15 | P285/40R17 | 1881 | | 185/60R13 | |
| 2698 | | | P245/50R15 | 1865 | P175/70R13 | | |
| 2682 | 205/70R14 | | | 1845 | 175/70R13 | | |
| 2673 | | 225/60R15 | | 1834 | | | 195/50R15 |
| 2659 | | P215/60R16 | 245/45R16 | 1685 | | P165/65R14 | |
| 2657 | | 205/65R15 | | | | | |

Note: These tables are based on maximum tire load capacity times 2 (two tires per axle), less 10% (for a reserve load safety factor).

*Rated load* = Reduced load for light trucks (approximately 91% of 1.1 rated load)

For example if you have a P235/75R15XL with a rated load of 2183 at 41 psi that you want to use on a light truck, you would reduce the rated load by dividing it by 1.1.

*Example:* $\dfrac{2183}{1.1}$ = 1985 at 41 psi

Remember to reduce the passenger tire rated load before considering the passenger tire a replacement for the OE tire. If the vehicle comes equipped with load range "D" or "E" light truck tires, you may find it impractical to consider passenger tires as replacement as they will not carry the load unless you upsize considerably.

## TIRE SIZES CAN CHANGE EFFECTIVE AXLE RATIOS

Changing tire sizes can affect a vehicle's rate of acceleration and possibly fuel economy. To keep the engines in today's vehicles at the desired revolutions per mile (rpm) range for optimum performance, specific gear ratios are chosen carefully. If replacement tire's rpm is different from the original equipment tire, the vehicle's effective gear ratio will change. This could alter the vehicle's intended level of performance.

### Tire Revolutions Per Mile

To estimate tire revolutions per mile (rpm), use the following formula: 20,800 ÷ Overall Tire Diameter = Tire rpm.

*Example: 20,800 ÷ 26.1" = 796.9 Tire rpm*

To properly determine how changing tire sizes will affect a vehicle's effective axle ratio, use the following formula. Refer to the preceding formula that estimates tire rpm.

> *Formula: New tire rpm x Original Axle Ratio = Effective Axle Ratio*
> *Original tire rpm*

What would be the resulting effect if the tires on a 1989 Chevy K Blazer with a 3.73:1 axle ratio were changed from P235/75R15's to 33x12.50R15LT Radial Mud-Terrain T/A tires?

*Example:* $\frac{630 \times 3.73}{720}$ *= 3.26 (Effective Axle Ratio)*

Changing the tire size on this vehicle as indicated yields a numerically lower effective axle ratio than the original axle ratio. This means that the Blazer will accelerate slower and may achieve better highway fuel economy. If the effective axle ratio were numerically higher than the original axle ratio, the Blazer would accelerate quicker, but might decrease its highway fuel economy.

## CHOOSING OPTIONAL AXLE RATIOS

How do you change a vehicle's tire size but maintain the vehicle's intended acceleration and fuel economy? There are two choices: You can order an optional axle ratio (if the vehicle is new), or install a different axle ratio. The following formula determines the correct alternate axle ratio. Refer to the previous formula in this section that estimates tire revolutions per mile (rpm).

*Formula:*

> *Original Tire rpm x Original Axle Ratio = Equivalent Axle Ratio*
> *New Tire rpm*

Using the same Chevy K Blazer from the preceding formula, here's how it works:

*Example:* $\frac{720 \times 3.73}{630}$ *= 4.26 (Equivalent Axle Ratio)*

Note: It is unlikely that the exact ratio will be available. Order the nearest ratio or change to a tire with a different diameter.

## PLUS 1 AND PLUS 2 SIZING

One of the best ways to move up to a higher level of performance is to utilize Plus 1 and Plus 2 sizing. As the chart illustrates, this concept achieves increased handling capabilities by mounting tires with wider section widths and lower aspect ratios to rims of 1, 2

and sometimes 3 inches greater diameter.

Plus 1 and Plus 2 fitments must also retain nearly the same overall tire diameter so that gear ratios and speedometer readings remain accurate. Equally important to proper Plus 1 and Plus 2 sizing is maintaining a load carrying capacity that is equal to or greater than that of the original tire.

A good way to remember this concept is to use the following rules of thumb. (These guidelines assume a base 70 Series tire.) PLUS 1 Rule of Thumb: Increase section width by 10 mm. Decrease aspect ratio by 10 points. Increase rim diameter by 1 inch. PLUS 2 Rule of Thumb: Increase section width by 20 mm. Decrease aspect ratio by 20 points. Increase rim diameter by 2 inches.

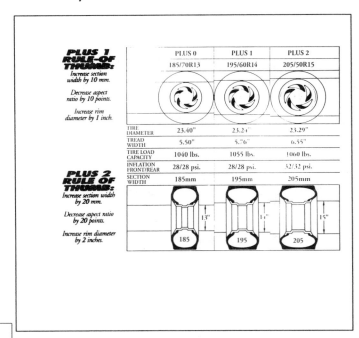

Looking more closely at the concept shows how it achieves greater performance benefits. Wider section widths and lower profiles give tires a wider footprint that increases the vehicle's steering response and overall cornering force.

The wider wheel widths that fit Plus 1 and Plus 2 tires strengthen their stability, also resulting in greater cornering force. It's important to select Plus 1 and Plus 2 wheels that meet recommended rim width range specifications. A wheel that is outside the recommended width range can curve the tire's tread surface, leaving you with less traction. It will decrease the tire's flexibility, increasing its susceptibility to curb damage. Properly mounting the tire may also prove difficult.

Knowing custom wheels will further assist you in achieving superior performance for your Plus 1 and Plus 2 application. Refer to the "Wheels" section for more information about custom wheels.

# . . . AND WHEELS

**BY JIM CLARK**

hen selecting wheels, remember these five points:
1. Mount tires only on approved rim widths. See tire manufacturer data for correct rim width range.

2. Always verify that the tire and rim diameter are the same. For example, an LT235/85R16 must be mounted only on a 16-inch rim.

3. When changing tire sizes, verify that the rim/wheel carries the adequate load and inflation pressure capacity. If the load and inflation pressure capacity are not identified on the rim/wheel (or are not identified for service conditions exceeding the rated capacities) consult the rim/wheel manufacturer to determine the capacity.

4. Never use high pressure compact spare tires with any other rims/wheels than those provided. Similarly, never use standard or snow tires, wheel covers or trim rings with a high pressure compact spare wheel.

5. Be certain that the replacement rims have an offset that is as nearly equal as possible to the OE rims or provides sufficient clearance without overloading bearings and suspension.

## HUB AND LUG CENTRIC

To meet your high performance expectations, you'll need to know as much as you can about custom wheels. Wheels are manufactured to center on a vehicle in one of two ways: 1. On the hub of the vehicle. 2. On the lug nuts.

The hub hole of hub-centric wheels is made to perfectly match the diameter of a vehicle's hub. For example, a hub hole that is 70 mm in diameter will fit perfectly on a 70 mm hub.
Automakers use hub-centric wheels because they provide a more accurate fitment. However, only the most expensive aftermarket wheels are hub centric.

70mm

When replacing a wheel, you must select a replacement with a bolt pattern or circle that matches that of the vehicle. A bolt circle is the diameter of an imaginary circle drawn through the center of each lug nut hole. This is true of all lug patterns—4, 5, 6 and 8. To determine the diameter of the bolt circle for 4, 6 and 8-lug patterns, measure from the middle of two holes that are directly across from each other. Using the 4-lug pattern as an example, the bolt circle is 100 mm in diameter. This is often referred to as "4x100 mm". Obviously, this is impossible with a 5-lug pattern. In this case, you must estimate the bolt circle diameter by measuring from the back of a hole on one side to the center of the closest opposing hole on the other side of the hub.

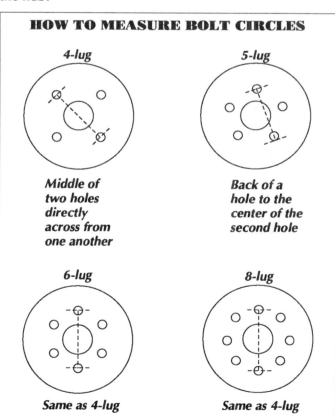

**HOW TO MEASURE BOLT CIRCLES**

*4-lug*

*5-lug*

Middle of two holes directly across from one another

Back of a hole to the center of the second hole

*6-lug*

*8-lug*

Same as 4-lug

Same as 4-lug

## RIM DIAMETER AND WIDTH

Before mounting the tire to the wheel, check the fit of the custom wheel to the vehicle. The diameter designation for both the tire and the rim must be the same. An LT235/85R16 must be mounted on a 16" rim only. WARNING: Never mount a tire of one diameter on a wheel of a larger diameter.

For example, while it is possible to pass a 16" diameter tire over the lip or flange of a 16.5" diameter rim, the tire cannot be inflated enough to position its beads against the rim flange. If an attempt is made to seat the tire bead by overinflating, the bead will break with explosive force, possibly resulting in serious injury to the operator.

When selecting wheels, you must also pay attention to rim width. The tire manufacturer's specifications will recommend a range of proper rim widths that will assist the tire/wheel assembly in meeting its performance potential. To achieve the best balance between ride, handling, and treadwear for highway vehicles, select a rim width in the middle of the manufacturer's recommended range.

To improve cornering traction and steering response, choose a rim at or near the maximum recommended width. How does a wider rim increase cornering and steering response? The wider the rim, the straighter the tire sidewall. (Conversely, using a rim width at the low-end of the range will cause the tire to balloon or curve out). If the tread and the rim are two points, the shortest distance between them is a straight line. The wider the rim width, the straighter the tire sidewall, and the quicker the steering response.

> *Example:*
> Tire size—P225/70R15
> Rim width range—6" to 8"
> Normal street use—Use a 7" rim
> Improved cornering—Use an 8" rim

For light truck tires that will be used off-road, select a rim near the minimum recommended width. The tire sidewall will balloon or curve out, providing additional rim and sidewall protection from rocks and other objects that could cause damage.

> *Example:*
> Tire size—33x12.50R15LT
> Rim width range—8" to 11"
> For maximum street performance—use an 11" rim
> For maximum off-road performance—use an 8" rim

In addition to selecting wheels with the correct bolt circle and rim width, you must also choose a wheel with the correct offset.

## WHEEL OFFSET

Offset is a measurement that most people know something about, but may not fully understand. Simply, offset is the measured difference between the wheel's mounting face where it bolts up to the hub and the centerline of the rim.

In other words, when the mounting face directly aligns with the wheel's centerline, the wheel has zero offset. When the mounting face is toward the wheel's centerline, the wheel has positive offset. Negative offset occurs when the mounting face is closer to the brake side of the wheel.

The offset of the rim is what locates the tire/wheel assembly in relation to the suspension. Front wheels usually have positive offset. Front-wheel-drive vehicles have high positive offset wheels which allow for proper clearance of the hub assembly within the wheelwell.

On front-wheel or all-wheel-drive vehicles, it is important to keep the front axle offsets as close as possible to the factory designed specifications. Offsets that do not meet these specifications can increase steering effort, steering wheel kickback when accelerating around a turn, and load on the wheel bearings. Using the proper positive or negative offset at the rear of the vehicle is important but less so than at the front where the bearing load situation is critical.

Negative offset wheels also affect handling. At the rear of the vehicle, they can increase its track, improving stability and handling. Excessive negative offset up front increases steering wheel kick-back and places additional stress on wheel bearings and the vehicle's suspension.

## MEASURING WHEEL REAR SPACING AND CALCULATING OFFSET

Rear spacing is the distance from the inside of the rim edge to the inside of the mounting face. When the offset measurement is not provided in the manufacturer's product literature, use the following procedures to convert rear spacing to offset:

1. Measure the rear spacing of the wheel, by laying it face down on a flat surface.
2. Then lay a straightedge across the inside edge of the wheel.
3. Measure from the wheel mounting face to the straightedge with a ruler (A), and record this distance.
4. Next, measure the total wheel width (B), and calculate the offset using the following formula:

$$Rear\ Spacing\ (A) - \frac{Total\ wheel\ width\ (B)}{2} = Offset$$

## MEASURING WHEEL REAR SPACING AND CALCULATING OFFSET

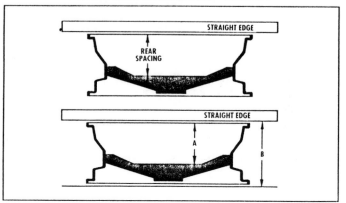

## CALCULATING THE OFFSET OF A MOUNTED TIRE AND WHEEL

To calculate the offset of a tire mounted on a wheel, follow these procedures:

1. Place the assembly face down on a flat surface.
2. Lay a straightedge across the inside sidewall of the tire.
3. Measure from the wheel mounting surface to the straightedge (C).
4. Then measure the tire's actual mounted section width (D) and use the following formula to calculate offset:

One solution in this situation would be to install a 235/60HR15 on the standard wheel or another aftermarket wheel that has an offset and rear spacing closer to the original specifications.

Few areas in the building of your truck will have as much impact on the final outcome as selecting tires and wheels. Custom wheels and tires do much to enhance the truck's appearance. With a thorough understanding of the processes used in selecting tires and wheels it should make the task easier and the finished vehicle a much safer and more enjoyable truck to drive.

$$\textit{Sidewall to Mounting Surface (C)} - \frac{\textit{Mounted Section Width (D)}}{2} = \textit{Offset}$$

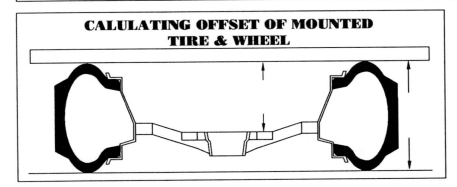

### CALULATING OFFSET OF MOUNTED TIRE & WHEEL

*Example:*

You want to install 15"x8.5" aftermarket wheels and 235/60HR15 tires on a 1989 Chevrolet Camaro. Here are the steps you should follow:

1. Check the fit. To do this you'll need to determine the aftermarket wheel's offset. The rear spacing measures 3.875", and the total wheel width measures 9.25".

$$\textit{Rear Spacing (A) 3.875"} - \frac{\textit{Wheel Width (B) 9.25" Total}}{2} = 0.75" \textit{ Offset}$$

2. Then measure the original 15"x7" wheel and P215/65R15 OE tire to compare offsets. The measurement of the sidewall to the mounting surface is 4.75". The mounted section width is 8.90".

$$\textit{Sidewall to Mounting Surface (C) 4.75"} - \frac{\textit{Section Width (D) 8.90"}}{2} = +0.30" \textit{ Offset}$$

In this example, a 0.75" offset wheel is replacing an original +0.30" offset wheel. The difference of 1.05" should alert you to the fact that the front wheel, wheel bearings and suspension will experience more severe service. The tire will be moved away from the car and toward the fenders, possibly causing interference.

When combined with the 1.5" additional wheel width, these offset differences indicate that the given tire and wheel combination may not be able to be used.

# BASIC BODYWORK

**BY JIM CLARK**

**B**uilding a hot rod truck utilizing sheetmetal that has seen a decade or more of service requires bodywork techniques different from everyday collision repair. The metal suffers from the ravages of rust and the stress of day to day truck usage.

De-rusting is usually the first step. Most areas have de-rusting services listed in the phone book, both chemical and sandblasting types.

After the metal is de-rusted, straightening, hole filling and tear repairs can be made. This entails welding and leading or filling with glass body filler. In badly rusted areas patch panels usually have to be welded in, after removal of the old material left in the opening.

Some replacement panels are available from specialty suppliers for the more popular classic trucks. Otherwise you will have to fabricate your own. The better the piece matches the original, the less filling will be necessary.

Once the base metal has been repaired, the finish work will follow routine leading or plastic filler practices, then followed by paint work at the shop of your choice.

Teaching how to become a bodywork specialist is far beyond the scope of this book, but the accompanying photos should give a working knowledge of the procedures involved in building a hot rod truck.

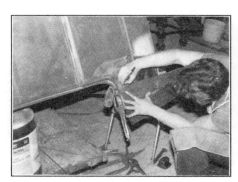

*It is quite often easier to cut out badly rusted areas and replace them with new metal, as is being marked up and fit here.*

*Panels should be tacked in place and welded in small sections, skipping around to avoid distortion of the surrounding sheetmetal.*

*After new patches have been welded in, a little heat applied to the seams and some picking with a hammer can save a lot of body filling.*

*To finish a panel, a picking tool is used on low spots. This one was made by welding very large nails onto a long piece of round metal rod bent into a deep U-bend. The top nail acts as a pointer to aid alignment of the rear picking rod.*

*After the low areas have been worked out, a body file is used to recontour the panel to its original form. File it with great care though.*

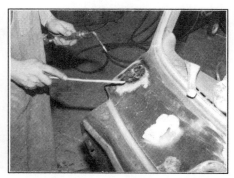

*Lead is the preferred method for filling a panel. The area is chemically cleaned, then lead is applied.*

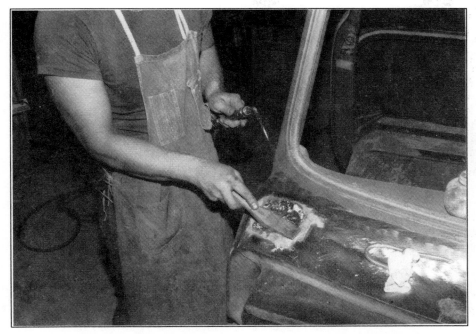

A wooden paddle coated with beeswax is used to place molten lead in the required spots, then it's filed to the desired contour.

Larger dents are worked out with a variety of different shaped hammers and backup dollies.

Dents are also removed by slapping them with this flat metal slapper file backed up with a body dolly.

Body filler should be mixed in small quantities and applied in thin coats to achieve the best results.

Sand the big areas into the basic contours with this big power body sander and coarse discs.

To prevent low spots, finish-sand metal or body filler with this type of inline sander or an orbital power sander.

The final step in repairing a damaged area is application of a protective coat of primer to preserve the metal until ready for paint.

# WRINKLE REMOVER

**BY JIM CLARK**

The manufacturer endowed your truck's outer skin with curves and creases, and these add strength and style to its appearance. Unfortunately, as time passes, you and others you encounter add new wrinkles to it in parking lot mishaps and some minor fender benders.

Major collision damage usually requires the skills of professional bodymen, but these smaller repairs can usually be made by a do-it-yourself enthusiast. All it takes on your part is some time and patience plus a few basic bodyworking tools.

Where access to the back side of the panel is available, the repair can be made by standard hammer and dolly techniques. Panels that have no access create a tougher problem. The traditional method for doing this has been to use a slap-hammer. A tool with a screw-shaped end that penetrates the metal to grab hold, then utilizes a sliding weight that, when pulled sharply outward against the handle, pulls the dent out. The tool removes the dent or crease, but leaves a trail of holes in the panel that then have to be welded up. This creates an extra repair job and leaves a potential corrosion point behind the blind panel.

A new tool has recently been introduced that makes it much easier to remove dents or creases in panels where access to the back side is blocked. The accompanying photos illustrate this new slap-hammer tool that spot welds pins onto the sheetmetal to serve as attachment points for the tool. It accomplishes the same task without making holes in the panel and those attendant problems created. See the photo sequence for additional details on the repair procedures.

Straightening out this hit-and-git parking lot mishap to the wheel opening restored the sheetmetal to like-new appearance. A number of power tools were used, but muscle operated versions can achieve the same results. However, buying one of the panel straightening devices would be cost prohibitive for anyone other than a pro. Local rental places may already have them if your budget is not set up to handle the $300 price range that these list for.

Minor sheetmetal repair is something that is more labor-intensive than demanding of professional bodyworking skills. Making these types of repairs is something most do-it-yourselfers should try. New tools like this panel straightener can make the finished job look better and last longer. So, go out and get rid of those ugly wrinkles.

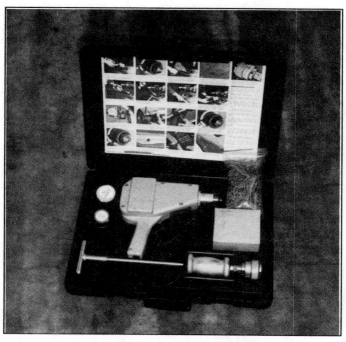

*This new tool spot welds pins to sheetmetal as attachment points for a slap-hammer type puller. This eliminates having to make holes in a blind panel where a dent has to be pulled out.*

*Begin the repair by removing all paint or fillers, down to the bare metal. Don't strip too large an area.*

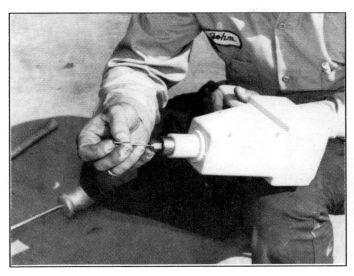

New style of dent puller spot welds pins to metal. Pin resembles a nail and is loaded in a spot welder, pointed end first.

The electrically powered spot welder attaches pull pins along the lowest point of crease or dent in panel.

A series of pins are spaced far enough apart to allow the attachment of slap-hammer style puller.

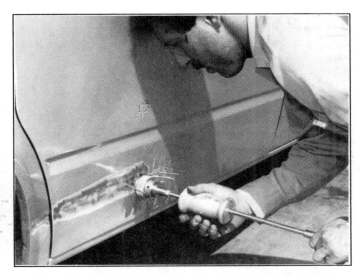

Here weighted slide is being used to pull dent. Weight impacts flange on handle when slid sharply outward on tool shaft.

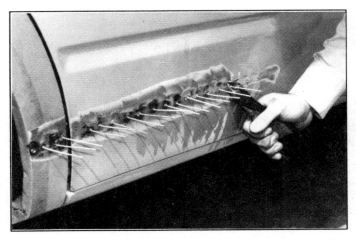

Pins are snipped off at their base with diagonal cutters after the dent in sheetmetal has been pulled out.

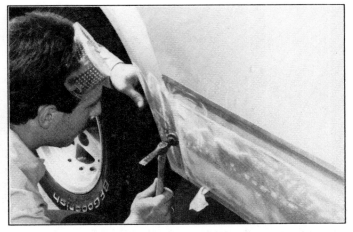

Remaining portion of pins is knocked off with coarse disc sander, then high spots worked flat with body hammer.

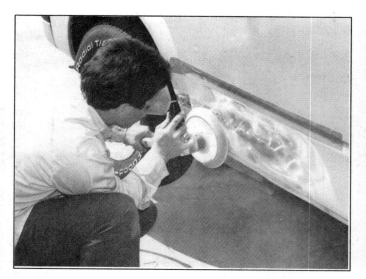

When satisfied with flatness of panel, sand entire area in vicinity of work site in preparation for applying body filler.

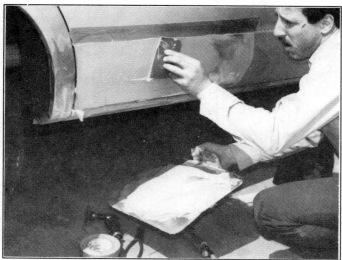

Duct tape protects paint areas from application of body filler. Smooth on an even layer, following body contours as closely as possible to reduce sanding.

Sand work area with large flat sanding tool to maintain a flat surface without high and low spots in the filler.

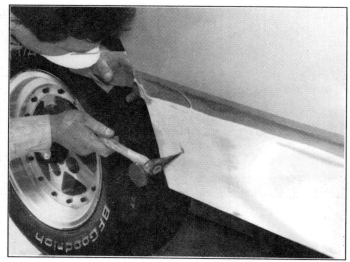

Sanding exposes high spots in metal panel. Use pick end of hammer to flatten them level with panel surface. Add more filler and sand as needed.

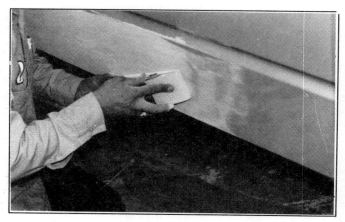

Tape placed along body contour line acts as guide for duplicating edge. Attention to these details creates top quality repair.

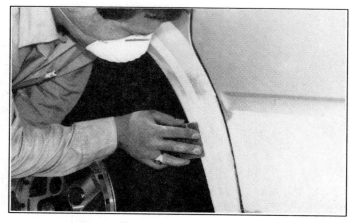

Block sand filler, feathering edges gradually into panel. Prepare surface for priming and finished paint.

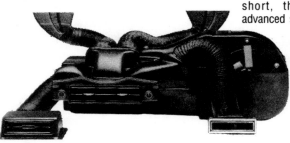

BY JIM CLARK

# FIBERGLASS REPAIR

**I**f you drive a truck that sports fiberglass accessories, you've probably experienced the slow torture of one of these pieces coming in contact with something solid. If you haven't you probably will, and it's not much fun. No matter how careful you try to be, if you drive on the street enough, odds are that something is going to break.

The scenario goes something like this: You ease your low slung cruiser ever so slowly out of a driveway that dips abruptly into the street. As you reach the bottom of the dip, a sound far more excruciating than nails on a chalk board drowns out the stereo and reaches your ears. "SCRRRAAAPE." Time seems to slow down, intensifying the pain. But, you're past the point of no return, all you can do is continue in the same direction and hope for the best.

Climbing out of the truck to survey the damage, your worst suspicions are confirmed. Hanging from the front of the truck is a cracked and scraped air dam. What will you do? A new air dam is out of the budget and your insurance deductible is too high to cover the damage. If the damage isn't too severe however (the air dam doesn't look like it's been through WWIII), you can repair it yourself at home for only a few bucks. The accompanying photo sequence shows how to accomplish this using an inexpensive fiberglass repair kit from your local auto parts or department store.

You can buy all the materials separately, but we've found that one of these simple kits is generally less expensive and has everything the do-it-yourselfer will need. We choose to use a basic Bondo brand fiberglass repair kit since it is a readily available brand name. The kit ran us $5.99 at a local discount parts store, and the only thing it didn't include was plastic body filler for the finishing work.

You won't need any elaborate tools to repair damaged fiberglass. Just a few common tools such as an electric drill with a coarse sanding disc, an

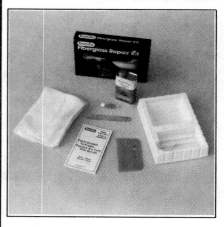

*This basic fiberglass repair kit from Bondo retails for under $10, and has everything you'll need for a complete repair job.*

*Fiberglass matte is cut to cover the size of the damaged area. Depending on the break, you may need several pieces.*

*After removing the damaged part from the truck, a coarse sanding disc is used to knock down the rough edges and remove paint.*

*Using a clean container, thoroughly mix the fiberglass resin and catalyst per the manufacturer's instructions.*

*Soak the fiberglass matte cloth in the resin, making certain the matte is thoroughly saturated. Be sure to wear rubber gloves for this part of the repair. Once dry, resin is hard to remove from skin.*

Apply the matte to the back side of the damaged area. Use a squeegee to remove excess resin from the area. Allow this to cure. Depending on the break, you may need to build up several layers for strength.

Turn the part over. If there is a piece of the 'glass missing, you will have to build up the hole with matte. Here we were able to save the broken piece and fill the cracks with resin.

Once the area is completely repaired, allow the resin to cure. You can then sand or grind off excess resin. Work from coarse to fine paper, following the contour of the surface.

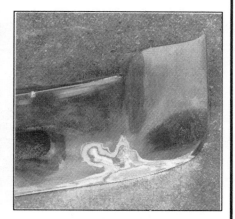

The fiberglassing part of the repair process is now complete. Notice how little finishing body filler will be needed. The repair is very strong, and should hold up for years to come.

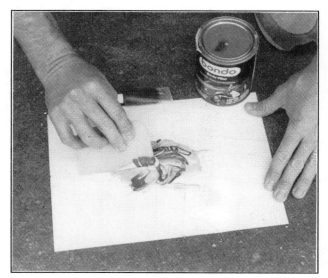

The next step is to finish the area with plastic body filler. This photo shows mixing of the filler and hardener per the instructions on the container. Mix thoroughly until it reaches a uniform color.

assortment of various grades of sandpaper, body filler and sandable primer. That's about it for materials.

The first step is to remove the damaged glass from the vehicle. This type of repair works equally as well on flares, wings and rear pans. We choose to illustrate the how-to process with a front air dam since they are the most vulnerable and likely to come in contact with foreign objects. The repair process can be handled in a Saturday afternoon, if you take your time and do it right the first time around.

Using a coarse sanding disc on an electric drill, grind down the damaged area to bare fiberglass, removing the paint and providing a clean working surface. Next, cut a piece of fiberglass matte slightly larger than the area to be repaired.

Mix the fiberglass resin included in the kit with the hardener, per the instructions on the package. Once thoroughly mixed, soak the cut piece of matte in the resin. We suggest that you use protective rubber gloves when working with fiberglass since it is hard to remove from skin. Place the saturated piece of matte on the backside of the air dam, covering the damaged area. Use a plastic body filler squeegee to remove excess resin. Allow this first layer of glass to cure for about an hour.

Turn the air dam over and work the front side of the damaged area. If the fiberglass is thick, you will probably have to build up successive layers of matte and resin until the area is filled. Cut the pieces of matte just large enough to fill in the damaged area. Sand the area flush with the surrounding surface. Once you have the broken area filled and patched with matte and resin, finish as you would any other bodywork.

Plastic body filler is used to fill in low spots that couldn't be worked out with fiberglass, as we've illustrated in the accompanying photos. Once it has cured, prime the area and block sand to a smooth finish. If there are any pinholes or minor imperfections, use spot putty to repair. All that is left is to prime again and prepare for paint. Paint the fiberglass part to match the truck, then reinstall.

We've included a fairly detailed photo sequence to illustrate how easy fiberglass is to work with. Take your time and don't try to rush the project. In a matter of an afternoon you can have the truck back on the road looking as good as new, and for considerably less than buying a new part. Just watch out for those monster speed bumps that were recently put in at the mall.

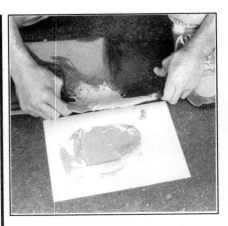

*Using a plastic body filler squeegee, apply the body filler to the area that needs finishing. Don't apply the filler too heavily because you will just be causing yourself extra work.*

*After allowing the filler to cure, use a cheese grater file to remove the excess filler. This is easiest if the filler is not completely set up. Be careful not to remove too much.*

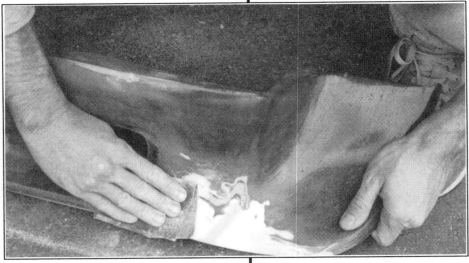

*Sand the repaired area smooth. It may be necessary to add another coat of plastic filler to obtain a smooth, flush surface. Use spot putty to fill any pinholes or minor irregularities.*

*Below- Here is the finished product, primered and ready for paint. Notice how well contour of the repaired area matches the original fiberglass surface. Nobody will ever know it was broken. This air dam can now be painted to match the truck and then installed.*

*Once the bodywork is complete, shoot the repaired area with sandable primer and prepare for paint. Then simply paint the piece before reinstalling it on the truck.*

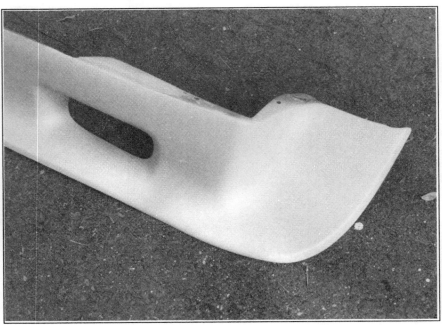

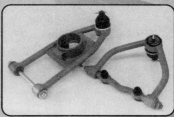

BY JIM CLARK

# FRENCHED TAILLIGHTS

Sometimes the simplest modifications are the most effective. Elimination of headlight and taillight bezels and frenching the lenses into the sheetmetal has become a standard custom feature on custom projects. To illustrate this, we followed the process of frenching the taillights on this '68 El Camino. With a minimum of sheetmetal work and with absolutely no changes to the wiring or electrical components, the appearance of the rear of the truck was substantially changed. The entire operation took less than a day to complete, and since all of the major components are stock the list of needed materials was minimal.

What was done was to set the stock lenses into the corners of the quarter panels at an angle. The first step was to enlarge the stock taillight cavities enough to position the taillight lenses where desired. Cardboard templates were then designed to set the lenses back in the cavity at the desired position. The cardboard templates were then transferred to sheetmetal and cut out using electric shears. Then the edge of a work table was used to form the necessary 90° bends in the new sheetmetal housings.

With the new frenched housings fabricated, they were positioned in place and then welded solid, using a wire feed MIG welder. The housings were made from 20-gauge sheetmetal, which approximates the thickness of the stock sheetmetal in the El Camino's quarter panels. Matching the thickness of the pieces to be welded together greatly reduces the chances of warpage.

After the new lens housings are welded in place, finishing the job is simply a matter of taking care of a few details. The welded area will probably need a light grinding before applying a thin coat of plastic filler and then priming. The housings must be drilled for the sheetmetal screws that hold the lenses in place. In this installation, VW fender welting was used between the taillights and the new sheetmetal as a finishing touch.

*To give the rearend of this '68 El Camino a custom look, the owner decided to french the stock taillight lenses into the quarter-panels.*

*Stock taillight openings were enlarged and then cardboard was used to mock up the new housings necessary for setting the lenses back into the openings.*

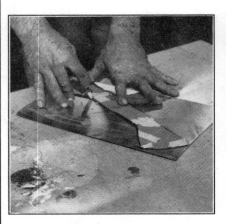

*Once satisfied with the cardboard templates, they were transferred to 20-gauge sheetmetal.*

*Electric shears were then used to cut the sheetmetal to size.*

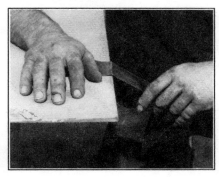

*The edge of a work table can be used to form the two 90° bends needed in the new housings.*

*The new housings were then mocked into place. You may want to mock-up both sides at this point (before any welding) to make sure that side-to-side symmetry is retained.*

*A wire feed MIG welder was used to tack and then weld solid the new taillight housings to the existing El Camino sheetmetal.*

*After all welding is complete, the reworked area is given a light grinding with an air powered die grinder.*

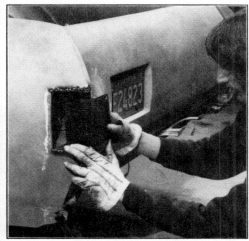

*At this point, the lenses are given a trial fit and the mounting hole placement is marked on the new sheetmetal.*

Although not an earth shattering change, frenched taillights is a back-to-basics customizing trick. It is a simple and neat modification that can be performed on a budget by anyone with basic welding skills.

*Holes for the sheetmetal screws that hold the lenses in place are then drilled.*

*After the lenses are trial mounted, they are removed and a light coat of plastic filler is applied to the area that has been welded.*

*The filler is then shaped, using a cheese grater, and finally a sanding block.*

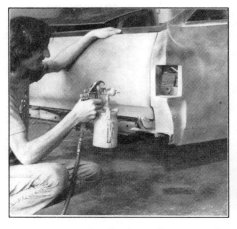

*Spot putty and a final sanding precede a coat of primer. Several coats of light grey primer are applied before a final darker guide coat is sprayed.*

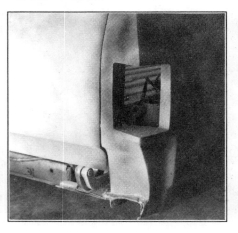

*The finished opening looks like this. It is a very clean and simple modification.*

*The stock taillight lens was then installed for the final time, using Volkswagen fender welting as trim.*

*The finished frenched taillights deviate from stock bodylines just enough to give a modified appearance, yet they still look like they belong. This is clean and simple customizing at its best.*

**BY JIM CLARK**

# Chopping Windshields

Chopping the top on a pickup truck is relatively simple, except for chopping the windshield. Instead of cutting, the glass can be ground down at the top, to reduce the chance of cracking due to stress at the corners. Both ends must be fit properly or the installed unit will break from body twist. Grinding is done with an upright belt sander. Installation takes about 40 hours for experienced pros.

Some shops cut the glass close to the finished size by removing one layer with a glass cutter and sandblasting technique, then cutting the remaining layer with the glass cutting tool. The cuts must be made with no hesitation in the stroke from one side to the other, or cracks can run off into the glass when breaking it off. Final fit with this process is also done by grinding the edge.

Both techniques can result in some broken windshields. A foolproof method of cutting this type of glass has not been perfected for the rod building enthusiast. If you want to chop the top you must consider this risk as part of the cost of the project.

*The finished windshield when reinstalled looks like it came from the factory this way, and with the truck's new lower proportions, it was worth all the effort and expense.*

*Once the sheetmetal work has been completed, the windshield has to be cut to fit the new opening. On most trucks, like this '56 Ford F-100, the bottom edge of the glass should fit into its original stock position. By installing the gasket and positioning it at the bottom, the top can be marked for removal of the excess material.*

*One method likely to achieve success without breaking the glass is the long and tedious task of grinding the top down on a belt sander. This can take up to forty hours, and still could end in disaster if great care is not exercised.*

# TILT FRONT END

**BY JIM CLARK**

**E**arly pickup truck hoods are not noted for their smooth operation or their alignment when closed. After years of use, the situation calls for replacement of the hinges, latches and rubber stops. This, however, only restores it to its original condition. A better alternative might be the conversion to a one-piece tilt front end.

This might seem like a major undertaking, but it isn't such a difficult project. A number of kits have been made to do this, simplifying the conversion. Shown in the accompanying photos are details of the procedures for producing a one-piece tilt front end on a couple of F-100 Ford pickups. The same techniques would work equally as well on other pickup models.

Before removing the complete front end from a running truck, mark a number of reference points on the fenders and hood where they meet. If you have already torn your truck down, it is necessary to temporarily reinstall the hood and fenders to establish your reference points.

Once the points are noted, and the sheetmetal is back out of the way, the radiator support bracketry and rods must be modified. By the way, if you haven't already done so, now is a good time to paint and detail the engine and the forward half of the chassis. From here on out all of it will be visible.

Unfortunately, there is no practical way to build a tilt front end without cutting the fenders. In this case the incisions were made 5-1/4 inches in from the lower rear corner. Because perfect alignment is a must, 3/8-inch holes were drilled in the hood and fenders and 5/16-inch bolts used to provide leeway for final adjustment. The hood and fenders are then bolted together in six

*A tilt front end makes servicing or repair simpler. Shown here are two examples that have both been converted in a similar way, one in a highly detailed form.*

*Both front fenders have to be cut as these were to clear the sides of the cowl when the front end is tilted.*

*When the front fender assembly is bolted together, some bracing should be constructed to support the sheetmetal in the area of the grille. One-inch square thin-wall steel tubing provides strength without adding too much weight to the front end. Small cables act as restraints to tilting.*

places (three on each side) with quarter-inch fiber spacers sandwiched between. Before cinching them up, the reference points should be verified.

The inner fender panels have to be cut to clear the firewall when the front end swings open. A conservative trim will get the job done. Up to this point, all of the cutting, drilling and trimming is done on loose sheetmetal and, for the most part, can be handled alone. But when it is time to reposition the assembly, you'll need the aid of a couple of helpers.

Use a one-inch block between the frame and the gravel pan to align the hood/fender assembly. Mount the hinges on the inner fender panels parallel to the frame.

After they have been secured, check the hood-to-cowl alignment. If all is well, drill two 1/8-inch pilot holes through the frame, then drill them out to 3/8-inch. Use 3/8-inch hardened bolts and self-locking nuts for hinge pins, and large flat washers between the hinges and the frame for bushings.

You may find it necessary to trim a half-inch off the front edge of the crossmember lip, but other than that, it's just a matter of loosening and retightening the nuts and bolts until you're satisfied with the fit of the assembly.

The final operations include the installation of adjustable late model hood bumpers to support the rear of the hood, luggage latches on the fenders to fasten the assembly when it is down, and quarter-inch plastic coated cables to limit forward travel and to support the assembly when it is lifted.

In the accompanying photos, the tilt front end shown is not a manually operated one, but a hydraulically actuated unit. Tilting of the assembly is performed by a 1953-'64 Thunderbird convertible top unit mated to a Mustang convertible top pump. It operates in the same manner as the system did when installed on the original vehicle. When installed as illustrated in the accompanying photos, it tilts the front end to the full extent of its travel, which is almost a full 90°. Regardless of which method is chosen, operation of the tilt front end is a fairly simple matter.

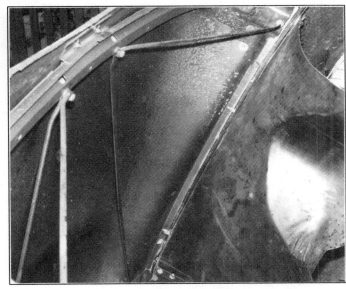

*At least three bolts should be used to hold the assembly together on each side, with fiber spacers sandwiched in between. Two additional support rods should be added to the underside of the hood to provide additional rigidity. When adding the new cross-mounted rods, make sure they clear everything.*

In order for the front end assembly to tilt, the inner fender splash aprons have to be trimmed back as they are in this photo. Some choose to eliminate them entirely, however this is not a very good idea if you drive your truck in adverse weather. Chrome fender welting trims the fender.

This photo of the remaining portion of the fender is still in primer, so you can see more easily how much of it remains bolted to the cowl. The sheetmetal strip added to the lower edge of the fender in this application is designed to fasten it to the tilt unit with a Dzus fastener.

Luggage type over-center clamps are a very inexpensive device used to latch the hood. To prevent the portion of the fender attached to the hood from scratching the cowl when tilting, add a small nylon roller to the bottom edge of the fender as a guide.

These hinges were part of a ready-made kit from SoCal Pickups in Buena Park, California. They are all that is needed to convert to a manual tilt front end. Owner of this truck, Jerry Thompson, fashioned the additional bracket to attach the hydraulic cylinder.

In order to get maximum tilt out of the front end assembly, a 1963-'64 Thunderbird convertible top hydraulic unit is used. With this combination of hinges and brackets, the unit is just the right length for this application.

A bracket must be fabricated to attach the cylinder to the frame, which will position it out far enough to clear the hydraulic line fittings and provide a pivot point with sufficient travel where the cylinder attaches.

Though not absolutely necessary, a centering device to align the tilt assembly will assure a better fit. This molded rubber bumper has a threaded stud which is adjustable, a nut welded to tubing, and flat stock complete bracket.

Receptacle for the hood aligning bumper was machined from aluminum, with a small ramp on the front edge to act as an aligning device for the tilt assembly. Ramp was welded on after the tapered cup was machined.

Looking up from beneath the truck, you can see how the hood-mounted bracket aligns with the cowl receptacle. Some sheetmetal and square tubing were formed into a bracket to mount it to the cowl. Original hood hinge mounting points were used.

Up under the front splash apron is a convenient place to mount the hydraulic pump for the tilting cylinders.

Radiator support rods remain attached to the cowl, but are moved to the radiator support from the valance area.

Tilting is controlled from switch mounted below the dash.

# NEW OLD REPRO PARTS

**BY JOHN LEE**

T here's some good news and some bad when you're considering an old truck as a rod or custom project. The bad news is that, being working vehicles, they've often been used hard with little regard for upkeep, especially when it comes to non-mechanical components.

The good news is that, structurally, they were built tough to take the abuse they got. The other good news is that help for dented and decomposed body parts is now readily available. Several firms are marketing a multitude of replacement parts, some in steel, some in fiberglass.

Among those making products for the popular Ford haulers of the '50s is Gibbon Fiberglass Reproductions. With their parts, you can rebuild or restore '48-'56 pickups or build a radical custom out of a '53-'56 F-100.

The '56 F-100 can be chopped 2 inches without cutting the wraparound windshield, and Gibbon's fiberglass top panel makes the job easier. They also offer stock roof panels for all 4 years, and 3-inch chopped ones for the '53-'55 models. Plus 'glass headliners you can upholster to finish off the truck's interior.

Gibbon replacement fenders are offered in stock configuration for all years, plus F-100 rears widened 3 inches for fat tires. Running boards are stock or smooth, or modified to fit with the widened fenders. They have a fiberglass back cab panel to convert the small window to a big window model.

Rolled front and rear pans, with and without license plate recesses, steel bed side, front and tailgate panels, emblems, weather stripping and many other parts are also in the catalog.

Fiberglass replacement fenders and running boards are being manufactured for popular Chevy pickups, as well. Dixie Truck Works carries them for all models from 1941 through 1959, plus stepside rear fenders for '65 through '72 models. They also have rear quarter panels and tailgate covers for '55-'57 cameos and doors

for 1955 models.

"Our '55-'59 fenders," says Wayne Hearne, "include reinforcement strips like the originals, with glassed-in mounting nuts and holes."

Dixie has reproduced several Chevy truck emblems and, with those of other manufacturers, can cover most emblems and letters for '55 to '72 models.

Coachworks of Yesteryear, in Oakland, Florida, offers a complete fiberglass 1936 Ford pickup kit or turn-key truck. The kit features hand-laid fiberglass components with a primer gelcoat finish. Doors are hung and latched (using a hidden hinge assembly), and a variety of accessories are available, such as Specialty

*Owner Steve Crooks is a Gibbon employee, and his '56 F-100 shows off many of the company's products.*

Power Windows and Classic Instruments components. Original headlamp assemblies and a stainless steel grille insert are ready for delivery. This kit has been engineered for a Ford Ranger chassis, but a reproduction chassis is also part of the company's offering.

Fiberglass replacement rear fenders for '55-'66 Chevy pickups are also manufactured by Bill Walski in Davie, Florida.

Using the Gibbon parts, the F-100 top can be chopped 2 inches without having to cut the windshield, which is a real advantage to the do-it-yourself builder. A replacement rear cab section makes it possible to convert a small rear window cab to a large rear window model.

Fiberglass stepside fenders are available in stock configuration or in 3-inch wider versions to accommodate fat tires. The smooth running boards are also widened to match these extra-wide fenders.

Steve installed '53 headlights in his truck. The front valance is rolled and has recessed licence plate mount.

Repro cargo bed sides and front panel are steel. Rolled rear pan features a recessed license plate area.

A fiberglass headliner insert makes it easy to upholster the overhead space inside the cab.

If you're into earlier trucks, Coachworks of Yesteryear offers 1936 Ford pickup body parts, including a dashboard stuffed with Classic Instruments.

The complete Coachworks of Yesteryear '36 Ford pickup body kit is ready for assembly and installation on a Ford Ranger chassis, or you can order up a turn-key truck on a reproduction chassis.

# LOUVERING

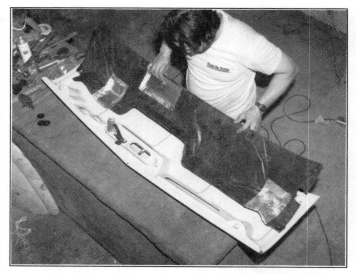

*The hood is unbolted and removed. Next, remove the insulation from the inside of the hood. This is done by popping out the plastic fasteners that hold the insulation in place.*

*Use a good quality paint stripper on the hood, and allow it to penetrate. Much easier to do now than after the louvering process.*

**BY JIM CLARK**

ave you ever considered punching holes in your truck's sheetmetal? Well, if you're looking for a traditional custom treatment that not only looks great but can be functional as well, that may just be the thing to do.

Louvers have been part of the custom car and hot rod scene for many years. Of late, louvers have made a strong resurgence as one of the trick things to do to a vehicle. The process of stamping a series of louvers in a sheetmetal surface such as a hood was originally done to ventilate the engine compartment or other area of the vehicle that was likely to retain heat. If your truck has a problem with overheating, you should seriously consider the practical function of louvers.

For the most part though, louvers are punched these days just for looks. The process is a fairly simple one. Louvers are punched by a louvering press, which stamps sheetmetal in a louver-shaped die. The die shears the metal on one side and stretches the metal into the shape of a louver. Simple as it may be, there are important things to watch for when buying louvering services.

The majority of louver presses in operation are the old style foot operated presses. The physical energy needed to punch out a louver is supplied by the operator's leg muscles. If you run a professional operation and punch hundreds of louvers every day,

you can imagine the drawbacks to this type of press. A better alternative is the heavy duty hydraulic press that delivers a consistent and uniformly punched louver every time. Since the operator doesn't have to step down on a pedal and physically punch out the louver, he is free to concentrate on the exact alignment and position of each louver.

When looking for a shop to do a louvering job, try to talk to other customers and see if they were happy with the service and quality of job they received. Also take a close look at some samples of louvers the shop has punched. Every louver should be uniform. The metal around the actual louver should not show any signs of distortion, rippling, creasing or stretching. These are signs of a worn or poorly aligned louver die.

Price is also an important consideration when shopping for louvers. Prices span a wide range, you should expect charges anywhere from 50¢ to $2.50 per louver. Also ask for the cost of the complete job. Some shops will tack on extra charges for paint stripping, cutting and welding hood braces back in, and other types of prep work. While other shops will include these services in the per-louver price.

As you can see by the accompanying photos, many sizes of louvers are available, as well as the new square style louvers. The angular lines of square louvers go well with many later model cars and trucks with angular lines. Since the Chevy van hood seen in the photo sequence has a more rounded overall design, traditional rounded louvers were chosen.

There are an infinite number of ways to layout a louvering job. Many people choose to design their own pattern. If you do, sketch it out on a piece of paper, then talk to the louver press operator about spacing and other necessary requirements. Most shops also have photo albums of louvering jobs they have done in the past. This is a good way to get ideas for your truck. If you don't have any idea what you want, you also

have the option of having the shop or press operator design the pattern. When you punch as many louvers as the pros do, you have a pretty good idea of what will work and what won't.

The accompanying photo sequence should give a good idea of what is involved in a typical hood louvering job. There is a lot more to it than just punching the holes. In fact, the actual punching of the louvers is the easy part of the job.

*With a scraper or putty knife, scrape away blistered paint. Remaining paint, if any, may need to be sanded off.*

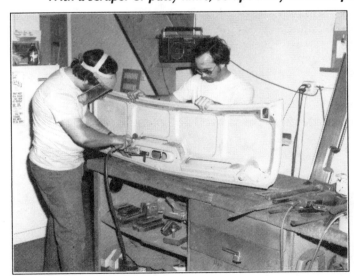

*Carefully cut away the inside hood bracing with a carbide wheel. Be sure to wear eye protection.*

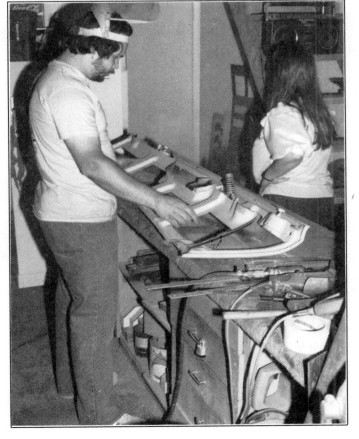

*Carefully remove the bracing. This section will be reinstalled later.*

The inside of the hood is sprayed with marking die. Next scribe the louver pattern on this surface.

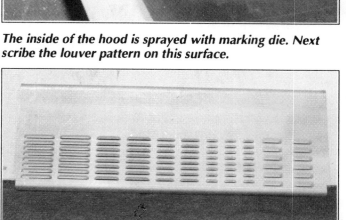

This tailgate shows the wide range of styles and sizes available. At the far right are the new square style louvers, popular with owners of vehicles having angular lines. The rest show different sizes of rounded louvers.

This is the part of the press that does the actual shearing and pressing of the louver, the two-piece die.

With the pattern laid out, the actual punching of the louvers is the fun and easy part of the job. Proper alignment is critical though.

Louver presses have come a long way. Many shops still use the old style foot operated press, but the one shown here at Seemore Louver Co., Fullerton, California is their own handbuilt hydraulic press.

Sand off the die (paint will not adhere) and weld the brace back in place. Avoid metal distortion by not concentrating heat in one spot.

After welding the brace in place, grind the welds smooth. Make certain that this bare metal surface receives primer and paint as soon as possible, to avoid rust. Shoot the entire hood with primer. Primer alone will not completely seal metal, repaint surface soon.

The hood can now be reinstalled on the truck. Make sure the hood is properly aligned before closing. The completed louvering job adds a custom look and also helps ventilation.

# FILLING AN F-100 COWL VENT

**BY RON CERIDONO**

H ave you ever had a project that just got out of control? This started out as just your basic driver type F-100, but something happened along the way. You see, I asked this friend of mine, Doug Morris, owner of Classic Auto Body, to help with the

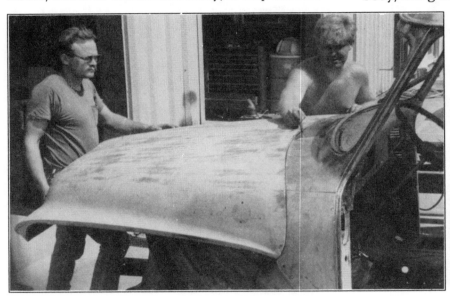

*With Doug Morris holding the hood, Tony LePore marks the shape of the F-100's hood on the pattern that will be used for cutting out a sheet metal patch. The original vent didn't fit the cowl particularly well, so a filler piece was cut from sheetmetal and formed to fit the hole, rather than just welding the stock vent closed.*

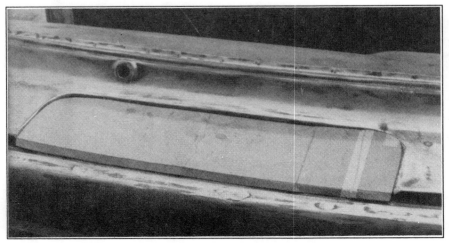

body work. I'd say, "Looks good to me," but Doug would shake his head, run his hand over the body and mumble things.

As the cab got straighter, we decided to get a little bit trick and fill the cowl vent. Now, on this particular body, filling the cowl is not as easy as most early cars because the vent rolls down in front where it fits the back of the hood. Under the watchful eye of a rather fussy bodyman, I decided to give the cowl vent a try.

First, a heavy paper pattern of the hole to be filled was made. The pattern was cut large enough to allow the front edge to bend over the vertical portion of the cowl.

Next, the pattern was transferred to sheet stock. The difficult part was going to be bending the lip on the front of the filler piece, and at the same time, matching the curve of the hood. The solution to that problem came in the form of a piece of scrap metal. An angle iron form was made that copied the hood shape. A little heat from a torch, and a few not so delicate whacks from a hammer, and the angle iron was shaped to match the back of the hood. The sheet stock could now be bent over the angle iron.

After cutting the sheet metal to size (allowing a little extra so the lip could be trimmed to fit) the filler piece was clamped to the angle, and the front edge was gently hammered into shape. The secret here is to go slowly, and work from side to side.

Once the front edge was bent, it was time for a trial fit. A little trimming was required, but after that was done, it fit perfectly.

A wire-feed welder was used to tack

*A pattern was cut to size, then the front edge was formed to fit the vertical section of the cowl that will be filled.*

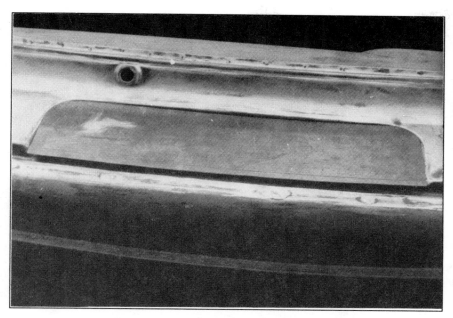

the filler in. Then it was time to check the fit again. The hood was installed to make sure the hood/cowl gap was consistent. Everything looked great, so lots of tack welds were made, then the spaces between the tacks were welded. Taking your time and skipping around to avoid concentrating heat in one area is important.

After some light grinding of the welds, a thin layer of body filler was applied. Some primer-surfacer, a little block sanding, and we were ready for paint.

Filling the cowl vent really cleans up the appearance of an F-100, and besides, it gives you a great excuse to install air conditioning.

*The shape of the pattern was then transferred to sheet stock. Arrow points out curved line where the filler will be bent at a 90° angle.*

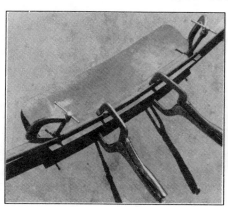

*A piece of scrap angle iron was curved to match the cowl and hood, then the filler piece was formed over it. The sheetmetal was hammered over the angle slowly and carefully to curve the lip.*

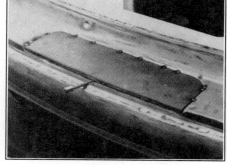

*The filler piece was supported from inside the cab and shimmed until it matched the shape of the cowl. It was then tack welded in place with a wire-feed machine. A punch was used to support the filler in the center until the front edge could be tacked.*

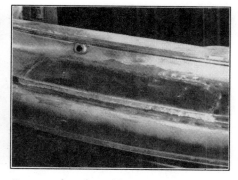

*Repeated tack welds were made until short beads could be run without fear of warpage. A disc grinder was then used to dress the welds.*

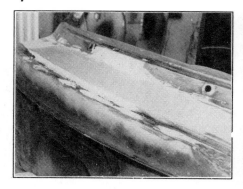

*A thin coat of filler was applied all the way across the cowl. As the shape of the filler and cowl were quite close, most of the filler was sanded off.*

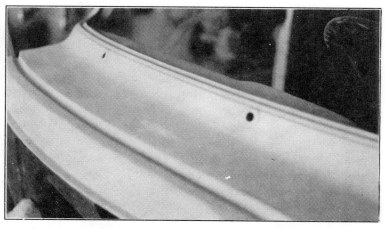

*Several doses of primer-surfacer were applied, then the surface was block sanded. Smoothed-up cowl looks so right, very few admirers notice it's been filled.*

# HEADLINER FOR YOUR HAULER

**BY JIM CLARK**

**T**he headliner is one item most rod builders shy away from installing, thinking it an impossible task. Headliners in cars are often large and intricate, but the ones in pickups should be far less intimidating. To illustrate this, we followed the installation of a headliner in the popular '56 Ford F-100 pickup.

The project begins with removal of the cardboard insert that is standard on the pickup. A tacking strip is cut from heavy door panel backing composition board, then drilled and pop riveted to the sheetmetal ridge around the roof inner panel. To provide a finished edge around the headliner, a welting strip is stapled or tacked around the entire opening.

In this model of pickup, there are already three headliner bows running from the front to rear of the top. They fit into holes drilled in metal supports in the cab roof. The Naugahyde was cut off the roll in one piece, large enough for the entire headliner. Three channels to hold the bows in the headliner were created by wrapping the material around the bows and sewing alongside them. The center bow was measured and marked out on the material before they were sewn. All three bows were mounted and stapling of the headliner began. The center bow is lined up on-center first and the headliner stapled along above the windshield. Smoothing and stapling continues around the top until it is all in place. A portable heat gun helps to draw the material in place and aids in removing wrinkles. All the excess material is trimmed off and a molding strip stapled over the exposed edge. This molding strip is folded over to cover up its staples.

Behind the seat is an area that contains the gas tank and a lot of ugly body seams, so inserts are cut from door panel board and covered with Naugahyde to match the headliner. These are held in place by metal screws. The headliner is held in place around the rear window with good fabric adhesive. To complete the job, all that is left is reinstallation of the rear window. It is held in place by the rubber molding and is actually quite easy to install. The trick to it is tying a small rope or cord around the

*Headliners like these add greatly to the appearance of pickup interiors, and they contribute to reducing the noise level. Though not usually thought of as a do-it-yourself project, the task is well within the scope of many rod builders.*

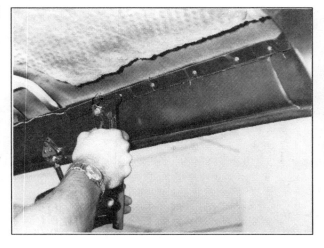

*Originally, this pickup had no headliner, just a cardboard insert. A tacking strip had to be pop riveted to the metal lip around the opening, to staple in the new Naugahyde headliner. Holes are drilled to accommodate pop rivets.*

Matching Naugahyde welting is stapled to the tacking strip to provide a finished edge around headliner. Staples are spaced about 1-inch apart.

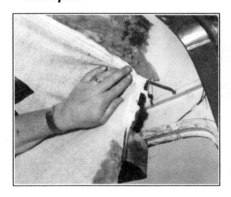

Three top bows provide support for headliner. They run across top inside of cab from front to rear. Bows push into holes in roof molding seams. Note addition of heat absorbing and sound deadening insulation between the top and headliner.

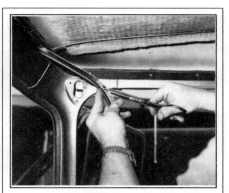

A trick used by upholsterers to make a smooth fit around corners is cutting small darts in the material where it will not show. Staples should be spaced closer in these areas to assure they do not come loose.

Bows run through sleeves sewn in one-piece headliner. Position of the bows is maintained by stapling headliner to tacking strip. Another trick to ease installation is wiring the two outer bows to each side of the cab. This stretches the headliner into position.

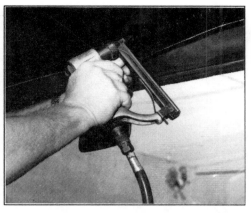

Stapling begins in the center of windshield at center top bow. Once secured, stapling is completed at one side, working out wrinkles and gaps as you go. Smaller staples are used here and spaced closer together.

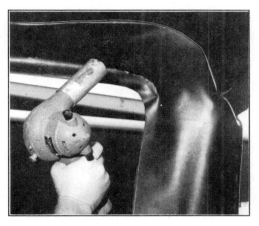

Naugahyde can be worked much easier with the aid of a heat gun. Care must be exercised not to get the gun too close, because the vinyl coating will melt under too much heat.

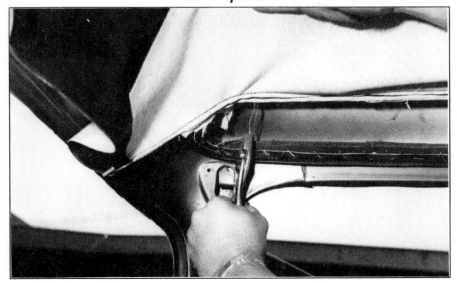

outside of the molding, putting the window in place, and then pulling the rope out from under the lip on the rubber molding, snapping it in place.

The pop riveter and staple gun have both simplified many upholstering jobs, making them possible for the non-professional, even though they were not formerly do-it-yourself projects. Armed with the knowledge of how it's done should make it much easier to find someone who can do the job right, if you don't feel like tackling it yourself.

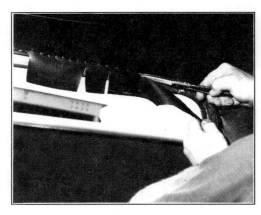

*Excess material should be trimmed off, being sure it is cut back past edge of welting strip. Edge should not be doubled under when stapling, because it would create an unsightly bulge around headliner.*

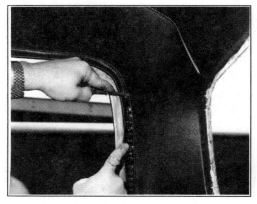

*Trim molding is stapled around edge of headliner, then folded over and locked to cover staples. Upholstery adhesive holds material to lip around rear window opening.*

*Area behind the seat is finished off by adding Naugahyde-covered composition board panels. They are held in place by metal screws in body molding flange.*

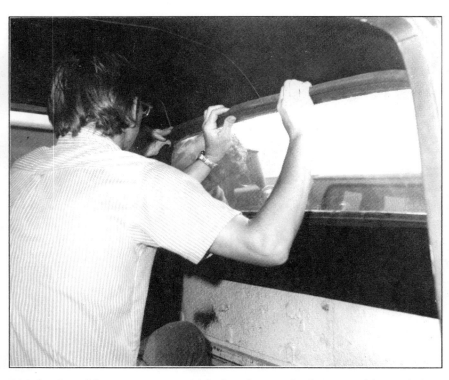

*Seat back cushion covers exposed fuel tank, so only short panel is needed under rear window. Window with rubber molding is set over lower knife edge in opening.*

*Replacement of the rear window completes the installation. Rubber molding is being pulled through into place by cord tied around molding prior to setting in place.*

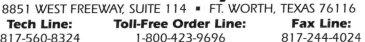

BY JOHN LEE

# 59-MINUTE TONNEAU COVER

Tonneau is a French word meaning "cask" which somehow came into use to refer to the passenger compartment of early automobiles. The tonneau (the proper French pronunciation is tu-NO) cover was popularized by the sports car set, who snapped fabric over their open cockpits to protect them from dust, rain and sun.

Today, the term is most commonly applied to pickup bed covers. Pickup tonneau covers are a specialty at Rob Penna's Lakewood Auto Upholstery, 7601 West Colfax Ave., Lakewood, CO 80215; (303) 238-8364. He's made so many of them, in fact, that he bet one of his employees he could whip one up from start to finish, single handedly, in less than an hour.

Actually, this job took longer because we kept stopping him to shoot pictures and ask questions. But the point is, this is neither a complicated nor time-consuming job. It does, however, require the use of a commercial sewing machine. Your wife's home model just isn't going to make it through three layers of vinyl.

If you're going to tackle this project yourself, look into renting a commercial machine for long enough to do the necessary stitching, plus any other upholstery sewing that could be done at the same time. Otherwise, pay your local trimmer to do the sewing for you. Buying supplies from him may help make him receptive. Even if you decide to have him do the whole thing, it shouldn't be too expensive. As an example, Lakewood Auto Upholstery's plain pickup tonneau covers start at $125.

The material Penna recommends is Arctic brand 40-oz. expanded vinyl with a 100% polyester back. It comes in a 54-inch width in nine standard colors. You'll need five yards to complete a full-sized pickup bed cover. This material is flame retardant and will withstand temperatures down to -30° without cracking.

Here are the other materials and

*Place the aluminum slider rail across the front of the bed and mark it at the inside of the bed rails, then cut the rail to length. The rail comes in 65 inch lengths, which should be just right for standard pickups. Center the rail on the front lip of the bed and drill a 9/64" hole about 4 inches in from each end, and one in the center. Attach the rail to the bed with sheetmetal screws.*

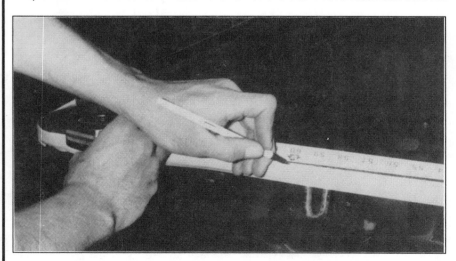

*Run a strip of 3/4" masking tape along both sides of the bed rail and across the tailgate. This gives you a surface to mark on and prevents paint scratches. Measure and mark on the tape where snaps will go. The first snap should be about 1 inch back from the front corner. Space the others at intervals from 4 to 7 inches, whatever figure works out evenly.*

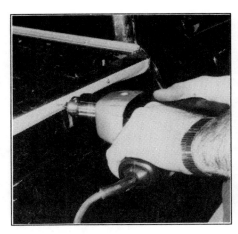

Drill a 9/64" hole at each mark on the tape. On this type of bed rail, the snap hole goes in the center of the rail. On a fleetside, center the snap at least 3/4" down from the top edge for strength. Place snaps on either side of the back corners, not directly on the corner. This gives the cover a place to break, making it easier to unsnap and lower the tailgate. Remove the tape after drilling, then attach the male snap pieces with the pop rivet tool.

The two halves of material are placed face to face and edge to edge. Then they are sewn together about 1 inch in from the edge.

The length of the pickup bed is measured. That figure is halved and one inch added to give the measurement from the center seam to the front and back ends of the cover. This line is marked across in chalk. Another chalk line is marked at one end of the cover 2 inches outside the first mark.

Beginning with a 5-yard length of vinyl 54 inches wide, Rob cuts it in half. These halves will then be joined together, side by side. The reason is, good quality vinyl material stretches only one direction, side-to-side. We want our tonneau cover to stretch the long way, front to back when installed on the truck.

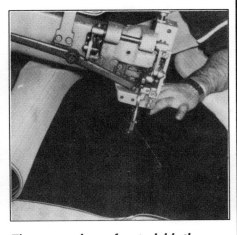

The upper piece of material is then folded back over, top side out, and the seam is top-stitched, sewn on the outside, or top.

tools you'll need: A 65-inch aluminum slider rail (available at a mobile home/camper supply outlet or from an upholstery supplier), shears, electric drill with 9/64" bit, steel tape measure, masking tape, file, hack saw, pop rivet gun and 1/8" x1/4" rivets, snap installation tool (inexpensive ones, or an attachment to fit your Vise-Grip pliers are available at a hardware store), general trim adhesive in aerosol can or brush-on form, sheetmetal screws, and three-piece snaps (cap, socket and body-side). Most tools and materials can be secured at a hardware store, but some may have to come from an upholstery supply house.

Take your time, measure carefully, and follow the accompanying step-by-step photos to make a tonneau cover for your truck. It will improve the appearance and increase security by keeping whatever you carry in the bed out of sight. As a bonus, you can expect gas mileage to improve because air flowing over the cab will not be trapped by the tailgate.

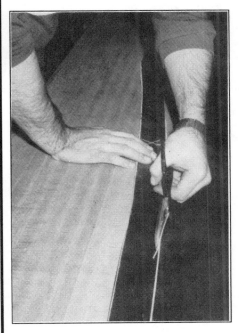

This 2 inch strip is cut off and trimmed to the exact width of the slide rail. This will be the welt to secure the tonneau in the front rail.

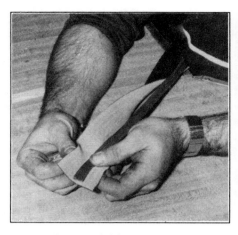

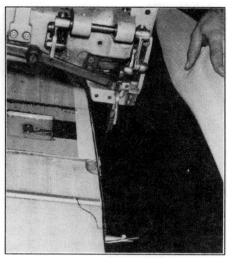

Seat welt material is used as a filler for the tonneau welt. The welt material is sewn into the fold in the vinyl strip.

Sew the welt onto the front edge of the cover on the outside (color side). Fold the front edge of the cover under and sew the full width, making a double row of stitches to hold the welt securely to the cover.

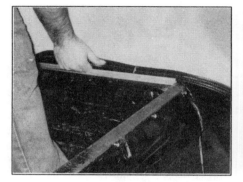

Now you can slip the welt into the slider rail. The aluminum slider rail gives a smooth, secure anchor for the front of the tonneau.

A helper is needed to pull the cover snug over the bed while the location of each snap is marked with chalk. All four corners are marked with chalk diagonally, between the snaps on either side of the corner.

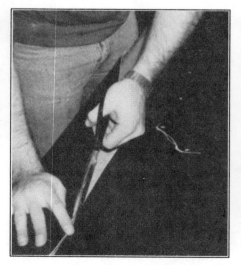
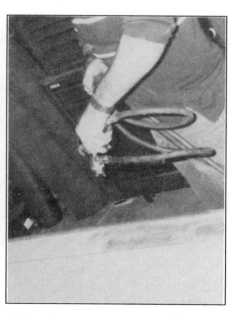

The corner lines mark the edge of the finished cover. With your straight-edge, make a chalk line 2 inches outside these marks. This leaves an edge to fold over for reinforcement.

Cut the material at these outer lines on both sides and the rear edge. Turn the cover over and mark a line 4 inches from the edge on each side. This line is a guide to which each edge will fold in.

Cover this 4 inch strip with general trim adhesive. Penna has it in a spray gun, you'll probably use an aerosol can.

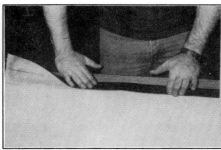

Fold the edge over to the guide line and press firmly into place.

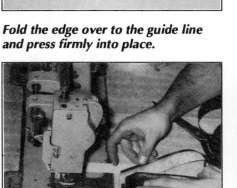

Now, a vinyl binding is sewn onto the edge all around. Sewing of the tonneau is now complete, and only the installation of snaps remains.

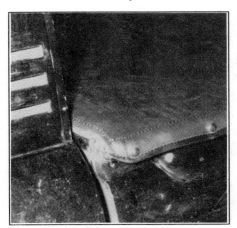

This is how the front corners should look when finished. Note the minimum of distortion between snaps, the sign of a good, tight job.

The finished tonneau cover gives this truck a smooth, clean look. If done correctly, a tonneau cover should look as if it has a board underneath supporting it!

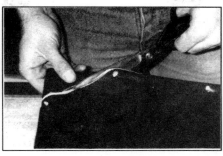

After all three edges have been folded and glued, cut the corners on the chalk lines.

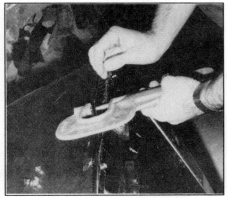

Put the cover back on the bed and pull it tight over the tailgate. Using the snap installation tool and self-punching snap caps and sockets, install the rearmost snap on each side rail first. Then go to the outer snaps on the tailgate, followed by the center and remaining tailgate snaps. Now recheck all other snap locations and remark them if necessary.

With the machine set about 1-1/2 inches from the edge, the cover is sewn around all three edges.

Moving to the middle of each side, install snaps, working from the center to each end. Adjust as necessary to keep a smooth, tight edge.

## BY STEVE DEMAICO

*Carolina Custom Machine*

# TAILGATE COVER

**W**hat we have done here is to give a custom appearance to a stock tailgate. Initially, the idea was to cut the center out of the tailgate and insert a flat louvered panel. Realizing that the welding involved would create some unwanted warpage and require some body work in hard to reach places, we took some careful measurements and chose the following method instead.

The plan was to insert a panel, but to weld it in places easily accessible to body work with the least amount of warpage — around the outside edges. A flat panel could have been made, but would have changed the features of the tailgate. A pattern was cut out and bent to fit the contour of the tailgate, with lips all around the outside edge to weld to the gate. These can be easily ground and filled and there should be no warpage on the inner parts of the insert. The louvers will provide a custom touch.

The latches had to be removed because they were in the way of inserting the panel (they are welded on the inside of the gate). After drilling the spotwelds out and cutting the welds, some shortie brackets were made up to weld inside the outer lip of the gate. This also cleans up the appearance of the gate as well as providing room for the insert.

*The subject for this project is a tailgate from a 1986 Chevy stepside pickup.*

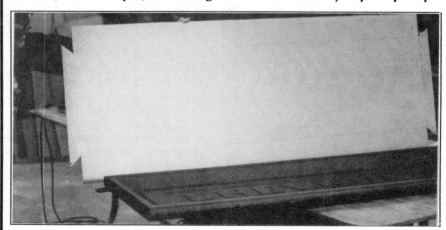

*After careful measurement, a pattern was made which was transferred to 22-gauge sheetmetal. This is done in such a way that the new piece will fit "inside" the original tailgate.*

*Before anything else was done, the flat piece of metal was given 75 louvers, following a theme carried over to the hood as well.*

*Every sheetmetal shop has plenty of tools. The brake is used to make sharp bends at each side, then top and bottom.*

*Top and bottom lips are bent, and where they meet the angled side piece, a bit of welding is needed.*

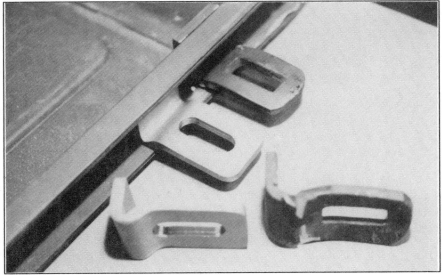

*The factory brackets stick through the tailgate and must be removed for the new panel. Shorty brackets can be made from bar stock and welded to the outside of tailgate side.*

*The finished insert in place, awaiting welding. This makes a quick and low cost way to customize any pickup. Obviously, any variation in the louver pattern will alter the final appearance.*

**BY JIM CLARK**

# EARLY CHEVY DOOR LATCHES

W e all know that mechanical parts wear out with extended use. Friction and the laws of physics take their toll on critical parts of a truck that you may never have considered. Owners of 1955-1959 Chevy and GMC pickups know this problem all too well. GM didn't skimp in those days when they built truck doors. They are very heavy by today's standards. But, after a quarter century of use, the lower hinge is generally well worn, causing severe door alignment problems.

The hinge is easy to replace or rebuild with a kit, but a greater problem is the damage caused by the worn out latch. The '55 through '59 latch lock mechanisms wear out as a result of the misaligned door. Until recently, replacement latches were expensive and hard to come by, so most owners resorted to replacing the latch with a rebuilt unit, or paying a premium for the NOS (new old stock) part.

Specialty parts houses have solved this problem by having these hard to find door latches reproduced. The new latch mechanisms look just like the NOS part, yet are stronger. The new latches are also less expensive than rebuilt or NOS latches. They retail for about $50 each and no exchange is required.

As you can see from the accompanying photo installation sequence, installing new door latches in a '55-'59 Chevy or GMC pickup (or panel) is a simple process. If the latch failed due to improper door alignment, you should also replace the hinges and possibly the striker plate. Making your door operate like new is a simple Saturday morning project.

The first step in changing the door latch and lock mechanism is to remove the inside door latch handle and the window crank handle from the door. This is a very simple process and should take just a few minutes to complete.

Next, remove the inner door panel from the truck. This is done by removing the series of Phillips head screws around the perimeter of the panel. With the screws removed, you should be able to pop the panel off.

With the inner door panel removed, you can see the door latch mechanism. This latch is worn out due to alignment problems from a worn lower door hinge.

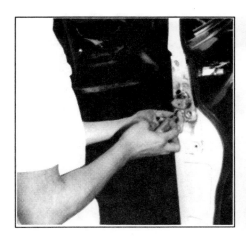

Remove the door latch by removing the three screws that secure it in place. The mechanism is detached from the actuating arm by turning it so the oblong hole lines up with the pin.

Once in place, reinstall the three mounting screws. The new latch will make your door operate like new. You may also need to replace a worn hinge if that was the cause of the latch failure in the first place.

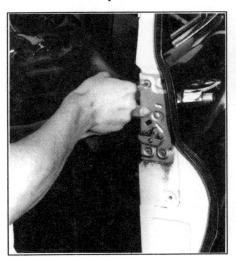

In this shot you can see how the latch releases from the actuating arm. With the old part removed, you can install the new replacement part by reversing the previous steps. Slide the pin into the actuating arm and align with mounting holes.

Left- Tighten down the three screws that hold the door latch in place. Check to make sure the latch operates properly before installing the door panel. Slide the handle on the shaft and try the latch by closing the door. Remove the handle.

Left- Next, reinstall the inner door panel. It is held in place with thirteen Phillips head screws. All that is left is to install the window crank handle and the door latch handle.

The last step is to install both the door handle and the window crank. Make sure they are in the same position as the other door. That's all there is to it. Your '55-'59 Chevy door will work like new.

BY JIM CLARK

# F-100 DOOR LATCHES

**M**uch of the work that must be done when renovating an older car or truck is simply manual labor. Pounding out dents, stripping old paint and repairing rust damage comprise the bulk of it. Some components are simply beyond repair, though. Items such as the door regulators on the 1953-'56 Ford F-100 pickups.

Three areas on the mechanism are prone to suffering the ravages of time and extensive use — the two actuating springs and the door handle mounting shaft. The springs either lose their tensile strength or succumb to rust. Damage to the shaft comes from use and even misuse, however. The splined teeth which engage the corresponding ones inside the door handle get stripped off.

Alternate methods usually employed to attach the handle include drilling a hole through the shaft and inserting a locking screw, or drilling the end of the shaft to accept a locking screw. Neither method works very well, or looks right.

Replacement shafts have been available for a number of years, but installing them in the old mechanism is quite a job requiring grinding off the mounting tabs and rewelding the retainer afterwards. SoCal Pickups of Buena Park, California was one of the first to supply the replacement shafts and was quick to realize how much better it would be for the do-it-yourselfer if they could just replace the whole mechanism.

Changing the shaft was not easy for them, even with their extensive facilities. Besides, that didn't solve the problem with the worn-out springs anyway. The logical solution was for SoCal Pickups to duplicate the original door regulator, as they have done with many other F-100 items that were no

*Designed as an exact duplicate of the original mechanism, the SoCal Pickups door regulator installs just like a factory replacement part.*

*Door regulator is held in place with three flathead machine screws which install in threaded mounting plate. Star washers on bolts insure they will not loosen after installation.*

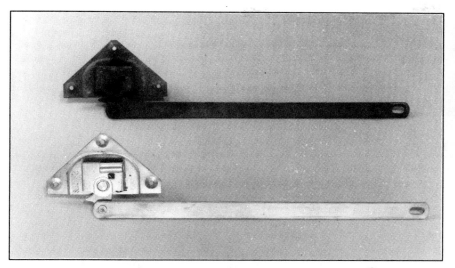

*A side-by-side comparison of the original and reproduction shows little variation between the two, however a few items have been strengthened in the reproduction.*

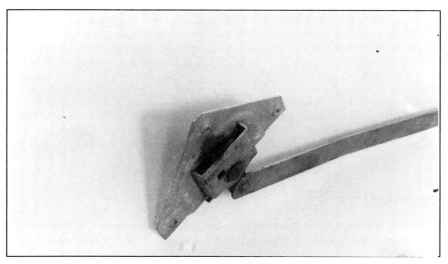

*Rust and time take their toll on actuating springs in door regulator. Here is an example of the kind of damage rust can do to one.*

*Rear view of mechanism reveals location of actuating springs.*

*New shaft in the SoCal regulator is a slightly improved duplicate of the original. Splined teeth are a bit more substantial yet accept stock handle as on original.*

*Splined teeth on the shaft get stripped off and various methods are employed to remedy the situation. These examples show some of those methods.*

longer available. Not an extremely difficult mechanism to duplicate, but one requiring a number of precision parts that had to function well together.

Cost of the complete unit is only about $25, a small price to pay to eliminate the hassle caused by a door handle that won't function. Installation is a simple do-it-yourself project as is illustrated by the accompanying photo sequence. There still may be no shortage of manual labor left in the renovation of your truck, but replacement items like this should make getting it on the road less of a long-term project.

# CHARGING SYSTEMS

### BY SKIP READIO AND DAVE McNURLEN

*Notice the difference in size between the late GM (left) and CS Series GM alternator (right). Compact size and high output are two of the advantages of the newer style alternator.*

## ALTERNATORS VS. GENERATORS

**C**harging systems can either be generator driven or alternator driven. There are advantages and disadvantages to each. The advantage of an alternator over a generator is that it can provide sufficient voltage to a battery even at an idle, whereas a generator must be spinning faster than it would at engine idle to produce a comparable amount of electricity. On the other hand, an alternator must have battery voltage present to operate. If the battery is dead and you were able to push start your truck to get it started spinning, the alternator still wouldn't charge the battery or provide enough electricity to fire the spark plugs. This is because without an externally applied voltage to get things going, the alternator just spins freely. Voltage must be applied to the slip rings in an alternator to produce a magnetic field in the spinning motor. This magnetic field is what will induce a current into the windings wrapped around the rotor and supply AC to the diodes. If there's no magnetic field, there's no output.

A generator, however, will start charging as soon as it's spinning fast enough. A generator needs no external voltage to get it operating.

Voltage regulators in a generator system are wired to the generator and the battery. No other wires are necessary for this charging circuit to function. Voltage regulators in alternator systems not only connect to the alternator, they also are fed by battery voltage via the ignition switch and most also employ an indicator (idiot light) as well. Without the switched power wire, the alternator cannot function.

Early GM alternator regulators are mechanical and are separate from the alternator, usually mounted on the firewall, fenderwell or radiator bulkhead in stock applications. Later model GM alternator regulators are housed right inside the alternator itself. These alternators put out more voltage than the mechanical units. This is due to the fact that these alternators are designed to work with maintenance-free batteries which require a higher charging voltage than the older style batteries which had to have the electrolyte topped off every once in a while. Using an older style battery with an internally regulated alternator usually results in boiling the water out of the battery faster than would be the case if an early (externally regulated) alternator were used.

## WIRING SCHEMATIC FOR "CS" SERIES ALTERNATOR

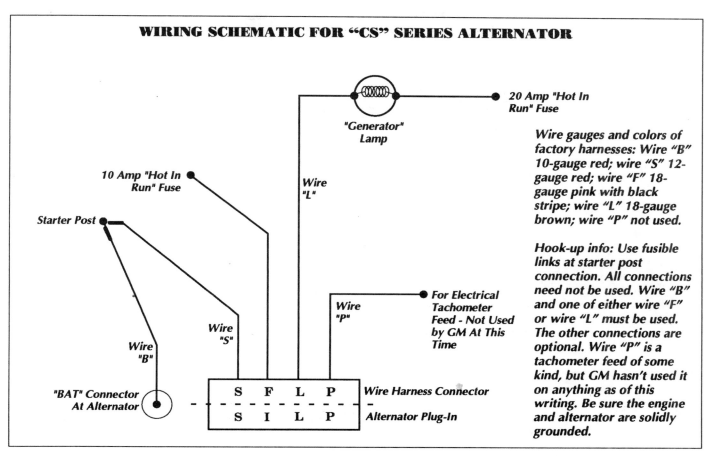

"Generator" Lamp

20 Amp "Hot In Run" Fuse

10 Amp "Hot In Run" Fuse

Starter Post

Wire "L"

Wire "B"

Wire "S"

Wire "P"

For Electrical Tachometer Feed - Not Used by GM At This Time

"BAT" Connector At Alternator

| S | F | L | P | Wire Harness Connector |
|---|---|---|---|---|
| S | I | L | P | Alternator Plug-In |

*Wire gauges and colors of factory harnesses: Wire "B" 10-gauge red; wire "S" 12-gauge red; wire "F" 18-gauge pink with black stripe; wire "L" 18-gauge brown; wire "P" not used.*

*Hook-up info: Use fusible links at starter post connection. All connections need not be used. Wire "B" and one of either wire "F" or wire "L" must be used. The other connections are optional. Wire "P" is a tachometer feed of some kind, but GM hasn't used it on anything as of this writing. Be sure the engine and alternator are solidly grounded.*

## GM WIRING DIAGRAM

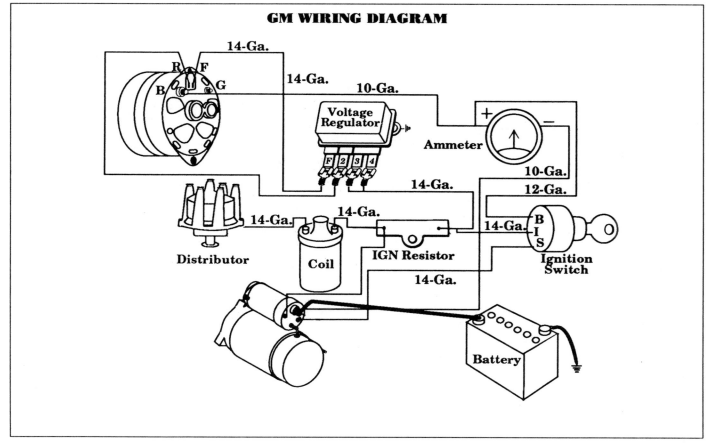

14-Ga.

R   F
B   G

14-Ga.

10-Ga.

Voltage Regulator

F  2  3  4

Ammeter

10-Ga.

12-Ga.

14-Ga.

14-Ga.

Distributor

Coil

IGN Resistor

14-Ga.

B
I
S

Ignition Switch

14-Ga.

Battery

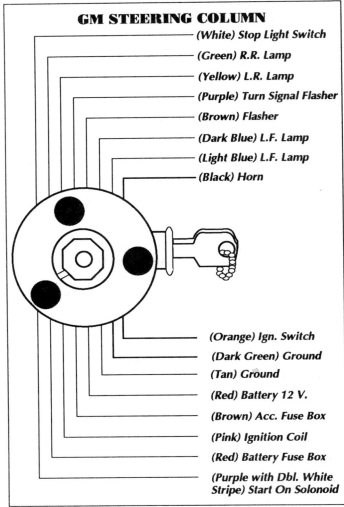

## GM STEERING COLUMN

— (White) Stop Light Switch

— (Green) R.R. Lamp

— (Yellow) L.R. Lamp

— (Purple) Turn Signal Flasher

— (Brown) Flasher

— (Dark Blue) L.F. Lamp

— (Light Blue) L.F. Lamp

— (Black) Horn

(Orange) Ign. Switch

(Dark Green) Ground

(Tan) Ground

(Red) Battery 12 V.

(Brown) Acc. Fuse Box

(Pink) Ignition Coil

(Red) Battery Fuse Box

(Purple with Dbl. White Stripe) Start On Solonoid

## EARLY GM ALTERNATORS

GM alternators with separate regulators can be connected in two ways. The factory configuration (with an indicator lamp) employs an external resistor (sometimes a special resistance wire instead) in parallel with the indicator lamp in the circuit. This circuit normally connects to terminal 4 on the voltage regulator. Regulator terminal 3 is connected to the ignition switch on the same terminal as that which feeds the ignition coil. Regulator terminal 2 connects to the terminal labeled R on the alternator, and regulator terminal F connects to the terminal labeled F on the alternator. Don't forget to ground the regulator.

The alternative method for wiring an external GM regulator is to connect both terminals 3 and 4 to the same wire from the ignition switch and eliminate the indicator lamp (idiot light), and use an ammeter or a voltmeter instead to monitor the condition of the charging system. Using a length of 10-gauge wire, connect the output lead of the alternator to the (+) terminal on the ammeter. With another length of 10-gauge wire, connect the (-) terminal of the ammeter to the same post on the starter solenoid that the battery cable is connected to.

## LATE GM ALTERNATORS

When using an internally regulated GM alternator, it is necessary to run only one wire to the regulator to energize it. This wire, like the other alternator/regulator systems, must come from the ignition switch. However, if it is physically connected to the same lead as the ignition coil, the engine will not shut off once it has been started. There is another terminal on the regulator, but it is hooked to the alternator output on a long wire in GM factory configurations. It can be jumpered back to the output with a short length of 14-gauge wire. This terminal will be the one farthest away from the alternator output stud.

The regulator energizing wire that runs back to the ignition switch goes to a terminal marked IGN 3. This terminal is in the lower corner of the GM column-mounted ignition switch in the smaller of the two plugs. The terminal is on the opposite end and opposite side from the coil lead on the IGN switch. The other two wires in this plug are for the key buzzer.

If you don't have a GM column, you can get a replacement ignition switch for an older Corvette at an auto parts store. The '57 Corvette ignition switches have two leads that are live only when the switch is in the run position, yet are separated when the switch is turned off.

Don't hook this wire to the ACC position because operating the radio while the motor isn't running will drain the battery as the alternator is also being biased at the same time.

The alternator's regulator-energizing wire can be run off the same ignition switch post as the coil, if an idiot light is installed in series with the switch and regulator. This requires a lamp socket with two insulated connectors. Neither of the wires on the lamp socket can be connected to chassis ground. To wire the idiot light, connect a length of 14-gauge wire from the IGN post to the base of the idiot light. Connect another length of 14-gauge wire to the internal voltage regulator.

## THE LATEST GM ALTERNATOR

GM has a new, smaller alternator that has been in use for the last few years. It's called the CS series and outputs between 80 and 120 amps, depending upon the model. The mounting system is close enough to the '70 and '80s style alternators that the earlier mounts will work with the new style alternators, and the pulley shaft size is the same as before. With their greater amperage output and small size, these units are ideal for trucks with electric cooling fans and powerful stereo systems.

The alternator pictured here came from an '87 Olds Calais with a 2.5 liter 4-cylinder engine, and it has a 100 amp output. The alternator harness came from the same model car. Most GM models newer than '87 use this style alternator, and amperage output is clearly stamped on the case.

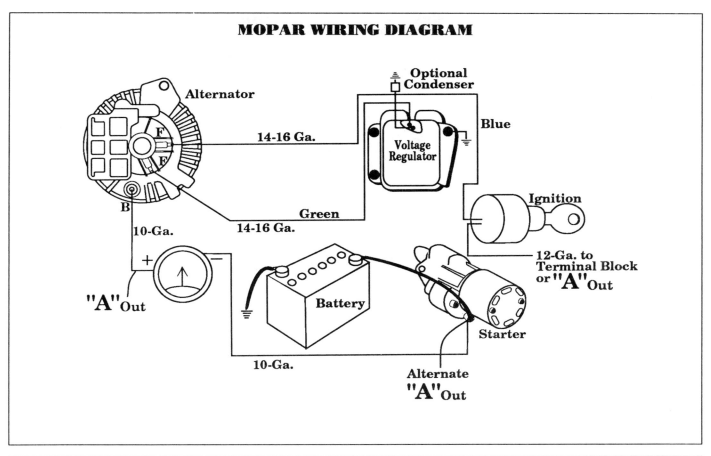

**MOPAR WIRING DIAGRAM**

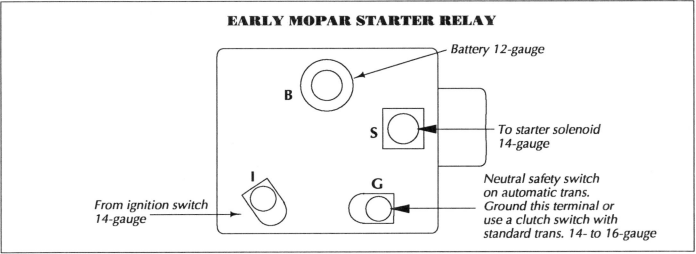

**EARLY MOPAR STARTER RELAY**

Hooking it up is easy, if you have the plug-in connector. Most dealers don't stock connector plugs, though some may have the "metri-pack" type terminals for the plug. A connector plug and terminal kit is available from Dr. K's for $7.50. When getting a plug at a wrecking yard, try to get as much of the wire harness as possible, to make splicing easier.

The best place to get an alternator is at a GM dealer, or look in the phone book under "Automobile Electrical Service" for Delco distributors. It might be a good idea to know the model and year of the car the alternator

originally came from, so the counterperson will have a starting point.

Used alternators are cheaper, but don't buy one expecting to overhaul it because you can't. These things are put together to be replaced as a unit. Only a minimum of disassembly should be attempted, such as swapping the drive belt pulley or reindexing the front half of the case for better connector plug alignment.

When connecting the alternator to the vehicle, you have a choice to make that depends on if a voltmeter, an idiot light, or neither of these is used. The main "Bat"

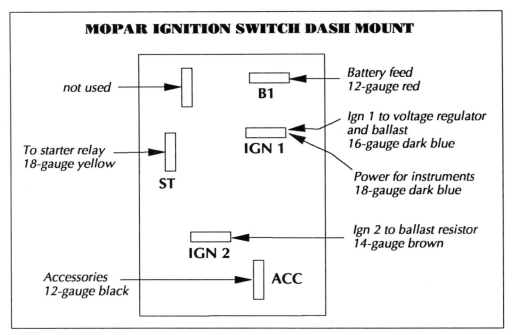

## MOPAR IGNITION SWITCH DASH MOUNT

not used

**B1** — Battery feed
12-gauge red

**IGN 1** — Ign 1 to voltage regulator
and ballast
16-gauge dark blue

Power for instruments
18-gauge dark blue

To starter relay
18-gauge yellow — **ST**

**IGN 2** — Ign 2 to ballast resistor
14-gauge brown

Accessories
12-gauge black — **ACC**

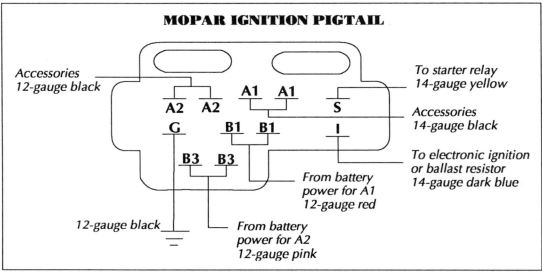

## MOPAR IGNITION PIGTAIL

Accessories
12-gauge black

To starter relay
14-gauge yellow

**A2 A2** **A1 A1** **S**

**G** **B1 B1** **I**

Accessories
14-gauge black

**B3 B3**

To electronic ignition
or ballast resistor
14-gauge dark blue

From battery
power for A1
12-gauge red

12-gauge black

From battery
power for A2
12-gauge pink

terminal on the alternator connects to the main starter post, or the positive battery terminal, whichever is closer. That's the easy part. On the four-wire connector plug, three of the connector labels match the connector labels on the alternator plug-in (S, L, and P). On the last one, they got tricky and labeled the plug F, while the plug-in on the alternator is labeled I. That will be referred to as the I/F terminal.

The I/F terminal (I on the alternator, F on the plug) is hooked to an "ignition on" circuit in the truck to start it charging. If an idiot light is used, hook the "ignition on" feed to the lamp (in series), and run that to the L terminal in the alternator plug. If the L terminal is used, be careful that a bulb is in the circuit, as the regulator will probably fry if the power is hooked directly there. The I/F circuit is designed for direct power, but the L circuit is not.

Some GM factory harnesses had connectors in both

the I/F and L circuits so the engine harness would fit more vehicles. When using one of those harnesses to hook up the alternator, the one not used can be eliminated. The S terminal can be connected to the same spot as the "Bat" wire. This lead tells the alternator how much amperage it needs to put out in order to keep up with demand. If the harness doesn't use it, that's okay; there's also a part of the regulator that can do that job on its own.

This leaves the P terminal, but it isn't used by any GM vehicle at this time. Shop manuals and other information say it's for a tachometer output signal, with no other information on calibration or signal output.

So, basically, if you want to slap one of these CS series alternators on your truck, bolt it up to the old bracket, hook the I/F circuit to an "ignition on" fuse or the L circuit to an idiot light, the "Bat" terminal to the battery or starter post, and hit the road.

Amperage rating is stamped into the front of the case. Here, 100A is equal to 100 amps of output.

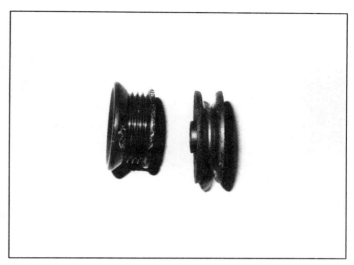

Even though the drive pulleys are different, the shaft size is the same for both the late GM and the CS Series alternators.

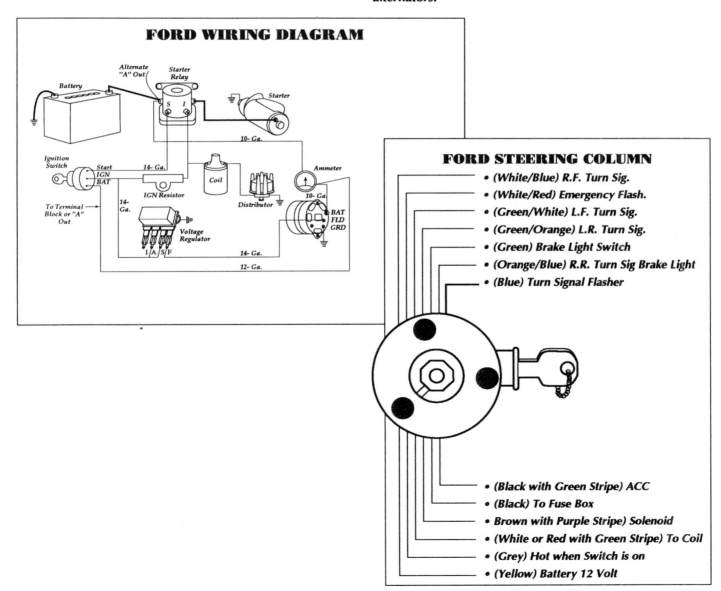

## FORD WIRING DIAGRAM

Battery
Alternate "A" Out
Starter Relay
Starter
S   I
10- Ga.
Ignition Switch
Start
IGN
BAT
14- Ga.
IGN Resistor
Coil
Distributor
Ammeter
10- Ga
To Terminal Block or "A" Out
14- Ga.
Voltage Regulator
I/A/S/F
BAT
FLD
GRD
14- Ga.
12- Ga.

## FORD STEERING COLUMN

- (White/Blue) R.F. Turn Sig.
- (White/Red) Emergency Flash.
- (Green/White) L.F. Turn Sig.
- (Green/Orange) L.R. Turn Sig.
- (Green) Brake Light Switch
- (Orange/Blue) R.R. Turn Sig Brake Light
- (Blue) Turn Signal Flasher

- (Black with Green Stripe) ACC
- (Black) To Fuse Box
- Brown with Purple Stripe) Solenoid
- (White or Red with Green Stripe) To Coil
- (Grey) Hot when Switch is on
- (Yellow) Battery 12 Volt

This is the harness plug for the alternator. The hold-in clip is on the other side. Note the S, F, L, and P stamped in the plug.

Three bolts hold the front and back halves of the alternator case together. If you must rotate the housing to get the alignment you need, pull only the front half loose. Don't pull the rotor out of the back half of the case.

The CS Series alternator installed. Note the ground wire from the alternator case to the frame. This eliminates any chance of a bad ground later.

# 6-VOLT TO 12-VOLT CONVERSION

## BY SKIP READIO

For various reasons, it often becomes necessary to convert 6-volt automotive electrical systems to 12-volt operation. Years ago, it was to allow for the use of the higher voltage for improved starting. Today, it has become necessary due to modern engines being transplanted into older trucks.

Converting the charging system, or changing the whole power plant, requires that the rest of the vehicle's electrical system be looked at.

• All lamps must be upgraded to 12-volt units.

• All instruments have to be isolated (power routed through a voltage reducing device) or replaced.

• Ammeters will have to have polarity reversed, because nearly all 6-volt systems employ positive ground, while 12-volt systems use a negative ground.

So, the ammeter will read backwards if it's not rewired.

• The heater motor must be isolated by a voltage reducing device, or replaced with a 12-volt unit.

If converting to 12 volts to simply improve starting characteristics, is will be necessary to change the ignition coil and install a ballast resistor in series with the coil and ignition switch (between the ignition switch and the coil).

Another consideration is that the factory radio won't work any more, because it's a positive ground device and you've just converted to negative ground.

There is one more alternative to improved starting. Many owners have used 8-volt batteries to improve starting, because none of the costly or bothersome component upgrades are involved. However, there are a few problems with this approach. First, you have to adjust the voltage regulator to put out 8 volts. This isn't an easy job. Yes, you can bend the tab and get the generator to charge higher, but to do it correctly requires: (1) An ammeter be placed in the circuit right at the generator, (2) The battery to be fully charged, (3) A voltmeter regulator be placed across the battery terminals, and (4) The voltage regulator be up to operating temperature. Most of these voltage regulator adjustment procedures are covered in older Motors manuals, and the like.

After doing this, the generator isn't capable of putting out enough voltage to charge an 8-volt battery. It requires nearly 9 volts to charge an 8-volt battery. While spending all this time trying to adjust the regulator, you're gradually wearing down the battery. How do you charge it back up again? Well, you can try a 12-volt charger, but I wouldn't recommend it unless something like a headlight bulb is wired in series with the positive charger cable to drop the voltage a bit. Put a voltmeter across the battery and make sure the voltage stays around 9 volts. Keep watching the voltage, because it'll change as the battery charges. Maybe you're starting to get the picture here. Charging an 8-volt battery is a real nuisance.

Another real nuisance is finding an 8-volt battery, especially when you're on the road. Farm Bureau stores are a good bet, as are honest-to-goodness battery shops. Auto parts stores will most likely have to order one for you.

If you only use the truck locally or for reasonably short periods of time, go ahead and install an 8-volt battery. Adjust your voltage regulator to keep the battery charged as best you can. Put together a special hookup for the battery charger to top off the battery charge when you get back home. You'll probably have to experiment a bit with different combinations of resistors, depending on the brand of battery charger you have, to get 9 volts out at the end of the wires, but it should be fine once you've worked out the variables.

If you plan on driving the truck for any length of time between charging times, switch to 12-volt electrics.

The first thing we'll cover here is what you have to do to the rest of the truck to get it to work with a 12-volt system. Then, we'll get into what you have to do under the hood to either convert just the charging and ignition system, or to convert to a later model motor with its associated electrical system.

To start off, all lights will have to be replaced. Headlights, parking lights, license plate lights, dome light, dash lights, under-hood light, courtesy lights, glove box light, etc.

Then, reverse the polarity of the ammeter. This is accomplished by removing the wires from the battery side of the ammeter and placing them on the generator/alternator side of the ammeter, and taking the wire from the generator/alternator side and putting it on the battery side. Only one wire should be on the battery side of the ammeter. This 10-gauge wire will connect to the starter solenoid on the same 3/8" stud as the positive battery cable. All of the other wires (10-gauge from the alternator or generator voltage regulator, 12- and 14-gauge wires to light and ignition switches, etc.) should be on the other ammeter terminal.

Most vehicles are constructed with ammeters having 10x32 studs on the rear. Some, however, employ an ammeter wherein the 10-gauge wire from the charging device to the battery just passes through a loop on the back of the ammeter. These are a bit more difficult to convert, as one half of the wire has to be removed from the harness so that it can be pulled back through the ammeter loop and fed back again in the opposite direction. This is the preferred way of reversing the polarity.

The wire can be cut and spliced, however, a soldered splice is recommended over a yellow crimp connector. Yellow crimp connectors are used for 10- and 12-gauge wire. Unless you have an expensive set of industrial crimping dies (they cost upwards of $130), I wouldn't recommend using a crimp connector in the charging circuit. Solder and shrink tubing or tape will make a much better connection.

## CERAMIC ENCASED VOLTAGE REDUCERS

Six-volt heater motors can be used, if a ceramic encased voltage reducer is placed in the wire feeding the switch or motor. If the heater switch has a lamp inside, placing the voltage dropping resistor between the ignition switch and the heater switch will allow you to retain the 6-volt bulb in the switch. Placing the resistor between the heater switch and the heater motor necessitates using a 12-volt bulb. It is worth pointing out here that 6-volt bulbs are getting a bit difficult to find, so the latter alternative might be the better of the two.

Six-volt windshield wiper motors and 6-volt electric fuel pumps can also be operated via one of these ceramic encased resistors.

## INSTRUMENT CLUSTER REGULATORS

Instruments should not be isolated with a ceramic encased voltage reducer. Because the output of these voltage reducers isn't sufficiently stable, a more precise means of voltage regulation should be employed.

Ford Motor Company and Chrysler Corporation have used instrument cluster regulators for years, to reduce voltage in their 12-volt vehicles to approximately 6 volts for their instruments. These ICRs (sometimes called IVR - instrument voltage regulator) are found on the back of the instrument cluster in most pre-computer-dash FoMoCo and MoPar vehicles.

ICRs/IVRs are used to regulate fuel gauges, oil pressure gauges and coolant temperature gauges. They are not used on the ammeter or voltmeter. You won't find one if there is a low fuel indicator wired into the fuel gauge, however, because the manufacturers rely on the low fuel bulb for the voltage regulation.

The ICR/IVR is a little (approximately 1" long by 1/2" wide) metal can with three contacts that plug into the back of the instrument cluster. One pin is part of the metal enclosure (or is connected internally to the enclosure) and connects to chassis ground via the instrument panel and/or harness. The other two are battery voltage in, and regulated voltage out.

Look for a vehicle with the same number of instruments as your vehicle, because ICRs/IVRs are designed to regulate a specific number of instruments, and one designed to operate a single instrument will provide the wrong voltage to three instruments. When you figure out which late model vehicle has a similar instrument cluster, head on down to your local parts store and they'll have a listing for the ICR/IVR for that vehicle. Most ICRs/IVRs are imprinted with "in" and "out" or similar indications on the two active pins. The third pin, as mentioned, must be grounded.

Idiot lights should be converted to 12 volts, and late model 12-volt senders should be installed in the engine block.

## ELECTRONIC VOLTAGE REDUCERS

Another means of reducing the voltage to the instrument cluster is to install an electronic voltage reducer. These devices provide a more precisely controlled voltage to the instruments and aren't load-dependent. In other words, the number of instruments controlled by the regulator has no effect on the voltage output to those instruments. Both Ron Francis Wire Works and Radio Shack market a pair of voltage reducers that will adequately regulate the voltage to your instruments.

The Ron Francis voltage reducers are designed specifically for installation in vehicles to control 6-volt equipment. One is rated for instruments only, while the other is powerful enough (15 amps) to control an electric fuel pump or something like a factory air conditioning solenoid.

Radio Shack units are designed to provide a range of voltages between 3 and 9 volts. The low-power unit (270-1560) is designed to plug into a cigar lighter and, while it is capable of 3-volt, 4.5-volt, 6-volt, 7.9-volt, and 9-volt operation, it can be wired into the system without using the cigar lighter, and set to 6 volts for powering instruments. The higher-powered Radio Shack unit (270-1562) provides only 6-volt or 9-volt outputs and is designed to be wired directly into the electrical system. While it doesn't have a current rating as high as the larger Ron Francis Wire Works model, it is quite adequate to handle vehicle instruments. I would recommend the latter model simply because it is a more compact unit and is less confusing from an installation standpoint, because you don't have to disassemble the cigar lighter plug and ascertain which wire is connected to the battery (the one connected to the center pin, usually fused as well) and which is connected to ground (the one to the side strap).

To connect any of these voltage reducers into your instrument circuit, first disconnect the wire that runs from the ignition switch to the instruments. The easiest place to disconnect the wire is usually at the ignition switch itself, because the wire is normally doubled up in the connector where it connects to the first instrument. The second wire in the connector runs to the next instrument and so forth. Between the ignition switch and the disconnected instrument wire is where the voltage reducer is installed. Follow the instructions packaged with the voltage reducer to get the proper colored wires on the proper points. Essentially, you'll have power and ground on the "in" side as well as power (to the instruments) and ground (to the dashboard) on the "out" side.

If original instruments are to be used with a later model motor, it will be necessary to adapt the original (or correct new replacement parts) coolant temperature and oil pressure senders to the new motor to ensure accurate instrument readings.

## UNDERHOOD WIRING

The following paragraphs assume that you intend to utilize some or all of the existing vehicle wiring. If the intent is to totally rewire, conversion isn't the issue any more, and you should refer to Tex Smith's book "How To Do Electrical Systems" for guidelines.

To convert the engine from 6-volt to 12-volt operation, replace the battery, generator and regulator with a 12-volt version. Nothing else is necessary, as both generator systems share a common wiring principle.

If converting to an alternator, it will be necessary to slightly modify the charging system harness. You need not destroy any of the original wiring to convert to alternator charging. First of all, remove the battery, generator and regulator. Lengthen the wire that previously connected to the voltage regulator "BAT"tery terminal. This wire will now connect to the output of the alternator. If mounting the alternator in the same place as the generator was mounted, bolt the aforementioned "BAT"tery wire to the "ARM"ature, where these two wires formerly connected to the regulator, and connect the other end (the one that used to connect to the armature terminal on the generator) to the output of the alternator. This will leave one wire in the old regulator-to-generator harness. This wire can be used to connect the new alternator regulator to the field of the alternator.

For most alternator applications, it'll be necessary to run an additional wire up to the alternator as well as running another wire from the ignition switch to the voltage regulator to energize the regulator when the motor is running. Unlike a generator, an alternator must have an ON/OFF switch function associated with its operation. Even the single wire alternators have this function, however, it is automatic, thus negating the need for the extra wires to excite the alternator. For all conversions, however, you'll have to make the modification to the length of the "BAT"tery wire.

If you intend to install a later model engine, you can still modify the regulator wiring harness in the same manner.

When upgrading the operating voltage, replace the ignition coil and add a ballast resistor into the supply circuit for the coil. Remember, when hooking up the coil, the distributor will be connected to the negative side and the ballast resistor will be connected to the positive side.

On Ford products, it is necessary to change the starter solenoid to a 12-volt unit. It is a good idea to try to use a 12-volt starter as well. Many people have used 6-volt starters in 12-volt systems, but long-term reliability suffers when the starter motor is driven with too much voltage for a few years. If the motor fires right up after one or two revolutions, the starter will last for quite a while. But if the motor is getting tired, and the starter has to grind for a few seconds, it's not going to last very long if you keep whacking it with 12 volts.

# WIRING TRICKS

**BY SKIP READIO**

### Ballast Bypass

Often times, especially in extremely cold weather, the starter draws too much current and there's not enough juice left fo fire the spark plugs once it passes through the ballast resistor. To compensate for this, auto manufacturers include a ballast bypass circuit in the starter solenoid.

On a FoMoCo system, the ballast bypass is on the starter solenoid. The post closest to the starter cable stud on the Ford solenoid is the ballast resistor bypass connection.

The ballast resistor bypass terminal should be connected with a 14-gauge wire to the coil, on the same post that the ballast resistor connects to. Actually, you can hook it to either the coil or the ballast resistor. You must make sure, however, that it is connected to the wire that runs between the ballast resistor and the coil.

What this does is put the full battery voltage on the points while starting the motor. Once you let go of the key and the starter disengages, the circuit opens up and you are now supplying the points with a reduced level of voltage.

If you're having trouble starting your stocker, add a manual bypass of your own. Connect a length of wire to each of the two resistor terminals. Run them out to a toggle switch or a push button switch. A push button is preferred. When cranking the motor over for a long time, the resistor will heat up. The hotter it gets, the more voltage it will drop, meaning less voltage is present at the coil. Push the button, and the resistor is no longer in the circuit, and there is now full battery voltage to fire the plugs.

### Ford Alternators and Idiot Lights

If you are using a Ford alternator and want to eliminate the idiot (indicator) light from the dashboard, there is a way to hook things up to accomplish this. Put a 500-ohm resistor across the two leads of the indicator light bulb socket when connecting the wire to the socket. In other words, run a wire to the bulb socket and the resistor from the ignition switch. Connect the other side of the resistor to the other wire on the bulb socket and connect these two to the regulator.

### The "A" Circuit

In cases in which an ammeter is included in the charging circuit, the common point for tying into power for the accessories is on the alternator side of the ammeter. If an ammeter is not included in the circuit, the point for obtaining power for accessories is at the starter solenoid. On our drawings, we refer to these points as "A" out.

# Engines

**BY DAVE MCNURLEN**

great thing about trucks is that with the exception of the '30s varieties, there's enough room under the hood to install just about anything. The limiting factors usually are: what engine is available to you at reasonable cost, how much money and time do you have to spend, and what do you plan to do with the truck after it's built.

In locating an engine, check your neighbor's yards, the back row of used car lots, food market bulletin boards, campus newspapers, bargain shopper newspapers, and your local paper. Any place where a car or truck could be bought cheap. Buying a complete running car is sometimes the best way to get your powertrain, as all sorts of little goodies come with it that your might have to scrounge later anyway. Lots of times, you can even get your original investment back selling off the parts you don't use.

What you're gonna do with the truck is important. An engine too large or too small can make an otherwise useful truck and enjoyable truck a real pain. Practicality, if you're planning on using it a lot, has to be considered.

Another thing to consider, if the original engine is still in it, is how would that engine work. Just because you're building a hot rod doesn't mean you have to rip out the motor the truck was designed around. Most truck engines are built tough, and can be rebuilt with little added touches to make them a lot of fun to drive.

There are numerous companies, including Egge Machine Company at (213) 945-3419, that can provide parts for even the most obscure engine. A nice running flathead Dodge or Ford 6, or a 2-carb Chevy 235 makes a sound not heard much lately, and they love to run down the highway.

For lightweight trucks, a four-cylinder engine will

work well. A modern Chevy four, made since the sixties, is still being used in some of GM's front wheel drive cars. There's the Chrysler 2.2, and a bunch of Ford fours to choose from. Toyota, Nissan, and other companies build engines that work well in a rod. And any factory fuel-injected four would be unusual, and very reliable.

There's always a Model A four, or even an early Chevy four. Speed parts are still out there for these, and they can make a nice powerplant, if you remember what you've got, and treat them accordingly. For instance, Model A four-banger interest is exploding, with various overhead valve conversion heads available, and even a complete aluminum block from Donavan Engineering. A Model A pickup hot rod with even a stock 4-banger is neat.

Sixes are plentiful. The big deal used to be swapping a 216 Chevy six for a big-cube GMC 6. When V8's came along, that slowed down. Now, several companies are making GMC and Chevy speed equipment available, and interest is returning. A GMC six will bolt in by moving the previous 216/235 front mounts forward one inch.

A call to Patrick's at (602) 836-1117 will fix you up with all sorts of early/late Chevy and GMC 6 stuff. Another source for these parts is the Stovebolt Engine Company at (503) 695-2571.

A 292 Chevy six will bolt in the same spot occupied by a 194, 230, or 250 inch 6, although it's a couple of inches taller. Leave the Chevy sixes with the integral head/intake in the wrecking yard. The earlier designs are much better. And don't forget that Ford sixes came as big as 300 cubic inches, with torque to match. Parts for these can be gotten from Clifford Performance Products, (714) 734-3310.

Six-cylinder intake manifolds are still available from Offenhauser, (213) 225-1307, among others. They have intakes for Studebakers, Fords, Dodges, and Chevy sixes.

V6s are now made by GM, Ford, and MoPar that make excellent medium-sized truck engines. Among the best are 231 Buicks, and 4.3 liter Chevys. With the complete engine weight just under 400 pounds, one of these engines with some hop-up parts can really scoot.

The early GM V6s were pretty anemic, such as the narrow degree 2.8 engines, and 229 cube 90 degree

# Engine Specifications

A= Width of engine, not including exhaust manifolds
B= Height of engine from bottom of pan to top of stock carburetor.
C= Length of engine from back to block to water pump pulley face.
D= Distance from water pump pulley face to back of valve cover, head or distributor over the top of the engine where firewall might hit.

| Engine | Displacement | WT | A | B | C | D | Starter | Oil Sump |
|---|---|---|---|---|---|---|---|---|
| AMC V6 | 232/258 | 525 | 24" | 26" | 30" | 25" | Left | Rear |
| AMC V8 | 304/401 | 545 | 21.5 | 28 | 29 | 21.5 | Left | Rear |
| Buick V6 | 196/231 | 380 | 24 | 25.5 | 23 | 21.5 | Right | Middle |
| Buick V8 | 350 | 450 | 23 | 25.5 | 29 | 21.5 | Right | Rear |
| Buick V8 | 430/455 | 600 | 23 | 27 | 29 | 22 | Left | Middle |
| Cadillac V8 | 472/500 | 600 | 23.5 | 29 | 30 | 28.5 | Right | Middle |
| Chevy 4 | 153 | 360 | 16 | 25.5 | 22.5 | 24 | Right | Front |
| Buick,Pontiac Olds, Chevy V6 | 194/250 | 415 | 16 | 25.5 | 30.5 | 24 | Right | Rear |
| Chevy Truck V6 | 292 | 430 | 16 | 28 | 22.5 | 24 | Right | Rear |
| Chevy V8 | 262/400 | 550 | 19.5 | 25 | 26.5 | 20.5 | Right | Rear |
| Chevy V8 | 396/454 | 635 | 22 | 29.5 | 30.5 | 23.5 | Right | Rear |
| Ford V6 | 144/250 | 400 | 17 | 26 | 29 | 24 | Right | Front |
| Ford V6 | 240/300 | 400 | 13 | 26 | 30 | 24 | Right | Front |
| Ford V8 Flathead | 221/225 | 540 | 26 | 26 | 30 | 30 | Right | Rear |
| Ford V8 | 260/400 | 460 | 20 | 25 | 27 | 22 | Right | Front |
| Ford V8 | 332/428 | 625 | 23 | 30 | 30 | 28 | Right | Front |
| MoPar V6 | 170/240 | 475 | 24 | 22 | 30 | 29.5 | Right | Front |
| MoPar V8 | 273/360 | 555 | 20.5 | 28 | 29 | 24 | Left | Front |
| MoPar V8 | 383/440 | 670 | 23.5 | 28 | 29 | 24 | Left | Front |
| MoPar | Hemi 426 | 690 | 28.5 | 28 | 32 | 24 | Left | Middle |
| Olds V8 | 330/455 | 600 | 21.5 | 27 | 29 | 24 | Left | Rear |
| Pontiac V8 | 350/400 | 600 | 22 | 26 | 28.5 | 20 | Left | Rear |
| Pontiac V8 | 455 | 630 | 23 | 28.5 | 29.5 | 27 | Right | Rear |

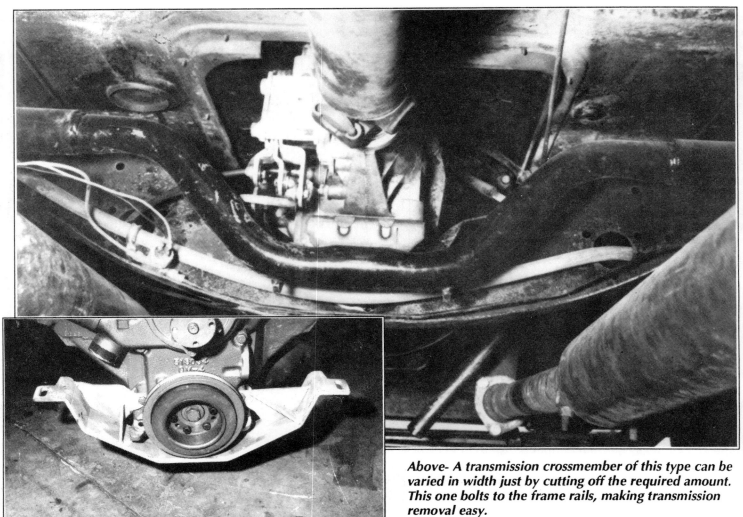

*Above- A transmission crossmember of this type can be varied in width just by cutting off the required amount. This one bolts to the frame rails, making transmission removal easy.*

*Left- A small block Chevy front mount in '50 Chevy pickup using early Ford type rubber insulators. This is a clean, simple installation.*

engines available in mid-sized cars like the Malibu. Even the earliest Buick 231's weren't that great an engine. But they are cheap and available, and sometimes that's more important. An engine like Ford's Taurus SHO V6 would be a good one, as would a Buick Grand National Turbo V-6, or the engine from a GMC Syclone pickup, if you could find one.

An engine often overlooked is the 500 inch Cadillac. It originated in the '74 Eldorado, and was used in the rest of the big Cadillac line from '75 up. In combination with the bulletproof Turbo 400 transmission they all came with, this is an ideal engine/transmission for someone who will be towing, or just has a heavy truck.

An example of this is a 1950 Chevy 1-ton panel truck that ran around in Texas. It weighed an easy 2-1/2 tons empty, and used this Cadillac engine/trans combination. Driven as a vendors vehicle to car events all over the country, it gave excellent mileage, even when loaded to the gills, and no trouble. Big Oldsmobile and Buick V8s are in the same class as the Cadillac, as are 440 MoPars, and 460 Fords. These engines will pull huge amounts of weight all day long, and never breathe hard.

Then there are the goofball versions of various V8s, such as 260 Oldsmobiles, 262 Chevys, and the 5.7/6.2 liter GM deisels. These engines are a lot more trouble than they're worth. The first two are too small, although anvil-reliable, and the last two are just plain trouble.

Smaller V8s, such as MoPar's 318/360, Ford's 302/400, and the Chevy small-block can be built to make gobs of reliable horsepower. Coupled to their respective automatic transmissions, they can get lost in the engine compartment of most any truck out there.

By far the easiest way to swap engines into your truck is to use the crossmember style motor mounts and transmission mounts available from various suppliers. They provide a strong, safe mount for the engine and transmission, and increase chassis strength by adding another crossmember. Another way is to buy pre-fabricated mount kits, sold at a lot of the same places. Or you can fabricate your own, from tubing, or flat steel plate.

TransDapt, (213) 404-2985, is one company that has a large inventory of mount kits, which include the crossmember or fabricated mounts, and any other engine/transmission mount insulators required.

# Transmissions

**BY RON CERIDONO**

t's safe to say that the substantial majority of hot rods that see regular street service have automatic transmissions. There are a number of explanations for this, both practical and fiscal. Modern automatics are not only strong and reliable, but are far more plentiful in V8 and V6 configurations than standard transmissions. Supply and demand being what it is simply means the greater availability of automatic transmissions makes them more affordable than the stick-shift variety. In addition, automatics simplify engine swaps in that there is no clutch linkage to deal with. A simple shifter and some sort of transmission cooler are all that is necessary.

In terms of strength, automatics can be modified to handle just about any engine that is streetable. Special valve bodies, altered shift points, improved friction components and increased internal hydraulic pressure are common modifications. All of these are worth looking into for ultimate performance applications. But for reliable street use, major modifications are not usually necessary.

When updating an older truck with a late engine and automatic transmission, or rebuilding the box in a later model automatic equipped truck, don't get carried away with race oriented shift kits, high stall speed torque converters, or manual shift bodies. Drag race prepped automatics on the street can be a real pain in the neck, literally. Head snapping shifts are hard on you and your passengers, not to mention your truck's drive train. Transmission modifications for all but the most serious performance use can usually be limited to a mild shift kit, an aftermarket torque converter, and most importantly an auxillary cooler.

Shift kits are available from a number of sources. They are easy to install yourself, or can be included by most shops during a transmission rebuild. The key to success here is to select a kit that is appropriate for the use of the vehicle. Discuss your plans for the truck, the engine/transmission combination being used, and your budget, with a transmission specialist or one of the mail-order transmission suppliers technical people. Then, follow their advice on which shift kit to use.

Torque converter selection is extremely important, and often the source of confusion. A common mistake is to install a converter with stall speed that is too high. In simple terms the stall speed of a converter is the engine RPM that can be achieved with the transmission in gear, the brakes locked, and the throttle floored. High stall

speed converters are great for the drag strip, they allow the engine to rev up and produce more power for a hard starting line launch. But unless your engine is equipped with a radical cam and needs to build a little RPM to get your truck moving, stick with a stock converter or an aftermarket unit with just slightly higher than stock stall speed. As with shift kits, talk to a transmission specialist or a performance converter manufacturer for advice on your specific application.

One item that must be included on any automatic equipped truck is a transmission cooler. Heat is the major killer of automatics, so make sure to install a cooler of sufficient capacity, and position it in such a manner so as to guarantee adequate air flow. If lack of space in front or behind the radiator dictates that the cooler must be located out of the air stream (under the cab as an example) fashion a sheet metal scoop to force air through the cooler.

When it comes time to select an automatic you can save money by starting out with a transmission that is suited to your needs. For high performance street use, heavy towing, or blasting down the 1/4-mile, it's much better to begin with a heavy duty transmission than make modifications to a light duty unit. The Ford C-6, GM Turbo 400, and Chrysler 727 are all virtually bullet proof, and are the way to go for high stress applications. Under normal operating circumstances, the lighter duty transmissions, such as the Ford C-4, GM Turbo 350, and the Chrysler 904, are more than adequate. But perhaps the best transmission option available today is the current crop of automatic overdrives. These transmissions feature a first gear low enough for good standing start acceleration, while their overdrive fourth makes for reasonable RPM when cruising on the highway

As an example of this, compare gear ratios between the commonly used 3-speed GM 350 and the 4-speed 700 R4 transmissions.

|       | 1st     | 2nd     | 3rd    | 4th     |
|-------|---------|---------|--------|---------|
| 350   | 2.52:1  | 1.52:1  | 1.00:1 |         |
| 700 R4 | 3.059:1 | 1.625:1 | 1.00:1 | 0.696:1 |

Now look at the overall gear ratios in first and high (third in a 350, fourth in a 700 R4) with a 3.55 ring and pinion

|        | 1st                    | 3rd                  |
|--------|------------------------|----------------------|
| 350    | 2.52 x 3.55 = 8.946    | 1.00 x 3.55 = 3.55   |

|        | 1st                     | 4th                   |
|--------|-------------------------|-----------------------|
| 700 R4 | 3.059 x 3.55 = 10.859   | 0.696 x 3.55 = 2.47   |

Obviously, when it comes to flexibility, automatic overdrive transmissions are hard to beat. Rearend gears low enough for good performance can be used, while the transmission's top gear will provide cruising (and mileage) capabilities. But with all this good news, you just know there has to be some bad.

According to automatic transmission expert Art Carr, of Art Carr Performance Transmission Products, 10575 Bechler River Ave., Fountain Valley, CA 92708, 714-962-6655, the weak point in all the overdrive automatics is the lock-up torque converter. The intent of the lock-up converter is to totally eliminate slippage within the converter at cruising speeds, thereby improving fuel mileage. But Art's experience has been that the lock-up components of the converters are prone to fail. His cure for the problem is to eliminate the original equipment style converter, and replace it with one of the non-lock-up variety. Art's specially designed and constructed converters will keep the engine within 200 RPM of a lock-up converter at cruising speed. Any mileage loss is negligible, while reliability is greatly improved.

Another method of dealing with GM lock-up converters is offered by B&M Automotive Products, 9152 Independence Ave., Chatsworth, CA 91311; 818-882-6422. Their Lock-Up Converter Electronic Speed Control allows the coupling point of the converter to be controlled by the driver. Another neat feature of this device is that it allows the installation of computer controlled transmissions in non-computer cars and trucks.

Non-GM fans have some automatic overdrive options too. Since Chrysler doesn't offer an automatic overdrive that is suitable for swapping purposes, Art Carr is making an adapter to install a GM 700 R4 behind big block MoPars. He also markets an adapter to put the GM 200 4R (a smaller 4-speed automatic overdrive) behind small block Fords.

Ford has two versions of the automatic overdrive, the manually controlled AOD, and the electronically controlled EOD. The AOD series is a prime candidate for swapping into early trucks due to its lack of electronic controls. Additionally, aftermarket manufacturers are developing shift kits and other performance components for the AOD.

On the other hand the EOD, while a well designed, rugged transmission, will not be a suitable candidate for swapping until a control system is developed to replace the electronics. But it's only a matter of time until that happens.

Of course there are other alternatives to the transmissions discussed here. The Ford FMX, the GM Powerglide, and the MoPar cast iron Torqueflite have all been used with varying degrees of success. But why use yesterday's transmission in today's hot rod? For reliability and performance, stick with the modern designs.

Now for those who would rather shift for themselves

a number of possibilities exist. If you want to swap engines and retain your truck's original transmission, adapters for a surprisingly wide array of engine/transmission marriages are still available. Offenhauser, 5232 Alhambra Ave., Los Angles, CA 90032, 310-225-1307; Trans-Dapt, 16410 Manning Way, Cerritos, CA 90701, 310-404-2985; and a number of other suppliers may be able to furnish what is needed. But the problem with most manual truck transmissions is that they are 3-speeds, or 4-speeds with ultra-low first gears, neither are well suited to hot rod applications. (The exception to this would be a 3-speed with overdrive.) An automotive 4 or 5-speed transmission is what will be needed.

GM, Ford, Chrysler, and AMC all used 4-speeds during the muscle car era, and beyond, so finding a transmission to bolt to a particular engine's bellhousing is not a problem. But be aware of the fact that all four-speeds are not created equal. Some of the early transmissions, such as the Borg-Warner T-10, lack the stamina for high performance use.

Another factor to be aware of is the difference in gear ratios between various manual transmissions Some feature a relatively high first gear with closely spaced gear sets, while others have lower first gears with wider spacing between the remaining gears. To make sure your truck performs as it should, take rearend gearing and rear tire size into account when selecting a transmission. High rear gears and large diameter tires will require a transmission with a low first gear to maintain reasonable performance.

As with automatics, manual transmissions have undergone considerable development in recent years. Both aftermarket and original equipment 5-speed are available, with gear ratios to fit a variety of applications. As with the 4-speed automatics, top gear in most of the 5-speed manuals is overdrive, a real advantage in most applications.

Clutch selection for a street driven truck is an important factor for overall driveability. A pressure plate with sufficient spring pressure to handle the loads imposed on it, while still having reasonable pedal pressure will be required. Again, the manufacturer is your best source of information on what is best for your specific application.

To operate the clutch some sort of linkage will have to be fabricated if none exists. Building the necessary linkage, or adapting the linkage from another truck is not particularly difficult, nor is installing a hydraulic actuating system. Hydraulic systems were used on mid-Sixties Chevy, GMC and International trucks, and are easily adaptable to others. But the simplest solution could well be the hydraulic throwout bearing. Available from Speedway Automotive, 300 Van Dorn, Lincoln, NE 68501, as well as other suppliers, the hydraulic throwout bearing simplifies standard transmission installations.

# Rearends

**A**hen considering a rearend swap for your truck, don't automatically think you have to go to the strongest thing out there. the strongest thing out there. A differential like a big, heavy Dana 60, or a Detroit Locker Ford 9-inch is nice if you've got a blown 702 inch big-block. But instead of over-building, what you've already got may be just fine.

Like when selecting an engine, you have to think about what you're gonna be doing with your truck. For instance, if you're thinking about a Pro-Streeter with a narrowed rearend, consider that you'll have a real rough time cruising down the rutted Interstates we've got with steamroller tires, bouncing back and forth in the grooves made by regular tires. And the ride usually suffers, with load capacity dropping to zilch. This is okay, if you know beforehand this is what you want, and can accept it.

Fitting a rearend requires precise measurement. You'll need 2 to 3 inches of tire clearance on the inside between the tire and the body/frame, to allow for body/chassis movement when turning or going over bumps. Same for the outside of the tire at the inner edge of the fender. A great way to figure out what width rearend you need is to put the wheels and tires you'll use in the fenderwells, with adequate clearance on both sides, and then measure the distance between the wheel centers.

When cutting the old brackets off the rearend housing, go easy on the heat. It's easy to warp an axle housing. One of the more common on-the-road failures is axle bearing failure from too much heat being applied when welding on new spring perches. In some cases, the axle housing warps from excessive heat, and puts additional strain on these bearings. A warped housing can be corrected by a good machine shop.

There are many rearends to choose from. Early Nova ('62-'67) 10-bolt rearends are 58-3/4 inches wide from axle flange to axle flange. Later Nova and Camaro up to '81 are 1-1/4 inches wider on each side, making them 61-1/4 inches flange to flange. Axles from under '78-up Malibu/Regal/Cutlass-style bodies are located in a four-link style, but can easily have spring pads welded on, and the extra stuff cleaned off the center housing. They have about the same width as an early Nova.

Late Z-28 Camaros and Trans-Ams had stronger 10-bolts in them, and most had disc brakes on the back.

These were the same width as earlier Camaros, with a wide range of axle ratios, including Positraction. The disc brake rearends have an integral parking brake built in to the caliper that sometimes makes it difficult to get back together when the pads are changed. And with any disc brake rearend, be sure your master cylinder has enough capacity for both front and rear disc brakes.

Ford 9-inch rearends came in passenger cars and standard models of pickups from '57 to '79, so most of you Ford guys are probably already set. Starting in 1963, Ford was nice enough to include a tag on each of these axles, bolted to the center pumpkin, that lists the ratio, the size of the ring gear, and if it has limited-slip. If the tag says 3.89, that's the ratio. If it says 3L89, it's a 3.89, and the "L" stands for "locking", or "limited slip". Or the tag might just have "NL" on it, which stands for "non-locking".

The one everyone used to want was under the '57 Ford station wagon with overdrive, as it was usually a 4.11, and the narrowest out there. Now, many companies can build you whatever width rearend you want. Peyton in Texas, (214) 923-1698, Moser in Indiana, (219) 726-6689, and Currie in California, (714) 528-2338, among others, can ship you anything from cut axles and/or housings, to complete differentials ready to bolt in.

Measurement-wise, mid-70's Mavericks and Granadas are 51-1/4 inches from inside backing plate to backing plate, with Galaxies about 4 inches wider. These all had a 5-inch bolt pattern, and Ford started putting disc brakes in the back about '75. When swapping center sections between housings, be sure there's a plug on either the housing or the center section. Ford sometimes moved this around. And remember that Ford axles had a varying number of splines, depending on axle type.

Most post-'80 Ford rearends are of the four-lug wheel pattern variety, and not very strong. That doesn't mean they can't be used, because most of them are wide enough for a truck. A rearend from an '85 Cougar is 4 inches wider between the backing plates than a '75 Granada. It would just be a case of having the axle available cheap, and then just redrilling the bolt pattern.

Mopar rearends from the mid-60's and 70's are like Ford 9-inchers, in that the center section comes out of the housing as a unit. They have a wide range of ratios available and are quite strong.

# DRIVESHAFTS

**BY RICH JOHNSON**

If you've done any engine/transmission swapping, you may need to come up with a driveshaft to fit the truck. But before heading for the machine shop, do some measuring. There is a huge selection of driveshaft lengths available, and surprisingly, there is a great deal of universal joint interchangeability. For example, the Volvo universal joint is a standard Chevrolet item.

You know the type of rearend you have, and you know the type of transmission. At the transmission output shaft and at the pinion, there are yokes that secure the U-joints in place. The critical bits of information about these yokes are the measurements across the semi-circular cups that receive the U-joints. They are not all the same. With a steel tape or a set of calipers, measure carefully the distance across the yoke cup right at the edge of the machined face, to find the size of U-joint that will fit. Be aware that the transmission output shaft U-joint yoke may not be the same size as the yoke at the pinion. The ideal situation is if the yoke cups measure the same at the pinion as they do at the transmission output shaft. This way, you only need to carry one extra U-joint in the spare-parts section of the tool box, and it can fit either position.

Some U-joints are designed with all four cups the same size, while others have two different sizes of cups on the same unit. There may be larger cups for the driveshaft attachment, and smaller ones for the yoke. The thing to keep in mind here is that the more unusual the U-joint, the more difficult it may be to find a replacement. If possible, design the driveshaft system to use the strongest and most commonly available components.

To determine the overall length of the driveshaft, measure the distance from the machined face of the rear of the transmission output shaft yoke to the machined face at the front of the pinion yoke. These machined faces represent the centerline points of the U-joint cups. This will get you close to the overall shaft length needed. Now shop the junkyards. Pay close attention to U-joint sizes. If in doubt, ask what universal joint might interchange with the shaft and rearend that you have.

While measuring, keep in mind the splined slip joint which allows the driveshaft to lengthen and shorten as the rear suspension works up and down. Although the slip joint has a built-in travel of several inches, it should ride just about in the center of its travel when the driveshaft is installed between the transmission and rearend, and the full weight of the truck is resting on the suspension. Take care to avoid inadvertently measuring the driveshaft length with the slip joint either pushed in or pulled out beyond its center of travel, otherwise you may end up with a slip joint that destroys itself when the suspension gets real active. If you are lucky, you'll find a shaft that fits. Sometimes it's a drop-in.

If you must have a shaft made, plan on paying from $60 to $150. Most communities have machine shops that can custom make driveshafts. They will cut and fit the tube, or install a new tube (using the measurements you supply), with a yoke that will fit the rearend. Have the shaft balanced while you are at it.

Note: You do not cut a driveshaft in two and butt-weld the pieces to the length you need! This might be OK for a dune buggy, but it doesn't cut it on a street-driven vehicle.

If you are building a truck with lots of horsepower, be sure to use the larger universal joints and a large diameter driveshaft tube. A good driveshaft shop will be able to advise you regarding the recommended tube diameter and U-joint size as it relates to your engine's horsepower.

BY TERRY STEAGALL

# HONEY, I SHRUNK THE TRUCK

**T**his is the story of how a 1948 Chevrolet Custom Cab 1/2-ton truck came to be equipped with 1985 S-10 Chevy truck running gear, including complete chassis, air conditioning, power brakes, power steering, door latches, hood latch, gauges, wiring harness, computer controls, steering column, seat and dash controls.

One question naturally comes to mind: How can a '48 Chevy 1/2-ton pickup be mated to all this late model downsized truck stuff? There is, after all, an enormous difference between the size of a late '40s pickup and a modern mini truck. The answer can be found in paraphrase of a popular movie — *Honey, I shrunk the truck.*

The 1948 body was reduced approximately 15% in every direction. Actually, the figure of 15% was only a guideline. Whatever looked right, or made the most sense was more important than the 15%.

The long wheelbase S-10 frame was shortened 14-1/2" between the axles. About 8" was cut off each end, and the hump over the axle was lowered 3-3/4" so the bed would have proper depth. It then had an X-member added, another rear crossmember, and was boxed.

The truck has a double firewall and floorboard, reinforced between the two with 1" square tubing and filled with foam board for sound and heat insulation.

Forty-three body parts were cut into more than 400 major pieces, then welded back together. As far as I know, this is the only vehicle in the world that has been chopped, channeled, sectioned, shortened, lowered and narrowed in every direction, using an original steel body.

Total investment is $5400, and approximately 4000 hours of labor. Every part of this truck is either old

*Yes, it is a 1948 Chevrolet pickup truck, and yes, it is smaller than an original. But if you want a copy, you'll have to build it yourself.*

*The basis for this entire project was a Chevy S-10. Here, the late model frame has had the hump over the axle lowered for bed accommodation, and a special X-member added for rigidity.*

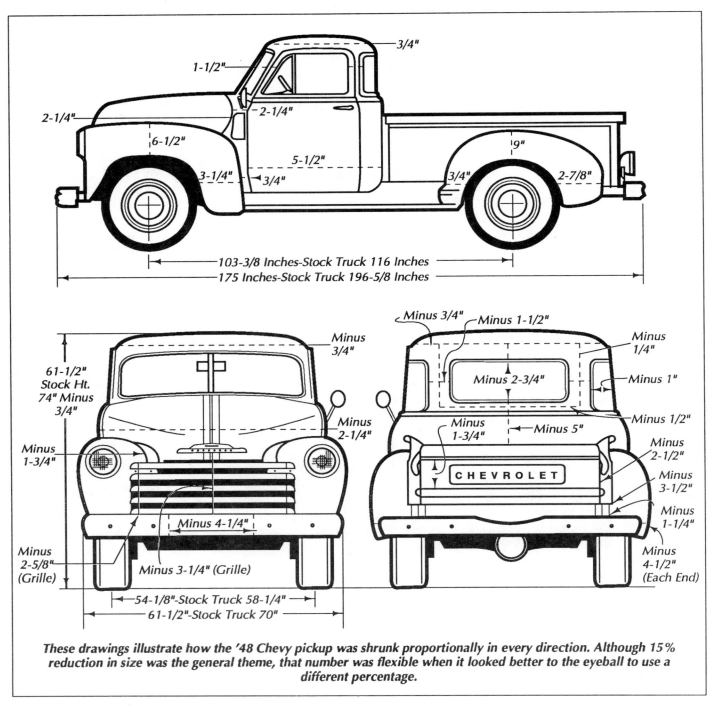

*These drawings illustrate how the '48 Chevy pickup was shrunk proportionally in every direction. Although 15% reduction in size was the general theme, that number was flexible when it looked better to the eyeball to use a different percentage.*

Chevy truck parts, late model Chevy parts, or parts my dad or I made.

Body modifications are as follows. The cab has been narrowed 5" and each fender narrowed 1-3/4" for a total of 8-1/2" narrower than stock. The top has been chopped 1-1/2" at window posts and 3/4" above the windows. Cab skin was sectioned 2-1/4" above fender and 3-1/4" at the bottom, for a total of 5-1/2". The 5-1/2" were removed from structural parts of the cowl between the door hinges. The back of the cab and doors had the 5-1/2" removed from the lower section. Running board to cab clearance was reduced approximately 1" for total

height reduction of 8-3/4".

Floor pan height was reduced 1-1/2" and cab and doors were narrowed front to rear 1-1/4". Height of side cowl vent was reduced 1" and top cowl vent was narrowed 1". Rear corner windows, when viewed from the rear, were narrowed 1" each. Rear center window was narrowed 2-1/4", chopped 1", and set back in the cab 1/2" closer to the beltline.

Hood and front fenders are 6-1/2" shorter than stock, and the rear fenders are 9" shorter than normal. The hood had the 6-1/2" taken off the rear portion, and the front fenders had the 6-1/2" removed at the center of the wheel opening.

A total of 2-1/4" was sectioned out of the hood height, to match the upper section of the cowl. The hood was narrowed 3-1/4" in the front by taking 1-5/8" out of each side at the area 1" from the middle seam, and tapering back to about 3/4" being removed from each side at the rear. Even though the cab was nar-

rowed 5", the hood had to be narrowed only about 1-1/2" at the back. The other 3-1/2" was taken up by the removal of the 6-1/2" in length taken off when the tapered rear part of the hood was amputated. The cowl area where hood and fender meet had to be tapered to match the new taper of the hood.

The front fenders had 3-1/4" of height taken out

*The cab was chopped, sectioned and narrowed. Just about everything that could be rebuilt to a smaller scale was attacked. A MIG welder was used to reduce panel warpage.*

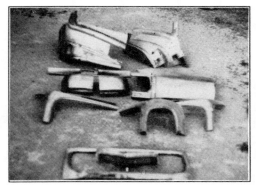

*After deciding that the new body shape needed to be approximately 15% smaller than original, Steagall went to work cutting apart the body. At this point, many builders would have looked for something else to do!*

*While the top posts were cut 1-1/2", the top panel was also lowered 3/4".*

*Cab height was reduced 5-1/2", and width was cut by 1-1/4". Cut through the door is to accommodate the section. A similar cut is through the cowl at the vent door location.*

*Window opening from another truck is fit inside stock opening to get the new smaller size.*

*Terry made a marking scribe jig from a piece of steel stock bolted to an old transmission case. With this he could scribe the exact line needed to cut.*

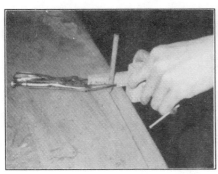

*Pencil line on inside edge of the fender shows where it is cut away 1", then the remaining lip is folded over 3/4" for a bolt flange to the bed.*

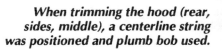

*When trimming the hood (rear, sides, middle), a centerline string was positioned and plumb bob used.*

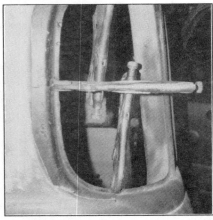

*A new firewall and flooring was made from steel. Special box for the heater squirrel cage was fabricated.*

above the molding at the bottom, and 5/8" of height taken off of the molding. The wheel opening is of a smaller radius than stock to match its reduced size, and also the 14" tires of the '85 S-10. Distance between the radius and the top of the fenders is 1-1/2" less than stock. The fenders are also 1-3/4" narrower than normal where they join the cowl and hood. Fenders were cut in 24 pieces, with 12 welded back together. The rear fenders are 9" shorter in length, 3-1/4" shorter in height at the front and 2-7/8" shorter in height at the rear, and are 1-3/4" narrower than stock at the front and tapered to 1-1/4" narrower than stock at the rear.

There were 3 radiuses on the truck that had to be altered. The cowl section, the back and sides of the top above the windows where 3/4" of height was removed, and the front fat portion of the rear fenders. Stock rear fenders have a flat vertical section at the front. Taking 3-1/4" out of this section leaves the rounded fat portion coming all the way down and looking odd, so the radius here had to be altered to regain the vertical flat portion before the bottom. This was done by making a new flange.

The bed sides and front were made from scratch out of 16-gauge steel, with original stock pockets (shortened 3-1/2") added on. The tailgate is stock Chevrolet stamping with 2-1/2" off each end, and 1-5/8" off the top and bottom. The rolls on the top sides and bottom of the tailgate are exhaust pipe tubing. Front and rear bumpers have 4-1/2" taken off each end. The splash apron behind the front bumper was cut into 12 pieces, with 6 welded back together.

Each grille bar, the chrome and the painted ones behind the chrome, were cut into 7 pieces, with 4 pieces being welded back together. Each end was shortened 1-3/4", and the middle was relieved of 3-1/4".

Gauges and speedometer are '85 S-10 units, mounted behind the repainted and renumbered '48 truck face plates.

All of the sheetmetal welds are butt welds, edge to edge, with the exception

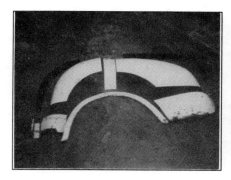

The rear fender was cut into many pieces and reshaped to fit the new smaller overall size, as well as the smaller diameter S-10 tires.

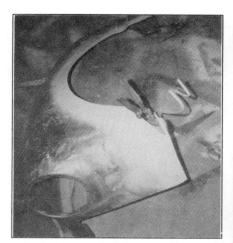

The new front fender wheel radius was raised 1-1/2" and then rolled under. At the front edge, 2-3/4" was cut from the fender bottom.

Front splash pan was cut into 12 pieces. About half of them were retained and welded back together to make a smaller unit.

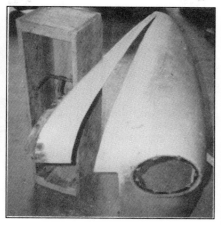

The front fender width was reduced by 1-3/4".

Rear lower section of fender was sectioned and trimmed to fit.

Inner splash aprons were fabricated from sheet stock. This was much simpler to make them fit original fenders and the new frame/ suspension.

of the rocker panel area of the floorpan. It is overlapped so it retains as much strength as possible. It was welded with a Lincoln SP200 wire feed MIG welder, and was almost all spot welded with ample time between spots to allow for cooling to keep the warpage down to a minimum. Filler used is very thin.

Every bit of this truck was built in my home shop, except the chrome plating and the Chevrolet emblem in the center of the dash. The emblem needed to be 4" shorter than stock, so I milled one out of cold rolled steel at a machine shop where I worked several years ago.

Shrinking and building this truck was right at a 2-year project, about 40 or 50 hours a week, every week. Some people say I must be a glutton for punishment, but I don't know what they mean. About 98% of the work I did on the truck was very enjoyable. To me, that's what street rodding is all about.

Dash is smaller and uses S-10 gauges inside original instrument faces. The dash plate was milled from steel stock to new dimensions.

BY RICH JOHNSON

# Chopped & Streched '40 Pickup

I f you like your classic pickup truck in stock condition, don't let Terry Steagall around it, because he has a habit of doing interesting things to vintage pickups. For instance, he built a scale downsized version of a '48 Chevy (seen elsewhere in this book), and now he presents us with this innovation -- a chopped and stretched '40 Ford.

This pickup is destined to become Terry's shop truck. He wanted to chop the top, but the tall guys at the shop would have trouble driving. So, it was decided that in order to compensate for chopping the top 3 inches, the cab should be extended a total of 6-1/8 inches to provide extra interior space.

Extending the cab 6-1/8 inches involved stretching the doors 2-1/8 inches, and moving the rear wall of the cab back another 4 inches. Even though the top was chopped 3 inches, the windshield was cut down only 2 inches. The additional inch of windshield was extended up into the front of the roof, to improve visibility for tall drivers.

The doors are hung suicide style on hidden hinges. The rear window framework was removed as a unit and the rubber lip was folded back 180 degrees, leaving the window area 1-1/2 inches larger in both directions. Tracks for a roll-up window were made and installed, so the rear glass can be opened and closed to improve ventilation.

With all the modifications to the cab, Terry decided that the hood would also need some work. It was sectioned to lower the front 1-1/2 inches. Functional scoops were fabricated and installed, to direct fresh air to the passengers. Fenders, hood and grille are welded together in such a way that

*Early in the game, the doors came off and were cut in pieces. The doors will be lengthened 2-1/8 inches and then reskinned. The window frame was cut down 3 inches to accommodate the top chop.*

*When all the parts and pieces were put back together, this is what Terry Steagall's '40 Ford pickup looked like. The top has been chopped 3 inches, the cab extended 6-1/8 inches, and the hood pancaked.*

*After severing the cab's rear wall, the window area was fitted with tracks and a roll-up mechanism for the rear glass. Glass area is now 1-1/2 inches larger in each direction than stock.*

*At this point, the rear wall of the cab was moved back 4 inches. Trial fitting was done to see what the finished stretch-job would look like. Another 2-1/8 inches of stretch was put in the doors.*

*Carefully shaped patches of sheetmetal were used to fill the 4-inch gap between the forward and rear areas of the cab. Note that the sheetmetal has been worked with a brake and English wheel to get the contours correct.*

they can tilt forward as a unit. This gives access to the engine compartment without any extra cuts or seams at the rear of the fenders.

To keep engine/exhaust heat and road noise out of the cab, Terry devised a double-skin floor and firewall. Then he sandwiched rigid foam insulation between the inner and outer metal skins. Cool and quiet!

Power for this chopped/stretched '40 Ford pickup is derived from a healthy 331 Chrysler hemi and TH350 automatic transmission. Ride and handling are delegated to the Mustang II independent front suspension, and a Corvette rearend.

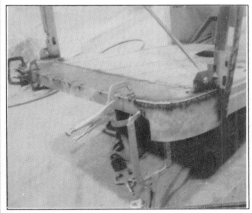

*With the upper portion of the cab extended, it was necessary to also extend the cab floor.*

Here's how the cab looks after all the sheetmetal patches are welded together. The rear window was cut away as a unit during the top chop, and is full sized. The rear glass roll-up mechanism is in place.

By using a pneumatic planishing hammer, weld seams are hammered flat, minimizing the amount of body filler that needs to be used later on to achieve a perfect finished surface.

Note that during the top chop and cab extension project, a length of reinforcing rod was tack welded inside the cab at the door to hold everything in alignment while the structure was apart. This is critical to getting everything to fit back together later on.

The skin has been removed from the doors for easy fabrication and installation of the hidden door hinges. These doors are hinged backward, so they open in suicide style.

To combat heat and noise, an aluminum floorboard skin was fabricated and spaced 1 inch away from the main floor, then foam insulation was sandwiched in between. The same was done at the firewall.

Toward the end of the project, parts were trial fitted. Eventually, the front fenders, hood and grille will be welded together in a single unit that can be tilted forward for access to the engine bay.

**BY JIM CLARK**

# REAR-DRIVE FLATBED '48

*Vehicle: 1948 Chevy Flatbed*
*Owner: David DeSure — Indian Wells, California*

**M**ost of us have favorite vehicles, usually more than one choice. When we finally get down to the building stage, one of these has to be selected and the work begun. That usually entails a series of modifications along traditional lines, inspired by others we have seen and liked. However, occasionally someone embarks on a rod building project that is a real departure from the norm.

That explains this very unusual '48 Chevy flatbed built by David DeSure of Indian Wells, California. He envisioned something more than just an updated pickup. It had to be truly one of a kind.

David had seen a lot of trucks with big engines, altered suspensions and wild paint, but his truck had to break some new ground. He decided on big power and a frame clip with modern suspension, only the clip was to come from the front end of a front-wheel-drive Oldsmobile Toronado, grafted onto the frame at the rear of the pickup.

To make his concept a reality, Dave took his ideas to friend Dan Condon who was experienced at building unconventional machines. Together they fabricated a frame extension that incorporated the Olds Toronado front clip, with a custom spring perch assembly to create the rear-drive, rear-engined flatbed pickup.

The cab and front sheetmetal remained stock in configuration, but the fenders were molded to the cab, side vents filled, door handles removed and custom running boards fabricated. On completion of the bodywork and

David DeSure's pickup turned flatbed hides a big 455 Olds rear engine package below that tilting rear bed. Subtle styling changes give no indication of the radically engineered chassis lurking beneath the surface.

Lightweight tilting bed was constructed from aluminum channel and diamond plate. Wooden slats surround bed on aluminum uprights. Custom made aluminum storage boxes mount on each side just in front of the wheels.

*Power for the pickup comes from this 455 cu. in. Oldsmobile Toronado engine and transaxle assembly. Complete unit from front of car was grafted onto rear of truck's frame, facing forward of course.*

*Rear suspension utilizes the front section of an Olds Toronado frame and engine package with custom made spring perches housing '70 Chevelle S/S 454 coil springs. Toronado disc brakes were retained and Gabriel shocks installed in the center of coils.*

chassis fabrication, Dan sprayed on the two-step bright red enamel, based on a '71 Opel red mixed by Victor at Big A The Paint Chemist in Indio. Finish work and detailing were done by Lalo, also located in Indio.

Up front, the stock suspension was replaced with modified Corvair independent coils and a Mustang II rack and pinion. Weight up front is considerably reduced with the engine at the rear, making this combination adequate for the truck.

Covering the engine in the rear is a handbuilt aluminum tilting flatbed actuated by pneumatic rams. A polished aluminum tank under the hood holds air for this purpose. The new fuel tank and battery are also located in the vacated engine compartment.

Inside the newly reupholstered cab, a pair of buckets from a Dodge Shelby provides seating for two. Air conditioning comes from a unit mounted behind the seats, blowing forward through ducts alongside the buckets.

For his effort, David's rewards include many "Best Engineered" trophies at shows, plus a one-of-a-kind vehicle to cruise around in. This flatbed doesn't see much duty hauling other than its passengers, but it hauls them in comfort unmatched by even the most modern of today's street trucks.

*Stock Olds Toronado T-425 transaxle with a 2.72:1 ratio transfers power to the wheels. Air-actuated cylinders tilt bed to provide access to engine and drivetrain.*

Cooling is provided by a radiator from the Toronado mounted crosswise behind the cab. Air is routed to it through ducting below the cab into the rectangular housing around the radiator. Bed support behind cab also has a latching mechanism to lock the bed in place.

Exhaust system is comprised of tubing connecting the stock manifolds to cross-mounted turbo mufflers with megaphone tips. Bed is hinged and pivots at the rear atop the rearmost frame crossmember.

Inside the vacated engine compartment reside the custom fuel tank, power brake cylinder and booster, battery, and polished fireman air tank, providing air to lift bed.

Seats are from a Dodge Shelby. Air conditioner is installed behind seats and blows forward from outlets between and at each side of the seats. Lieras' in Indio, California stitched up the matching carpet and vinyl covering the door panels and cab interior.

Stewart-Warner gauges beneath dash supplement the stock clusters on renovated original dash. Late GM Vega tilt wheel connects to Mustang II rack & pinion controlling modified Corvair independent front suspension setup.

Diamond plate panel at rear has dual brake/taillights high on each side and a large brake light in the center shaped like a Chevy emblem. HOT ROD vanity plate is real Nevada registration. Rear wheels are custom made 15x15 Centerlines shod with Mickey Thompson Sportsman radials.

**BY JIM CLARK**

# LUCKY MISFORTUNE

**Vehicle: 1956 Ford F-100**
**Owner: Bob Rice — Bakersfield, California**

**S**pending many hours on the road in a pickup truck can give you a lot of time to formulate plans for your ideal truck. Bob Rice of Bakersfield, California was afforded this opportunity while driving out to

service big rigs on road calls for his electrical system repair business. The shop where he reconditioned electrical components and maintained his small fleet of service trucks also provided the necessary facilities for Bob to build his dream truck.

The project started like many others do. A suitable pickup ('56 Ford F-100) was acquired and some minor modifications made to enhance its performance and appearance. Then a major traffic mishap destroyed the entire front end of the truck. This misfortune was transformed into an opportunity though.

Bob took the truck to his shop where he stripped away the damaged items and began building his ideal truck. New sheet metal was acquired

*Power for the F-100 comes from a '75 Chevy 350-small block V8. It is topped with a 650 cfm Holley carb on an Edelbrock Torquer manifold. Exhaust exits through custom tubing headers. Wheels are 15-inch Zenith wires fitted with BFGoodrich T/A radials.*

*Front axle is a 2-1/2 inch dropped Ford unit mounted via Ford leaf springs with reversed eyes. Brakes are '66 Mustang discs. Square tubing crossmember has attachment points for stock Chevy motor mounts.*

Chevy 350 V8 bolts to the Lake-wood scatter shield/bellhousing. Mid-'50s Chevy transmission mounts support the assembly via attachment to custom crossmember, fashioned from U-shaped channel. A third crossmember of straight U-shaped channel supports the rear of the GM Muncie 4-speed trans.

Air conditioner compressor mounts low on the left side opposite the alternator. This keeps the hoses low, eliminating the usual maze crossing the top of the engine compartment.

Stock steering box has been replaced by a unit from a '69 Dodge van. A popular conversion that bolts in place of stock unit on trucks with beam axle up front.

The one-piece tilt front end leaves the radiator freestanding in the compartment. Dual support rods, attached to the firewall, combine with the lower brackets to hold it in place.

Ample clearance between frame rails allows the alternator and air conditioning compressor to mount low at front of engine.

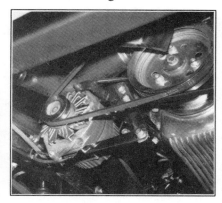

Custom bracket mounts GM alternator low on right front corner of engine. This cleans up the top end, eliminating much of the clutter.

Universal joint joins '69 Dodge steering box to Lincoln Continental Mark IV steering shaft.

and bolted onto a new tilt front end framework. The frame was extended, incorporating the tilting hinge mechanism into the extensions.

Up front, a 2-1/2 inch dropped axle and Mustang disc brakes were installed, utilizing stock front springs with reversed eyes. A '69 Dodge van steering box and Lincoln Continental Mark IV steering column were used to update the steering system. At the rear, a 9-inch Ford rearend with 3:50:1 ring and pinion was installed, utilizing the F-100 rear springs. Bob chose Zenith wire wheels, 15x8's for the front and 15x10's for the rear. These are shod with BFGoodrich T/A radials.

Power for the truck was enhanced by installing a 350 cid Chevy small block V8. Modifications to the engine included a Crane cam and ported heads, Ed Pink aluminum rods and TRW pistons, Edelbrock Torquer 4-barrel manifold with Holley 650 cfm carb and Mallory ignition. For a transmission, Bob installed a GM Muncie 4-speed. It bolts to a Lakewood scatter shield and is controlled by a Hurst floor shifter.

In addition to the power tilting front end, Bob added a number of other unique modifications. One of the most unusual is the squaring off of the bed by removing the top slanting portion of the side panels and adding rectangular tubing. Square tubing in the bed corners and a smooth tailgate create a flush edge to accommodate a tonneau cover. Below the tailgate, a rolled pan houses dual taillights and a recessed licence plate mount. Red Firemist metallic acrylic enamel was applied by the owner.

Inside the cab, custom upholstery covers a Lincoln 6-way power seat and door panels. Analog gauges were installed in the dash after the stereo tape player and CB radio were moved inside the glovebox.

The transformation took place during Bob's off hours over a 4-year period. In addition to the large number of awards that the finished truck has received, Bob has the satisfaction of knowing that he built the truck himself. The traffic mishap ended up being a blessing.

Convertible top cylinder performs power tilting of front end. Rod travel is long enough to allow tilting from fully-closed to open 90-degrees.

Front frame horns were extended to accommodate the hinges on the tilt front end. They disappear into the openings in the frame extensions.

Motor for the convertible top mechanism used to tilt the front end mounts on brackets along the outside of frame rail.

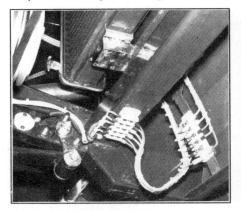

A pair of terminal strips serve as connection points between the main wiring harness and lighting harness on the one-piece tilt front end. This separation allows removal of front end and slack for tilting. Custom bottom mount on radiator sits atop front crossmember.

Where hoses pass through the firewall, a chromed plate covers any openings and serves as a mounting point for fittings joining braided steel lines. Much cleaner looking than rubber hoses and spring clamps.

Monroe 50/50 shocks were installed via stock front mounts. Tilting cylinder attaches to frame just forward of top shock mount.

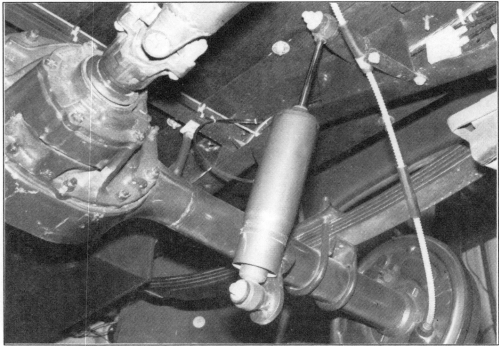

Compensation for added load in the rear is provided by a set of Gabriel Hijacker air-adjustable shock absorbers. Custom brackets were welded to the 9-inch Ford rearend housing and frame boxing plate.

Air to inflate the shocks is always available, due to the 12-volt air compressor mounted alongside the frame rail, beneath the bed. This also can be used to air flat tires.

Custom built fuel tank holds 26 gallons. It mounts between the frame rails in place of original spare tire carrier. Rolled rear pan shields it from view.

Rolled rear pan fills the gap between the bed and bumper. It also serves as a location for sunken license plate mount and dual round recessed taillights.

Right- The slanting portions of the bed side panels were removed and replaced with rectangular tubing. Tubing is also added to the corners, squaring off the top of the bed. Bed wood was replaced with mahogany separated by chromed divider strips.

Original instrument cluster is augmented by a full array of analog gauges, including a Sun electronic tach. Air conditioner mounts beneath center. Complete column assembly including cruise-control were taken from Lincoln Continental Mark IV.

Raised pleats and vinyl cover the Lincoln 6-way power split-back bench seat. Door panels and headliner were done in a matching pattern. Shifter is a Hurst floor-mounted 4-speed model.

"FOR SOME REASON IT'S JUST NOT CATCHING ON."

"HEY, NOBODY SAID ROBOTS WERE PERFECT!"

BY RON CERIDONO

# PRETTY AS A PICTURE

**Vehicle: 1929 Ford Pickup**
**Owner: David Thacker—Fullerton, California**

**A**rt can take many forms, and can be expressed in any number of ways. As an example, David Thacker's artistic abilities can be seen in drawings used on T-shirts and Bonneville posters,

photography that has appeared in a number of magazines, and most recently, this Model A pickup.

David's current creation rides on a chassis based on a TCI frame. Front

*Pretty as a picture is David Thacker's ultra clean '29 Ford pickup. It has that just-right stance of a mild hot rod, without going overboard with cosmetic alteration.*

*Thacker sacrifices the '32 in order to finance the building of his '29 truck. Actually, this is what everybody's garage should look like!*

Before the body was installed, it was easy to get a close look at the engine and transmission. Even though the rocker covers read 283, the engine is actually a Chevy 305 of 1983 vintage. Induction is via Weiand manifold and QuadraJet. HEI provides the spark, and the tranny is TH350 that is commanded by way of Gennie Shifter.

Thacker employed a TCI frame for this project. Michelin rubber surrounds Solid wheels at all four corners. Tire sizes up front are 165x15, while the rears are slightly larger at 235x15.

Out back, the Ford 9-inch rearend is equipped with 3.25:1 gearing, and is positioned by Deuce Factory triangulated 4-bars, with coilover shocks to ease the bumps.

Dropped tube front axle with reversed-eye spring and 4-bar suspension gets the front down low. Vega provided the steering unit, and a combination of disc and drum brakes came from JFZ and Ford, respectively

suspension consists of a dropped tube axle with a reversed eye spring, with the now standard 4-bar system keeping everything in place. A Vega steering gear provides directional control, while fore and aft braking is provided by a combination of JFZ discs and Ford drums respectively.

In the back, a 9-inch Ford rearend is positioned by Deuce Factory triangulated 4-bars with coilovers to soak up the bumps. At all four corners are powder coated Solid wheels, wrapped with Michelin rubber, 165x15 front, 235x15 rear. Ford hubcaps and trim rings finish things off.

Power for the pickup is provided by a 305 Chevrolet of 1983 vintage. The small block has been topped by a Weiand manifold and a QuadraJet carburetor. Spark comes from a GM HEI and sound effects are courtesy of a Pete Jackson gear drive. To add some under-hood sparkle, there are chrome valve covers and air cleaner. A Gennie shifter equipped Turbo 350 sends the power through an aluminum driveshaft to 3.25 rear gears.

After the running gear was completed, attention was turned to the sheetmetal. Dan Fink was called on to build the hood and a rolled rear pan, while the cab was worked over by the guys at Bitchin' Products. The reproduction pickup bed was supplied by Antique Auto Sheetmetal.

Once the truck was completely assembled, it was sent to Roger Ward's Bad Paint Company, in Ottawa, Kansas. There it was taken apart, painted with a special mix of yellow Dupont Cronar enamel, then put back together.

Upon its return to California, the '29 was outfitted with a Rod Tin interior and top, a Magoo dash with VDO gauges, and Vintage heat and air. Mike Maris was charged with running the wires to make things work.

David has been in and around hot rodding as a writer, photographer, and magazine editor for a number of years, and has had a string of fine cars. This Model A pickup being the eighth he's built.

**BY RON CERIDONO**
*photos by Vicky Davidson and Tim Frazier*

# Rock 'N Roll Ride

**Vehicle: 1940 Dodge Pickup**
**Owner: Dave Hurtt -- Salt Lake City, Utah**

**D**ave Hurtt was thumbing through a "cars for sale" publication, looking for something interesting, when he discovered this 1940 Dodge. As the marketing director for a rock 'n roll radio station, Dave's ride couldn't be some mundane look alike econo-box, and this pickup struck him as having the potential to be the unique rod he had always wanted. A deal was made, and the Dodge had a new home.

Right from the start it was decided that the MoPar front end would receive major modifications. The most striking is removal of the stock headlights from atop the fenders, and installation of '37 Ford units low in front. Lots of people scratch their heads over that one. Other changes include removal of all trim, three grille openings, and the front bumper. Dzus fasteners attach the hood side-panels, replacing the original latches.

The cab has had its share of changes too. Frameless V-butted glass replaces the stock windshield. Door handles have been removed, access is gained by lowering the power windows with hidden buttons, and using the inside handles. A neatly frenched antenna by Jack Harris is behind the passenger door. Running boards have been smoothed by hammering the original diamond tread flat.

Bringing up the rear is a custom made pickup bed, 12 inches shorter than the original. Stock rear fenders are attached to the abbreviated box, the right one has had a Porsche gas tank door installed. To finish off the rear, a panel was fabricated to fit below the bed. Trick taillights were done by Steve and Mike Hansen, and are simple utility trailer lights placed behind milled slots.

When it came time to pick a color for the truck, Dave decided he wanted something that would remind him of the blue-green Chevy pickup he learned to drive in. But the right color just couldn't be found. That changed

*The Dodge had 12 inches removed from its wheelbase, making it sort of a '40s mini-truck. A completely new bed was fabricated to fit the MoPar's reduced dimensions, stock rear fenders were retained.*

*The interior is unfinished, but that hasn't kept Dave from putting the miles on. The necessities for comfortable traveling are all in place, tilt-tele column, stereo, CB, power windows and air. Razoo upholstery is on the list of things to do.*

The Sig Erson cammed .030 over 327 Chevy supplies the urge for Dave's over the road exploits. The original Dodge radiator was modified and handles the cooling chores quite well. The firewall mounted master cylinder operates Chevy drum brakes.

Custom built bed features an integral tailgate. Trick slotted taillights are matched by miniature versions used to light the license plate. Rectangular exhaust tips empty through notches cut in the rear pan.

Painted Keystone wheels are used along with Goodyear rubber. The tires were won as a door prize at a rod run. The crowd at the event determined what order the prizes would be awarded. Dave won four tires, If the order hadn't changed he would have had a '34 Ford roadster. But hey, they are nice tires.

one day at the supermarket, when he found the colors he wanted on a can of Gillette Foamy shaving creme. J. P. Flynn of Salt Lake City mixed and sprayed the custom paint and scallops.

Underneath all the modified sheet metal are enough ponies to make the MoPar roll as well as rock. A 327 Chevy, bored .030 over, is fitted with a Sig Erson cam and ported and polished heads. A Rochester QuadraJet supplies fuel by way of an early Corvette manifold. Ignition is via stock HEI system. Chrome valve covers and air cleaner, plus lots of paint detailing finish things off under the hood.

Backing up the small block is a shift kit-equipped Turbo 350. A 2800 rpm stall speed gives the truck plenty of low-end response, and a Nova 12-bolt rearend equipped with 3:08 gears provides for highway cruising.

To get the Dodge in the weeds and make it ride and handle like it should, Bob's Rod and Custom of Logan, Utah was called on to install a Nova subframe. The rear frame rails were bobbed and replacement stubs fabricated to mount the rearend on GM springs. In the process of modifying the frame, 12 inches was removed from the wheelbase.

Goodyear Eagles surround Keystone wheels, which came from a Corvette Dave sold. The new owner didn't want them, so Dave lowered the price and kept the wheels. After repeated unsuccessful attempts to sell the them at swap meets, he gave up, painted the chrome rims and gold centers, and they went on the truck.

Creature comforts such as air, cruise control, power windows, and a tilt column are part of the interior package. VDO gauges are mounted in a custom aluminum panel.

The Dodge had only been on the road three days in its present form when we photographed it, and a number of things are still scheduled to be completed. Upholstery is yet to be done, and a hard tonneau is planned. Dave is even debating the installation of a blower.

Like they say, it's only rock and roll, but we like it!

Nose down stance comes from a Nova subframe and a custom rear frame section. Up front, scallops blend into a pin stripe that wraps around the back of the cab. Original sculptured detail lines in the fenders have been accentuated with painted highlights.

BY BURLY BURLILE

**O**ut here in "Hole In The Wall" country, famed outlaws Butch Cassidy and the Sundance Kid made history holding up stage coaches and robbing banks. Their reign of treachery began in the late 1800's and ran into the new century, a time filled with all kinds of new-fangled gadgets. Local rumor has it that Butch didn't really die in that shootout in South America, but returned to Utah and lived in quiet solitude until his death in the late Thirties. It's even possible he had the chance to ride in a vehicle, perhaps like this early Dodge owned by Bob and Louise Eames.

This street rod is a 1916 Dodge Screenside Delivery, a commercial truck which found great popularity in the rural state of Utah. Bob originally paid $300 for the truck and in the ensuing years has spent $3500 restoring it to the present condition.

To start, Bob and friend Dick Hall cherried out the existing body shell and located replacement sheetmetal where metalwork could not save it. The frames on early Dodges were boxed and are very sturdy, so no modifications were necessary. It was simply prepped and painted black. At the front, a '56 Ford half-ton axle was dropped six inches by Mordrop for a definite in-the-weeds stance. The spindles and brakes were altered to accept '49 Chevy pieces and the steering box changed to a reversed Chevy II unit.

The rear axle, a '67 Chevy II assembly, was attached to the stock

*Behind that grille is a late model Dodge 225 cid slant six with Holley Economaster carburetor and Accel ignition. Note the '56 Ford half-ton front axle, which was dropped six inches by Mordrop, giving the truck a definite in-the-weeds stance. Spindles and brakes were altered to accept '49 Chevy pieces, and the steering box is a reversed Chevy II unit.*

# 1916 Dodge Screenside Delivery

**Vehicle: 1916 Dodge Screenside Delivery**
**Owners: Bob and Louise Eames — Roy, Utah**

*When it comes to hot rod trucks, this 1916 Dodge Screenside Delivery is about as unique as they come. A resto-rod in the finest sense of the word, the bodywork was restored to original condition, while definite hot rod stuff took place underneath.*

*Rear axle is a '67 Chevy II assembly, attached to the stock quarter elliptic leaf springs and Monroe shocks. The driveshaft was shortened 18 inches, fabricated from a MoPar front and a Chevrolet rear section.*

*Upholstery is done in deep saddle brown Naugahyde, and deep pile carpeting. Stewart Warner gauges and wiring were installed by Dennis Williams, with room left over for plenty of dash plaques.*

*Running board tool boxes have been restored to original condition, but a few licks with a pinstriping brush added a bit of accent.*

*It's the neat little original equipment details, like the wing windows and sideview mirror, that make this vintage rod such a treat to see.*

quarter elliptic leaf springs and Monroe shock absorbers. Rotation from the '65 Torqueflite transmission was provided by a driveshaft that was shortened 18 inches, fabricated out of a MoPar front and a Chevrolet rear section. Power comes from a later Dodge product, a 225 cu.in. slant six engine of stock dimensions. The carburetor is a Holley Economaster and ignition is by Accel. A Hayden transmission cooler keeps the ATF at the proper temperature. Many of these components have been chrome plated for the "show" as well as the "go" modes.

All the custom woodwork came from the hands of Fred Christiansen, who fabricated the many bows and runners from Philippine Mahogany. Interior appointments were the craft of M.B.'s Upholstery and were done in deep saddle brown Naugahyde, and deep pile carpeting. Stewart Warner gauges and wiring were installed by Dennis Williams.

Dick Hall applied the special effects R.M. yellow lacquer that gives a definite glow to the Screenside's appearance. This helps to highlight the original 1916 Dodge accessories, such as the running board tool box and side vent wings. The taillight and headlights are stock '16 items, but the wheels once graced a rare Buick Skylark. Even the starter crank is original, but with the low stance, it would never be able to make one full revolution.

Whether or not Butch and Sundance ever got the chance to enjoy a ride in someting like this is irrelevant. It's enough to know that a truck such as this has been preserved and upgraded for our enjoyment. When you're out in Hole In The Wall country, look this one up.

*All the custom woodwork came from the hands of Fred Christiansen, who fabricated the many bows and runners from Philippine Mahogany. The screenside approach to delivery trucks has been lost to progress, but this fine example keeps the memory of the past fresh, while including mechanical advancements in the form of hot rod equipment.*

BY CALVIN MAULDIN

# C-Cab Woodie

**Vehicle: Model T Ford C-Cab**
**Owner: David Roberts—Denison, Texas**

**I**n this new high-tech era of rod building, the use of such exotics as carbon fiber and aluminum billet have become commonplace. To be different, Texas rod builder David Roberts opted to use one of man's oldest building materials on his project. Wood. Red oak to be exact. One of mother nature's most durable and difficult-to-work-with products ever made from a tree.

Before all the sawing and hammering could commence, a foundation had to be built to hold all the good wood stuff. Using C-channel for the frame rails, a '70 Opel GT front suspension was attached, with the back of the chassis being completed by adapting the entire rear clip from a '73 Jeep. Steering was taken care of with the addition of a Datsun B-210 unit. A stock Chevy 350, with a Turbo 350 automatic were bolted in for dependability and plenty of stump pulling power (couldn't resist that).

Building a wooden body requires a high degree of patience and skill. And, one would think, a stack of blue prints would be necessary to complete a project as intricate as this one. That's not the case here. Using only one simple sketch for reference, David eye-balled the C-cab's entire construction.

What goes into the handcrafting of a one-of-a-kind project like this? Well, for

*Over a year's worth of toil went into this expression of the hot rodding philosophy. This truck is different, to be sure. It's not red, there's no billet aluminum to be seen, and the body won't rust anytime soon.*

*You've got to compromise somewhere. David Winchester stitched up the interior to provide the soft seating that red oak cannot offer.*

*When was the last time you saw wooden headlight buckets? Untold hours were expended creating these lathe-turned pieces.*

*Independent front suspension is out of a 1970 Opel GT, while rack and pinion steering is a Datsun B-210 item.*

*This puts true meaning in the word dashboard. Though not completed at this time, the finished piece will no doubt be a knockout.*

*Piano-hinged tailgate is a work of art, hardware store latches hold it closed. Taillights are over-the-counter trailer items. Notice the beautiful way the red oak fenders flow up and over the tires. If you're in the mood for a challenge, try making curved oak fenders!*

starters, Miller's Cabinet Shop of Denison was called upon to custom mold over 600 feet of tongue and grooved red oak strips. They would be stacked together to form the body's main panels. To keep all of the wood in place once it had been fitted together, over three pounds of nails and screws were used, along with a gallon or two of Elmer's best. Time, a year's worth of it, was required. As a matter of fact, the body was tacked together and taken apart three times before the final assembly, to get it looking "just right."

Though the C-cab is most unusual, and not like all the rest, to be sure, its owner-builder is typical of most rodders. He wants to sell the truck to make way for his latest project, a full-fendered, Model T style boat-tail speedster. Of the red oak variety, naturally.

*The rear position of the chassis was made by adapting the entire rear clip from a 1973 Jeep. One thing is for certain — you aren't likely to see another truck like this one anytime soon.*

BY DAVID G. FOX

I Like a lot of quality builders, Kurt Scheider has a bit of a problem. As the owner of Kurt's Hot Rod Shop in Phoenix, he frequently has a car under construction for himself, but seldom has a finished hot rod to drive. Every time one gets close to completion, someone who just has to have it steps up with enough money to take it from him.

This truck had been sitting in the back of Kurt's shop, just a collection of parts from a project someone else had started, but never finished. Once the decision was made to begin construction, it didn't take long for Sterling "Jethro" Allen to massage the metal into shape. The chassis was powder coated and fitted with a small block Chevy, Turbo 350, and an early Corvette independent rear suspension. Up front was a Walker radiator over a four-bar-mounted Super Bell with a Magnum disc brake kit.

The pickup was almost completed, lacking only striping, color sanding and buffing, when a fellow from Luxembourg came along. He couldn't live without it.

Before being shipped overseas, a B&M supercharged Chevy 350 was installed under the hood. The four-bolt block was bored .040 over, fitted with a Competition Cams stick, forged pistons and heavy-duty rods. Seventy-six-cc heads with a little port matching work yielded a 9.0:1 compression ratio. The blower runs a maximum of 6 pounds of boost. The rest of the drivetrain was left as it was. Kurt described the total package as "not really trick, but enough to melt the tires." That's what the new owner wanted. It must be universal that some people just can't have enough horsepower.

The astute observer will note that something looks a little different in the proportions of this topless '28, but may not quickly identify what has been changed. The bed, according to tradition, has been shortened three inches, but at the front, not the back. That had to be because the cab has been lengthened three inches behind

# 28 Roadster
# Pickup

**Vehicle: 1928 Ford Roadster Pickup**
**Owner: Kurt Scheider — Phoenix, Arizona**

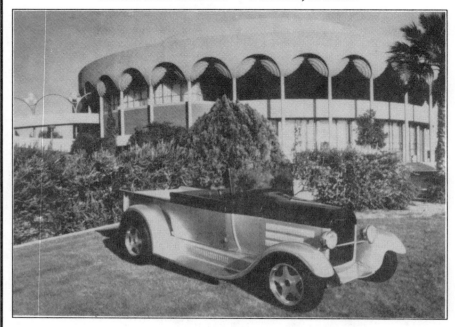

*Can you imagine building such a beauty and then letting it go to another owner? This low and lovely '28 Ford roadster pickup is a prime example of early hot rod pickups at their best.*

*The bed has been shortened three inches at the front, because the cab has been lengthened three inches behind the doors to provide more interior room.*

*The chassis was powder coated and fit with a fully chrome plated early Corvette independent rear suspension. Ford Probe taillights and third brake light are tastefully integrated into the super clean body.*

*A small block Chevy 350 was installed under the hood. The four-bolt block was bored .040 over, equipped with a Competition Cams stick, forged pistons and heavy-duty rods.*

*Custom touches include a rolled rear pan, smooth running boards, and a trick grooved steel bed insert. Five-spoke Riken wheels add to the clean, high-tech appearance.*

the doors to get more room inside. Other custom touches include a rolled rear pan with Probe high brake lights modified for primary use, a third Probe light in the back of the cab, smooth running boards, and a trick grooved steel bed insert.

When Kurt told folks he was going to split the square little body in two with color, they all told him he was nuts. A few hours spent on a computer graphics program helped Kurt design a paint scheme that proved all the critics wrong. The upper hue on the cab, hood, and shell is 1988 Chrysler Dark Cherry, the rest is 1990 Ford Light Titanium. Both are PPG pearl base coat/clear coat urethane applications by John Mastrangelo.

Upholstery in the extended cab was done with vinyl intended for boat use, to try to create something that would survive in the Arizona sun. All of those rolls and folds were finished with French seams by Mike Collins. The dash and steering column were given a coat of matching flat paint to complete the monochromatic look inside. VDO gauges were used, and the steering column, shifter, and parking brake handle are modified '65 Mustang items.

So, another neat hot rod, another satisfied customer, and it's on to other projects. But Kurt let us in on a second reason why his cars end up sold before he gets much of a chance to cruise the highways in them. He and able associate Bob Jensen build machines to be used as well as look beautiful. When you do that, you know they are going to rack up some nicks and scratches along with the miles. By selling them, he doesn't have to watch.

*Upholstery was done with marine quality vinyl to survive the intense Arizona sun. Dash and steering column received a coat of matching flat paint for a monochromatic look. VDO gauges were employed, and the steering column, shifter, and parking brake handle are modified '65 Mustang items.*

BY CALVIN MAULDIN

**W**hen Tim Babbit bought a '66 GMC 1/2-ton in 1985 and brought it to his home in Cartwright, Oklahoma, his intentions were to tinker just a little with the stock 283 to fine tune the mill, and maybe add a little paint on the semi-wrinkled body panels. Well, as you can see, good intentions oft pave the road for building super slick show trucks. Here's what happened.

The Jimmy was Tim's daily driver for two years, and was worked on as time and coins permitted, but the 1/2-ton pickup couldn't haul home any show gold. Then in 1989, while working at his dad's body shop, Babbit decided to try out some ideas that had been cluttering up his mind.

The 283 was pulled, bored .030 over, outfitted with a Performer camshaft, Performer intake, Quadra-Jet carb, and Accel ignition goodies. To get the attention of the white glove and clipboard guys, all the engine bolt-ons and underhood pieces were covered with chrome, plus the top of the radiator tank was polished to a high luster mirror finish. Plumbing was taken care of utilizing braided hoses.

While the body panels were being slicked, Tim took the hood to H.P. Lawson of Waco, Texas for some louvers. Old H.P. punched 136 of 'em in the bonnet and 26 more in the rear rolled pan. Other custom work is a sunken license plate box, shaved tailgate, and a frenched antenna.

After the '66 was covered in Ditzler Mars Red acrylic enamel, the finishing touches were added. And what touches! They include an oak bed floor, blue dot taillights, Dodge pickup tailgate chrome, some blue pinstriping by David Guymon, Pep mirrors, a black vinyl hard bed cover, and some white Naugahyde on the stock seat, stitched by Dorthy Frassier of DeLeon, Texas. Finishing out the interior, everything was painted white (with a dab of red), including the 1989 GMC steering wheel. A Panasonic AM/FM

# TIM'S TINKER TOY

*Vehicle: 1966 GMC*
*Owner: Tim Babbit — Cartwright, Oklahoma*

*It's hard to believe, but some of the truck guys consider '60-'66 GMC's to be ugly ducks. But with some thinking and just the right details, ducks become swans.*

*Clean is the word to best describe the rear of this red Jimmy. Latches have been removed from the tailgate. The rear pan has been rolled and punched. Check out the recessed license plate box. Tailgate trim is a blend of late model GMC and Dodge goodies. Simple, but neat.*

*Ever changing, Tim's GMC has been dropped another two inches since this photo was taken. Overall appearance is definitely of eye-catcher quality. Understated, yet fine.*

*Kinda makes you want to drag up the cooler and have a formal tailgate party, doesn't it? Oak lined floor is accented by the red painted slide strips. GM seatbelt buckle assemblies keep the tailgate fastened securely. Sure wouldn't want to haul hay in this baby.*

casette with 6x9 Pioneer speakers mounted under the seat can play rock 'n roll nonstop.

To get the 1/2-ton riding at the proper altitude, 1-1/2 coils were cut from the front, and four leaf springs were removed out back. Prime 228, 15x8-1/2 wheels were decked out with P225/60x15 Sears GT Radials which provide an ample footprint. In all, the red Jimmy sits comfortably low without dragging the mufflers on highway stripes.

So, did all the hard work net any gold? How about 14 first place trophies, 3 seconds, and a Club Choice award its first season out! Tim's Tinker Toy is continually being refined. If he keeps it up, he may have the same problem as Ivan "Iron Man" Stewart — where the heck do you put all the trophies?

*Under the hood is an environment more sanitary than some restaurants. Once again, Tim has sent more parts and pieces off to the platers since this shot was taken. The way the truck is always in a state of flux, we might have to do a sequel.*

*As a famous person in the magazine business once said, "Just plain pipe racks." That term pretty much says all that needs to be said about the '66 GMC's interior.*

**BY RICH JOHNSON**
....................................................
*photos by James Handy*

**B**ob Miller is a fat kinda guy. No, we don't mean it *that* way! It's just that he is the type of fellow who likes fat fendered stuff well enough to join a club named the Fat Bunch. At age 50+, Bob has been involved in the love of street rods since the early '50s. A list of his previous rides is revealing. In addition to a few other cars, he has owned three '41 Ford coupes, and a '46 convertible. See what we mean about Bob being a fat kinda guy?

Originally, Bob bought this '41 pickup for $400. Then he spent some 15 years building it into what we see here. Power comes from a '47 Ford flathead that was bored .060 over, yielding a total displacement of 255+ cubic inches. The heads were polished and the block relieved, then an Isky 3/4 cam was installed and the valve-train was upgraded to Johnson adjustable solid lifters. Isky springs close the valves tightly each cycle. An Eddie Meyer Hollywood intake manifold has been topped with a pair of Stromberg 97 carbs. Exhaust is routed by way of a set of Fenton headers, through turbo mufflers.

Gear selection is the duty of a 1977 T-10 4-speed transmission that has been upfitted with altered stock shift linkage. The final member of the drivetrain is a '57 Ford station wagon 9-inch rear axle, stuffed with 3.56:1 gears. Spring packs for both the stock '41 front axle and the rear unit have been treated to Teflon between the leaves.

Steering, from wheel to box, is totally stock '41 Ford, except that the column was chromed. But the brakes have

# Fat Bunch '41

**Vehicle: 1941 Ford pickup**
**Owner: Bob Miller — Yuba City, California**

*Relatively stock body is beautiful despite the fact that it wasn't even chopped, channeled, sectioned or reworked in any way. It has a classic styling that is just fine the way it came from the factory.*

*Although the truck looks low, it is riding on stock front and rear leaf springs, which have been treated to Teflon between each leaf. Tires are 215x14 in front and 235x15 in the rear, stuffing the wheelwells full of rubber.*

*Hand-rubbed oak cargo bed adds a touch of class. It's things like this that bring home the trophies from area shows.*

*Classic flathead styling, with enough chrome and polish to encourage the use of sunglasses. The '47 Ford V8 was bored .060 over, stacked with an Eddie Meyer Hollywood intake manifold and topped with a pair of Stromberg 97's. Fenton headers route the exhaust.*

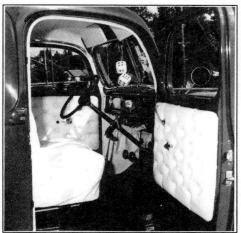

*Button-tufted white Naugahyde upholstery brightens up the interior in Fifties style. Fuzzy dice are the crowning touch.*

undergone some updating. Front binders are '73 Chevy discs, and the rear units are '57 Ford drums. Tru Spoke wheels (14x7 front, 15x8 rear) are wrapped with Armstrong radials (215/70R14 up front, 235/70R15 in the rear).

Body and frame are basically stock, but somehow everything looks better than Ford ever intended back in '41. Of course, it helps to have a bunch of chrome under the hood, the engine painted red, the chassis painted black, and endless-depth of red lacquer paint everywhere else. A hand-rubbed oak cargo bed adds a distinct touch of class. Then there's the button-tufted white Naugahyde interior, complete with fuzzy white dice hanging from the rearview mirror. It looks dynamite! The stock dash has been fitted with King Seely 12-volt instruments, and a Sears sound system was installed.

Along the way, a number of custom parts had to be made and creative installation performed. Among them were the triangulated 4-bar rear, alternator and air conditioner brackets, placement of the air outlets, controls and evaporator, as well as the radio beneath the seat.

Besides the pure enjoyment Bob gets from driving this piece of automotive artwork, he has garnered a stack of awards from numerous shows. Friends Ben Collins and Mike Overton can also take pride in the workmanship. Ben rebuilt the crossmember and put in the T-10 4-speed, using an Offy adapter, split the wishbone and built a new floorpan. Mike helped out with making the rearend fit, fabricated all-aluminum pulleys, air cleaner, and did the aluminum and stainless welding.

It's good to have friends like this when you're a fat kinda guy.

**BY RON CERIDONO**

# Purple
# Pickup

**G**eorge and Vicki Arbuckle wanted a ride that would attract attention. What better way to accomplish that than a chopped purple '48 Chevy pickup.

Originally, this project had been started by the Arbuckles' neighbor, Bob Gillum. Bob had begun to built a

work truck when his buddy, Dave Kinnaman, suggested they chop the top. That sounded like a neat idea, but after the lid was lowered other

*Purple '48 rides on 14x8 ET mags, shod with 60-series rubber. Cargo bed floor was done with yellow poplar planks and stainless steel strips. A race type fuel cell is mounted below the bed. A unique adaptation of Trans-Am taillights was used at the rear.*

*Interior is done in light and dark gray velour. Climate control is by way of a Superior heating and cooling unit. Stewart-Warner gauges are installed in a custom aluminum panel.*

*A GM power brake unit and tandem master cylinder mount to a handmade aluminum firewall. Chrome valve covers and air cleaner, along with lots of paint, detail the complete underhood scene.*

***Vehicle: 1948 Chevy Pickup***
***Owners: George and Vicki Arbuckle — Elwood, Indiana***

*George spent many hours in the garage to get this Chevy to its present condition. Dave Kinnaman, Bob Gillum, and wife Vicki provided valuable help.*

*Use of a Studebaker grille causes lots of double takes. Turn signals are mounted in the grille, with driving lights below. A small chin spoiler is molded into the lower pan.*

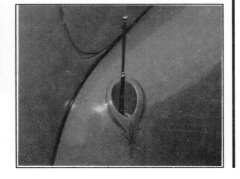

priorities (like a new baby) put the Chevy on hold.

One year passed with the truck sitting in a barn, then Bob decided to sell. A deal was made, and George hauled the pickup home in pieces, convincing himself on the way that this would be a quick project. One thing led to another, as they often do with hot rods, and 2-1/2 years passed before the truck was on the road.

Since the top had been chopped 4 inches, it was decided to continue the fat 'n smooth look. Door handles were removed, hood corners rounded, and headlights frenched. Up front, a Studebaker grille was used, because it was hanging in the garage and needed a home. Louvers were punched in the hood and the tailgate, and the rear was finished off with inverted Trans-Am taillights. The folks at East Side Parts in Elwood, Indiana mixed up their own version of purple to cover the exterior.

Inside, seating is provided by Chevelle bucket seats, separated by a hand-crafted console. To provide cruising comfort, a GM tilt column, power windows, and air conditioning were added. Stewart-Warner gauges supply necessary information.

Under the hood, we find a stock 400 cu.in. small block Chevy. Power is delivered to the leaf spring suspended Pontiac rearend by a TH400 automatic transmission.

To get the front down, and still provide the desired ride quality, a frame clip from a 1973 Pontiac Ventura was grafted to the original rails. Disc brakes and power steering are additional benefits of the chassis update.

The Arbuckles' goal was to build a rod that attracted attention, and we think they've succeeded.

*A tunneled antenna on the right front fender is just one of the many small details that accent this custom/rod pickup.*

BY JOHN LEE

**T**he '67-'72 series of Chevrolet pickups picked up where the '53-'56 Ford F-100s left off as customizing favorites. From high riding four wheelers to ground scraping low riders, mild street to pro street, they've been modified every imaginable way.

Wally Reinke of Imperial, Nebraska, thought one done with early customizing techniques would give him a unique ride, and he's right. In the process, he and Doug Reinke, his nephew, tried out some new tricks that are worth passing along.

When Wally traded an El Camino for the truck, Paul Hutchinson had already chopped the top 4-inches. Wally and Doug took the next step by suiciding the doors using Kenworth truck latches and International Scout hinges. A reworked grille opening now hosts two sets of Corvette grille teeth mounted on a 1/8-inch aluminum bar. Rectangular quad lights were pirated from a '77 Buick Regal.

Frenching and painting the bumpers lends a rolled pan effect front and rear, and the hood and tailgate are punched with 232 louvers. Twin '59 Cadillac bullet taillight lenses are set into housings on each rear quarter panel, and a power antenna is tunneled on the right flank. One of the neat stock styling touches of these models is the flared, radiused wheel openings, which show off chrome Cragar SS five-spokes backed by plastic discs painted body color.

Speaking of color, it's '79 Chrysler Spitfire Orange urethane trimmed with pinstriping by Todd Hayes. Triple-cap lakes pipes, smoked glass, peep mirrors and spotlights complete the image.

Wally converted the utility box for people-accommodation by building a rear-facing rumble seat that makes into a bed. Storage compartments were also built into the carpeted box. The tonneau cover is secured by Velcro strips and can be rolled back to any desired point.

The gray velour trimmed in orange that Arlene Ahrens stitched for the

# Fantasy

**Vehicle: 1968 Chevrolet C-10 Pickup**
**Owner: Wally Reinke—Imperial, Nebraska**

*With a little bit of imagination and a lot of talent, this is what can be done to a '68 Chevy pickup. Wally Reinke pulled a bunch of nice custom tricks out of the hat when building Fantasy. Two sets of Corvette grille teeth rest on an aluminum bar. Quad headlights, 4-inch top chop, louvered hood, and lakes pipes are only the beginning.*

*Bumpers painted body color almost appear to be molded in. A pair of '59 Cadillac taillights nest in 3/4 tunnels, allowing the lights to be seen from the side as well as from the rear. Spitfire orange urethane paint was highlighted with pinstriping by Todd Hayes.*

*Doors were suicided, utilizing Kenworth truck latches and International Scout hinges. Grey velour upholstery is trimmed with orange piping for accent.*

*A '74 pickup was stripped of usable mechanical parts including the 350 engine. Edelbrock Elite air cleaner and valve covers, and a matching Night Prowlers battery cover top off the engine, rebuilt with a .030 overbore. Mallory electronic ignition, Holley 650/Weiand combo and Jackman headers pull duty here. A custom-built fan shroud and radiator cover, braided hose covers and chromed accessories accent the engine compartment.*

*Tonneau cover pulls back to reveal a bed-mounted rumble seat, for fair weather cruising with friends. Carpeted cargo box also features custom-built storage boxes.*

interior closely matches the bed's vinyl. A Bose stereo plays tunes, and Wally even has a viewer from a '50 Pontiac to help him find traffic lights above the chopped windshield!

A '74 pickup was stripped for usable mechanical parts including the 350 engine and Turbo 350 trans, rearend, front disc brakes, seat, power steering and tilt column. Chassis lowering was accomplished by C'ing the frame and installing 4-1/2-inch blocks in back and substituting 3-1/2-inch dropped spindles and coil springs from a 6-cylinder for a 5-inch drop in front.

An Edelbrock Elite air cleaner and valve covers and a matching Night Prowlers battery cover top off the engine, which was rebuilt with a .030 overbore and stock lower end. The cam is a Chevy RV grind, working in concert with a Mallory electronic ignition, Holley 650/Weiand combo and Jackman headers. A custom-built fan shroud and radiator cover, braided hose covers and chromed accessories further accent the engine compartment.

As Nebraska late-model rep for the KKOA, Wally is showing the way for truck customizing.

*Graphics tell the story on the louvered tailgate. Dual exhaust tips peek out from beneath, and a pair of Appletons highlight the pickup.*

BY RON CERIDONO

# Pick A Pair Of Pickups

**Vehicle: 1934 Ford Pickup**
**Owner: Bo Huff -- East Carbon, Utah**

**W**hat we have here is a difference of opinion. Two interpretations of what should be done to one of Henry's haulers to make it into a hot rod.

Jerry Wilson took the subtle approach when constructing his version of a hot rod pickup. He began with a '34 that was found in a garage under a pile of mattresses and other debris. After a seven-year pursuit the complete but rough Ford was his.

Originally the plan was to get the old truck running, paint it, and use it as a beater. But Jerry, with a number of other rods to his credit, couldn't hold himself back once he got going. He pulled the truck apart, down to the bare frame, and started from the ground up.

The rebuild was begun by boxing the frame and updating the suspension. A Super Bell axle positioned by a split wishbone and stock spring was used up front. For sure stopping GM disc brakes were installed. Steering is by way of a Mustang box. Out back, '54 Chevrolet leaf springs hold a GM positraction rearend.

Making this pickup haul is a 350-cubic inch Chevrolet LT-1 that, like most everything else, was built by Jerry. Backing up the potent small block is a B&M Turbo 400 Jerry bought in a crate. After calling B&M to investigate the origin of his find, he was told it had been built in 1972 and contained all the trick internal goodies. It had been built to hold some serious horsepower, but never was used.

Once the chassis was done, it was time to get the sheetmetal straightened out. The 27 years the pickup spent with its previous owner had not been easy ones, so virtually every panel on the truck needed attention. Jerry returned the body to like new condition, then widened a set of fiberglass fenders for the rear. To keep the lines the same as original, the running boards were widened with a tapered insert to fit the width of the stock fenders in the front, and the widened fenders in back. Bringing up the rear is a homemade

*Definitely a homebuilt, Jerry did virtually everything himself, spending a grand total of $6,102 to get this '34 to where it is now.*

*Bob Hampton was there to lend a hand with the body work and then laid out the flames. Chassis was painted with $18-a-gallon red enamel Jerry picked up from a tractor/equipment supply store.*

*The original bed was pretty well thrashed, so new sides were made from sheetmetal. Rear fenders are widened Wescott glass items, and running boards have been widened in the rear to match.*

*In front of the owner-built replacement firewall sits a stout Corvette LT-1. The 350 features 4-bolt mains, steel crank and TRW pistons. Ignition is by Mallory Unilite, carburetor is a Holley 750.*

*Mustang steering is used along with mid-sized GM disc brakes, Super Bell axle, and a split wishbone. Wheels at each end are by Weld.*

stainless steel tailgate on modified hinges.

When it came to choosing colors for the truck, Jerry thought long and hard before deciding on what he calls a '50s style theme. He shot the DuPont Corvette Arctic White basecoat/clearcoat himself, then asked Bob Hampton to help lay on the orange and yellow flames. After a few check-out miles sitting on a milk crate, upholstering chores were handed over to Wayne Alderman of Butte, Montana.

We asked Jerry if he had any future plans for the truck. He said "Yeah, heat and air... and lots of driving."

*Wayne Alderman and Jerry stitched up the interior. Tilt-tele column is out of an Oldsmobile Tornado. Jerry used the emblem from an early Ford hubcap in the center of the Olds wheel to confuse the troops.*

*Taillights were made from Lincoln side marker rings, Buick Rivera lenses, and Chevy Nova boxes. Tailgate is stainless steel.*

# Pick A Pair Of Pickups

T he second half of our dynamic duo is Bo Huff's pickup. Bo elected to take the hit-ya-right-between-the-eyes approach when building his '34.

No doubt about what we're dealing with here, channeling the body over the frame gives the Ford that unmistakable '50s hot rod look. The image is helped further by a 6-inch top chop. Inside the close confines of the cab is a chromed '33 Chevy dash, a custom built console, and a Panasonic sound system. Period perfect maroon and white tuck and roll was done by Deor.

Continuing the '50s approach, a Model T tailgate was punched full of louvers and hung between similarly ventilated and chopped Model B bed sides. Below the gate are blue dot equipped '39 Ford taillights and a homemade nerf bar. Inside the abbreviated box is a seat, designed for two really close friends, which conceals the battery and gas tank.

Frame modifications are as extensive as those done to the body, but of a more modern nature. The '34 rails have been shortened, narrowed, and boxed. Up front, a 4-inch dropped axle, reversed eye stock spring, and 4-bars are found. Brakes are disc and steering is from a Datsun 210. The rearend is a '77 Corvette assembly that has been fully chromed and mounts to the chassis with a homemade crossmember.

Sitting in front of a louvered and chromed handbuilt firewall is a Corvette 4-bolt main 350 built by Paul Candelario. The small block has been topped by an Edelbrock manifold, holding a trio of chromed 97's. A Turbo 350, built by J&S transmission of Price, Utah, delivers the power to the 'Vette rearend through a custom built chromed driveshaft.

At all four corners are wide-white-

*Little doubt exists about the look Bo was trying to create. Early rod styling conceals current rod building chassis trends.*

**Vehicle: 1934 Ford Pickup**
**Owner: Jerry Wilson -- Twin Falls, Idaho**

*Chrome wheels with bullet equipped baby moons hold wide-white Firestones. Bed sides have small fins molded into the rear above the tailgate.*

*Pete and Jake's shocks attach to a 4-bar equipped dropped axle. Grille shell is a '32 with a custom made insert, and fits between visored Dietz headlights.*

*Lakes plugs hook to Sanderson headers. Check the old timey molded/flared door hinge.*

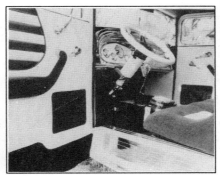

*A '33 Chevy dash has been cut to fit, chromed and filled with Classic Instruments. Gennie shifter hooks to a Turbo 350.*

wrapped chrome wheels. The unique hubcap treatment was created by installing handmade bullets on baby moons.

Like we said before, what we have here is a difference of opinion. Two different methods of personalizing a pickup. Jerry and Bo's pickups may be as different as night and day, but the one thing they have in common is, they're both hot rods.

*Passenger seat in the pickup box hides the fuel tank and battery. Pinstriping is by Jerry Crimm.*

*Peeking out from under a bobbed bed is a fully chromed '77 Corvette rearend. Complete exhaust system has been plated as well.*

BY JIM CLARK

# THE BLOWN RANGER

*Vehicle: 1978 Ford Ranger*
*Owner: Jim Biller*

**P**ro Street vehicles use massive tires, big engines, wheelie bars, and trick paint to mimic their racer cousins. Though there are 1/4-mile drag trucks to emulate, this look has not been accepted by truckers until very recently, and then in just a few instances. Could be that after the country sees Jim Biller's nasty Ford the trickle may turn to a flood.

Jim bought the Ranger new in '78 with visions of making it into a custom cruiser. As a result, the body still boasts many custom touches. Up front we encounter a 10-tube grille flanked by smoked and etched headlight covers, all hovering above the fiberglass chin spoiler/fog light combo. Frank and Roger Bogner created the oak bed rails and trim as well as the classy oak floor boards. Biller installed a polished beer keg as a reserve gas tank for flash. Dave Samm applied the black lacquer and then highlighted it with flames of candy red, orange, and tangerine accented by blue pinstripes. Samm also airbrushed the "Blown Ranger" name on the spoiler and the Ford logo on the tailgate.

Jumping inside, we find a bench seat covered in black vinyl and Skanda cloth. The dash is well stocked with gauges including a full array of factory pieces augmented by a Sun tach and fuel pressure gauge plus a digital clock. If music is required, Jim can turn to either his Craig AM/FM stereo or a tape player. Should ventilation be needed on those muggy Ohio days, a removable sunroof resides in a padded headliner. Etching graces the windows. A handbuilt switch panel, map light, aircraft dome lights, fire extinguisher, and a wood rim Grant GT wheel round out the accessories.

No doubt about it, the truck's a looker. But the powertrain is what gets you doing the old double take.

*Bigs and littles are definitely a hot rod statement, and these consist of massive 33x13x15-inch McCreary tires on 10-inch Weld wheels out back, with tiny 3-1/2 inch wheels up front for the F-78 Firestones.*

*A 10-tube grille and smoked headlight covers dress up the front, while a chin spoiler is emblazoned with the truck's name, "The Blown Ranger."*

*A profile shot clearly shows the down-to-business stance of this '78 Ranger. With a "just right" rake, a blower sticking through the hood, and wheelie bars out back, nobody is going to mistake this for anything less than a serious performance truck.*

*A polished beer keg was instaled in the cargo bed to serve duty as a reserve fuel tank. Oak cargo bed floorboards match the custom built oak bed rails and trim.*

*In case there were any doubts, this is a true hot rod truck. One doesn't generally need a drag 'chute and set of Moroso spring-loaded wheelie bars just to get the groceries!*

*Powertrain is dominated by a mildly built 302 V8, topped off by a 6-71 GMC supercharger over an Offenhauser tunnel ram. The Holley 750 cfm carb inhales through a polished Mr. Roadster scoop.*

Dominating the engine bay is a 6-71 GMC supercharger. The Dyer's Street Charger is underdriven 12% and mated to an Offenhauser tunnel ram via a 1-inch spacer. Dual 750 cfm Holleys suck air through a polished Mr. Roadster scoop. Most of the 302's internals including the crank, rods, and 9.1:1 pistons remain stock. Bronze valve guides and a 3-angle valve job help the Windsor heads.

Jim decided to pitch the stock cam and go with a hydraulic from Competition Cams with .456 lift and 216 duration. A double roller chain and Comp Cams springs keep the valves off the pistons. The factory electronic distributor was recurved to pass spark through Blue Max wires. Burnt gasses are evacuated by Doug's headers and dual glass packs. A heavy duty oil pump circulates the oil out of a 7-1/2 quart pan, through dual filters and into the engine. The little C-4 automatic was strengthened at Norwalk Trans Service. An early model valve body, B&M deep pan, and a Trans-Go shift kit help it stand the gaff. Biller installed a driveshaft safety loop just in case. Puttin' the ponies to the pavement is left to a 9-inch Ford rearend packed with 3.90 gears and capped by massive 33x13x15-inch McCreary tires on 10-inch wide Weld Wheels. Tiny 3-1/2 inch Welds with Firestone F-78's up front handle directional changes. Moroso spring-loaded wheelie bars and a parachute are there in case things start to get out of hand.

There you have it; one man's vision of the perfect pickup. Jim and wife Linda do put the miles on the truck too. Traveling to the Street Machine Nationals, the P.F.C.A. Ford meet and numerous local events, the Ranger pulls down 12 mpg. Now that's ridin' the range in style.

*Interior has been upgraded with a Sun tach and fuel pressure gauge, plus a digital clock. Tunes emanate from a Craig AM/FM stereo, while Jim enjoys the comfort of a wood rim Grant GT steering wheel.*

**BY JIM CLARK**

# THUNDER TRUCK

**Vehicle: 1956 Ford F-100**
*Owners: Matt and Andra Bradley — Thornton, Colorado*

Ford enthusiasts will really appreciate this stunning green 1956 big back window F-100, belonging to Matt and Andra Bradley of Thornton, Colorado. A look under the pickup's hood reveals an unexpected surprise, a Ford Y-block V-8 with all the right speed equipment to give small block Chevys a run for their money.

Wanting to improve upon the F-100's powertrain, but retain the Y-block nostalgia, Matt swapped the original engine for a 1963 vintage Thunderbird 312 cid Y-block. Forged pistons, a full race cam and solid lifters were added to help the Y-block handle the heavy breathing of a 4-71 GMC supercharger. The Jimmy blower is mounted on a Cragar intake manifold. Notice the rare 3-belt Cragar blower drive set-up, which is overdriven by 20%. Fuel is supplied to the engine by two dual-feed AFB four-barrel carburetors, which are supplied by an electric fuel pump with a fuel pressure regulator.

An Accel coil and Mallory distributor ensure that the healthy powerplant receives all the firepower it needs. To better handle the exhaust gases from the huffed Y-block, Matt installed a set of chrome plated Sanderson headers which dump into turbo style mufflers. From there, the exhaust exits through '57-'58 era full length chrome plated bed pipes. The crowning touch to this excellent example of Ford engineering is a set of original 1957 Thunderbird valve covers.

The F-100 retains its stock 3-speed column shifter and stock tranny. The rearend houses 3.90:1 Spicer gears for excellent acceleration off the line. 1953 to '56 F-100's look great lowered, with meaty rubber filling up those large round wheelwells. To achieve this, a 3-inch Mor-Drop straight front axle and spindle kit were added to drop the front, and the rear was lowered 2 inches. Teflon is used between the springs for a quiet smooth ride. Fat Remington radials are mounted on

1953 to '56 F-100's look fantastic lowered, with meaty tires filling the wheelwells. To accomplish this, a 3-inch Mor-Drop straight front axle and spindle kit were installed to drop the front, and the rear was lowered 2 inches.

Matt installed a set of chrome plated Sanderson headers which dump into turbo mufflers. From there, the exhaust gasses exit through full length chrome plated bed pipes from the '57-'58 era.

*Matt swapped in a 1963 vintage Thunderbird 312 Y-block with forged pistons, a full race cam and solid lifters. A 4-71 GMC supercharger is mounted on a Cragar intake manifold. Note the rare 3-belt Cragar blower drive set-up.*

*A 1963 Chrysler power bench seat with rolled and pleated black leather upholstery offers comfort, and the door panels are also upholstered in rolled and pleated black leather. A wood rimmed steering wheel replaces the stock unit, and a dash full of Stewart-Warner gauges keep Matt informed about the engine's vital signs.*

*Rich '75 GMC metallic green paint is highlighted by 3-color pinstripes and flames from the steady hand of Bernie Johnson. The chrome was brought back to life by Denver Bumper.*

*Teflon is sandwiched between the spring leaves for a smooth and quiet ride. Fat Remington radials are mounted on Cragar SST wheels, 7x15's in the front and 10x15's in the rear. The rearend houses 3.90:1 Spicer gears for snappy acceleration.*

Cragar SST wheels, 7x15's in the front and 10x15's in the rear.

Matt relied on the talents of Merle Rhodes to whip the F-100's body into shape. E&T Auto then applied the rich '75 GMC metallic green paint. It is highlighted by 3-color pinstripes and flames from the steady hand of Bernie Johnson, and plenty of chrome plating by Denver Bumper. The bed also received a fresh look, with new redwood slats and a bed tarp by Larry McDaniels.

The interior is just as clean and functional as the rest of the truck. A 1963 Chrysler power bench seat with rolled and pleated black leather upholstery supplies plenty of comfort for those hours behind the wheel going to and from truck runs. The door panels are also upholstered in rolled and pleated black leather, and Larry McDaniels gets credit for the headliner. A wood rimmed steering wheel replaces the stock unit, and Matt added a dash full of Stewart-Warner gauges to monitor what's going on in the engine compartment. The sound system features an AM/FM stereo tape deck, and a CB radio allows Matt to keep in touch with other truckers on the road.

Matt gives special thanks to his wife Andra, and their friends who helped with the project. With a blown T-bird Y-block under the hood, the Bradleys have one of the most unique examples of the classic '56 F-100 around. Matt feels they have both a mover and a cruiser. We'll second that.

**BY JIM CLARK**

**A**fter owning a fairly diverse number of machines ranging from fast Corvettes to wild altereds and roadsters, Darryl Witt has definitely found a vehicle he's comfortable with...the outrageous crew cab dualie shown on these pages. And why are we so sure he's comfortable with this choice? The fact that this is his fifth crew cab in a row might have something to do with it!

Darryl is an avid racing fan and participates in motor and watersport events under the handle "Sterile Darryl Racing." Here, you can find him assembling any number of different racing machines at varying times depending upon his mood and the time of year. His stable currently includes a drag bike, a turbo/nitrous funny bike, a Curtis blown alcohol picklefork hydro, and several double-engined street bikes. His latest project is a Class 1 Unlimited off-road buggy.

The brilliant red dualie serves as both tow vehicle, support vehicle, and everyday transportation for Darryl and his wife, Denise. The 1980 GMC crew cab also serves as excellent advertising for Sterile Darryl Racing due to the eye-catching Porsche India Red paint by Mario's Classic Colors in Chatsworth, California and pinstriping by Tim Bartee of Designs and Lines in Placentia. Adding an extra special touch is the gold-leafed "Sterile Darryl" lettering on each side, the handiwork of Walt Prey of Chatsworth.

Many fine touches have been dealt this machine at every quarter. Perhaps one of the most noticeable is row after row of louvers which have been punched into the hood and tailgate by Dennis of Seemore Louvers in Fullerton, California. A total of 402 louvers grace the hood alone, and each of these is individually pinstriped for effect. Other exterior refinements include a chromed Stull tube grille, rectangular headlights, and a rear tonneau cover by A-1 Canvas in

# HOT ROD DUALIE

*Vehicle: 1980 GMC Crew Cab Dualie*
*Owner: Darryl Witt*

*Darryl Witt, operating under the handle "Sterile Darryl Racing," owns quite a variety of toys including the 1980 crew cab dualie shown here.*

*The crew cab's windows have been darkly tinted for a distinctive look and to keep sun glare to a minimum.*

Lots of pinstriping and lettering is found on the India Red truck. Artwork was handled by Tim Bartee and Walt Prey.

A total of 402 louvers are found on the truck's hood alone, and each of these has been meticulously pinstriped. Louvering was handled by Dennis of Seemore Louvers in Fullerton, California.

Darryl replaced the stock GMC grille with a trick setup from Stull Industries that includes an array of chromed tubes and quad rectangular headlights. Note the louvered front license plate—neat!

Beneath the hood rests a 454 cubic-inch mill outfitted with an Engle cam and lifters and a Pete Jackson gear drive. More than enough power is generated to smoke the dualie's tires impressively.

Upland, California. The whole works is brought closer to the pavement courtesy of a lowering job performed by Art Snyder.

Beneath the impressively louvered hood one finds a 454 cubic-inch mill bored .030 over and equipped with such goodies as an Engle cam and lifters and a Pete Jackson gear drive. More than enough power is produced to smoke the truck's Michelin 875-16.5 meats and chromed GMC 16.5 reverse rims whenever Darryl decides to really get on it. The inside of the engine compartment has received a fresh coat of India Red paint and lots of contrasting pinstriping for a nice effect.

The interior compartment is pretty mild in comparison to the wild exterior. Here, Darryl kept things basic by sticking with the truck's stock instrumentation and seating, but added personal touches such as louvered dash panels and pinstriping for a custom look. A leather European-style steering wheel and a Wink mirror enhance driving comfort, while darkly tinted windows eliminate sun glare and add a distinctive touch.

Darryl is quick to point out that many friends and associates have helped him with his crew cab, and extends special thanks to Joe Taran, Art Snyder, Tony Ledford, Dennis of Seemore Louvers, and numerous other friends. He continues to refine his trick truck (Showtime Marine in Upland is currently preparing 23 karat gold lug nuts for the wheels!), and the machine continues to get better and better. All of which is the very essence of hot rodding and customizing a truck.

Interior refinements are minimal, but do include a handful of louvered dash panels accompanied by some pinstriping. A leather wheel and Wink mirror are also found here.

**BY JIM CLARK**

# CANADIAN CUSTOM

*Vehicle: 1978 Chevy*
*Owner: Rod Collett*

**W**hen former Canadian resident Rod Collett decided to put together a new street ride, he had to give it some thought. He had already owned some pretty impressive machinery, including a Roadrunner, Nova SS, Chevelle SS, and a Cutlass, so it had to be something pretty special to get him motivated.

What Rod came up with was something unique that holds special meaning. He special ordered a new '78 Chevy Silverado with all the factory whiz-bang effects, from electric windows and door locks to power everything and tilt steering. Once the basic machine was in his hands, he began a long process that would see the pickup customized three different times, until the desired result was finally attained. This truck is Rod's version of luxury at its finest...his "Canadian Cadillac," which he calls out to the world with his "CanCadi" personalized plates.

The stock high riding truck was lowered some 8-inches overall, with the removal of the rear leaf springs and the modification of the front coils. To accentuate this long, low look, Rod bolted up a set of Tru-Spoke Classic wire wheels and BFGoodrich T/A radials that tuck nicely inside the wheelwells. Hidden beneath the truck are chromed Gabriel shocks at all four corners, a chromed front sway bar, and many other chromed undercarriage parts. All suspension work was handled by Collett's Brake & Wheel Alignment in Bloomington, California.

Subtle body modifications were performed that come together to make this custom truly beautiful. Rod had the door handles and roof gutters shaved, the emblems removed and filled, and the stake pocket holes filled. He even went so far as to relocate both the primary and auxiliary fuel tank inlets

When Rod Collett set out to build himself the smoothest street cruiser possible, he pulled out all the stops! His '78 Chevy Silverado is really wild with just about every known amenity.

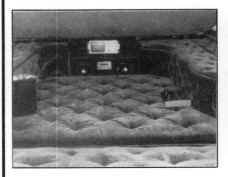

*Beneath the plushly upholstered rear tonneau rests an incredible interior that really wows 'em at the shows (no wonder he's won eight 1st place trophies). Here we find plenty of button-tucked velour at every quarter.*

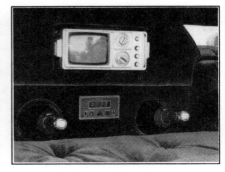

*The forward part of the pickup bed boasts a velour covered cabinet housing a built-in television, digital clock, and even a wine rack. A TV antenna is found topside at the front of the tonneau.*

*The tonneau cover is hinged so that two-thirds of it can swing upward to expose the nifty bed upholstery. Highlighted on the tonneau is the outline of a maple leaf — a sign of Rod's Canadian heritage.*

*Above- Attention-to-detail and subtle customizing are found everywhere on this pickup, from the etched windows and windwings to the shaved door handles and filled fuel inlets and emblem holes.*

*Inside the engine compartment, we find a shimmering and brilliantly detailed 350 powerplant. Much chrome is found here including hood hinges and springs, Moroso air cleaner and valve covers, pulleys, alternator, and much more. Other engine modifications include an Edelbrock Sp2p manifold, Carter 625 cfm carb, Blackjack headers, and stainless steel braided lines and hoses.*

*This pickup's cab is replete with button-tucked velour everywhere, from the seat and headliner to the door panels and dash. Ron Mangus and Gary Contrerras are responsible for this interior wizardry. Other additions include a Pioneer AM/FM/ cassette deck and a Personal leather steering wheel.*

*Rod has added many other fine touches in the interior including a louvered glove box door, louvered ash tray, and louvered panels on the doors. Everything combines to make this a fabulous custom pickup.*

inside the wheelwells, and then had the fuel tank doors filled on the body. Rod added a chromed tubular grille with rectangular headlight up front, a custom fabricated rear Plexiglas lense with a "Silverado" callout at the rear, and opera lights on the cab sides. All of this is handsomely shown off with a Camaro Blue paint job, with dual stripes applied by Tracy Larson of Fontana, California.

The TV antenna located just behind the cab exterior should be taken as a hint that there is more to this truck than meets the eye. Lifting the velour button-tucked tonneau cover reveals a super plush pickup bed that is not to be believed. Here we find button-tucked velour everywhere, along with a velour covered front cabinet boasting a television equipped with Atari, a digital clock, and even a wine rack. The sides of the bed offer upholstered wheelwell boxes with built-in stereo speakers.

Inside the cab, Rod had Ron Mangus and Gary Contrerras do a fantastic job with the button-tucked velour. Everything is covered from the seat and headliner to the door panels and dashboard. Complementing this plush decor are items such as a Personal leather steering wheel, Pioneer stereo, plush floor carpeting, and rows of louvers on many interior components.

This machine not only looks good, but also travels at a fast clip, courtesy of a well appointed 350 V8 backed by a B&M equipped Turbo 350 tranny. Many fine touches have been employed here, including an Edelbrock Sp2p intake and Carter carburetor, Moroso valve covers and air cleaner, stainless steel braided lines, and lots of chrome.

Rod Collett's efforts have netted him one fine pickup, along with eight 1st place show trophies, to date. Needless to say, he is extremely happy with his creation after reworking it three different times, and we certainly can't blame him. It's an international show winning attraction.

BY TODD KAHO

# RADICAL STEP SIDE

*Vehicle: 1979 Chevy Step Side*
*Owner: Bill Stull — Corona, California*

**W**hen you own a company which manufactures automotive specialty and performance parts, people expect you to drive something a bit unique. Corona, California's Bill Stull is a good example. Bill is the owner of Stull Industries, which you may recognize as the company that makes those excellent tube grilles seen on the front of custom vans and trucks. Bill's latest venture is a business called Pick-Up Parts Co., which is devoted solely to the truck end of the automotive market.

Even if you know all this background information, you're still likely to be a little stunned when Bill rolls up in his yellow and black, chopped top step side. It's a knock-out! The truck, built to showcase accessories from Pick-Up Parts Co., is sponsored by Stull Industries. Bill purchased the truck new in 1979 for $6000, and now, he has over $20,000 invested. If you've already examined the accompanying photos, you know where that money went.

Until just recently, the step side was powered by a turbocharged 400 cubic inch big block Chevy. That powerplant has been swapped into the Crew Cab Bill is currently building, and replaced with a blown small block Chevy. After a "ride around the block," I can honestly say that if anything, the pickup is even faster than before.

The 350 cubic inch V8 was built by Ed Pink. Ed reworked the heads, added a high-performance cam and cam gear drive, a 6-71 blower topped off with a single 850 cfm Holley 4-barrel, and headers with turbo mufflers round out the performance package. The 350 is backed by a built Turbo 400 automatic which is shifted by a B&M Quicksilver shifter.

The pickup rides very close to the pavement. It was lowered with a Stull Industries lowering kit, and the frame was notched. Front and rear anti-sway bars keep the pickup's attitude very flat and neutral through the corners. Stull

Built to showcase some of the accessories available from Pick-Up Parts Co., Bill Stull has invested more than $20,000 in the building of this radical step side Chevy.

Bill louvered everything in sight, including the tailgate, rolled rear pan, and even the roof panel. A rigid tonneau cover was upholstered in black with yellow stripes to match the body graphics.

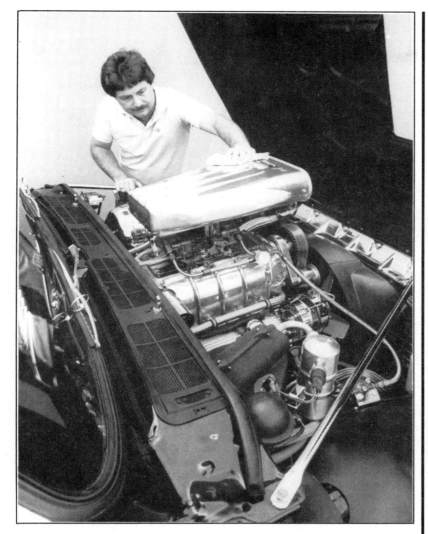

*A blown small block Chevy V8 powers Bill's ride. Built by Ed Pink, the engine features reworked heads, a high-performance cam and gear drive, a 6-71 blower with single 850 cfm Holley, headers and turbo mufflers.*

*A fiberglass one-piece tilt front end from Pick-Up Parts Co. was installed for easy access to the engine compartment. Note louvers in roof panel and even in the plexiglass side window.*

*The interior is upholstered in black Cadillac cloth, covering the Kamp bucket seats, dashboard and door panels. Stewart-Warner gauges fill the dash, and a Pioneer sound system plays the tunes.*

Industries traction bars were used in the rear to keep all that supercharged power to the ground. Bill added polished alloy Streaker wheels, 15x8 in the front and 15x10 in the rear and BFGoodrich Radial T/A's at all four corners.

To say that the body has been radically altered is quite an understatement. Bill did all the bodywork himself, except for the top chop which was handled by none other than the master, Dick Dean. Bill installed a Pick-Up Parts fiberglass tilt front end, which now has a Mr. Gasket bug catcher sticking through it. Bill louvered everything in sight. The step side fenders, stepwells, tailgate skin, rolled rear pan, and even the roof panel have been louvered. If that isn't enough, Bill also had louvers punched into the Plexiglas side and rear windows.

Bill is also responsible for the application of the flashy yellow paint scheme. Three tones of bright yellow graphics were used over a subtle yellow base coat. Naturally, the front end features a Stull Industries square tube grille and smoked Plexiglas headlight covers. The outside mirrors are electrically operated Tornados. Even the rigid tonneau bed cover is trick. It has been upholstered in black with yellow stripes which match the graphics on the body.

The inside of the pickup is just as impressive as the outside. The interior is upholstered in black Cadillac cloth. The Kamp seats, dash and door panels have all been covered with the high grade material. Stewart-Warner gauges were added to the dash, along with a louvered and chrome plated glove box door and ash tray. Another nice touch adding to the luxurious feel of the interior are the Pick-Up Parts Co. oak armrests. The sound system features a Pioneer AM/FM stereo cassette deck and Pioneer speakers.

Bill Stull has built a very neat calling card for his Pick-Up Parts Co. It's an attention grabber that'll rip the pavement from under its rear tires at will. Seems like a sound investment to us.

**BY JIM CLARK**

**W**hen discussing just why he built his '76 Ford pickup, Olin Allen of Falls Church, Virginia, agrees that the scarcity of customized late model Fords did have some appeal and the Flareside shortbed trucks do lend themselves to a variety of bodywork

# FLAMED FLARESIDE

*Vehicle: 1976 Ford Flareside*
*Owner: Olin Allen — Falls Church, Virginia*

*Wild looking daily transportation! Olin Allen purchased this truck new, and made mods while using the truck as a daily driver. His reason for selecting this '76 Ford Flareside as a project was because that was what he had.*

changes. But in his case, Olin points out those weren't the prime considerations. He built his Ford primarily because it was what he had. Olin had purchased the truck new and had made a number of small changes while using the vehicle for daily transportation. The end result was a lowered mild-custom with a black paint job and a wild set of flames.

A couple of years ago, the urge hit to redo the truck and the decision was made to go all the way this time. Olin took the truck to Dimension Louvers in Waldorf, Maryland where most of the bodywork was performed. The top was chopped 6 inches and the front end was converted to a hydraulically operated tilting model, while the doors were given the suicide hinge treatment. Other body changes include a flattened tailgate, filled rear pan, frenched license plate and a general dechroming.

*The 6-inch top chop really brought the truck low, and it was taken down even more by installing a set of Mor-Drop lowered twin I-beams with a 3-inch drop. The rear was lowered by removing leaves from the springs and shortening the shackles.*

*Body mods include shaving the doors, building a flat tailgate, filling the rear pan, frenching the license plate, and dechroming the entire truck.*

*A set of Cragar S/S wheels add classic sparkle. Measuring 14x6 in front and 15x10 in the rear, they are surrounded by BFGoodrich tires up front and Posi-Traction rubber out back.*

With the major bodywork complete, the pickup was delivered to Richard Glymph in Silver Spring, Maryland. Richard's job was to finish up the bodywork by making the whole package perfectly straight before applying the paint. Many hours of block sanding and priming preceded spraying, with the Ford Canary Yellow lacquer and the multi-colored flames. The exterior was finished off with the addition of 14x6 and 15x10 Cragar S/S wheels mounting BFGoodrich and Posi-Traction tires.

The underside of the truck received its fair share of modifications as well, the most striking of which is the lowering job. Olin purchased a set of Mor-Drop lowered twin I-beams that had been dropped 3 inches. The rear was lowered by removing leaves from the springs and shortening the shackles. Other mechanical modifications include a factory 406 tri-power unit added to the otherwise stock 390 powerplant, Cyclone headers and a tilt and telescoping steering column added from a Cadillac. The upholstery is the work of E&T Auto Top in Falls Church, Virginia and features pleated burgundy Naugahyde with yellow and orange graphic panels.

The finished version of Olin's truck represents not only one of the nicest Ford pickups in his area, but one of the finest custom pickups anywhere. It is a street-driven car show winner that should set an example for Ford enthusiasts throughout the country.

*Under the hydraulically operated one-piece tilt hood is a fairly stock Ford 390 V8 that has been treated to a 406 tri-power unit and Cyclone headers. Obvious dress-up goodies include braided hoses and aftermarket valve covers.*

*Doors were given the suicide treatment, and handles shaved. Burgundy Naugahyde interior is accented with yellow and orange graphic panels.*

175

**BY JIM CLARK**

# RADICAL RANCHERO

*Vehicle: 1979 Ford Ranchero*
*Owner: Dirk McConnell — Orange, California*

**R**ancheros aren't the most popular trucks to customize, but when they're done right they can be some of the most stunning. Case in point — this '79 Ranchero belonging to Dirk McConnell of Orange, California. A member of

Rancheros Unlimited, Dirk, with the help of friends Jim Larr and Jeff Swank, invested three years in the building of his Radiant Ranchero.

Dirk kept the bodywork to a minimum, shaving the emblems to provide a clean, unobstructed surface for a wild custom paint job. "H" Street Custom in San Bernardino, California is responsible for the paint. The base color is a black Imron. A combination of blue, magenta, yellow, orange, purple, red and charcoal graphics were added in lacquer, then cleared with urethane. The result is an eye-catching paint scheme that will attract more than its fair share of attention. The finishing touch was the addition of a chrome-look "Ranchero" identification on the tailgate.

To set off the paint, Dirk added four Tru-Spoke wire wheels, 14x7's in the front and 15x10's at the rear. The rear

*Ford Rancheros may not be the world's most popular truck to turn hot rod tricks on, or to customize, but this example of a '79 by Dirk McConnell shows just how much potential these vehicles have. Grass trimming stance was achieved by lowering all around and installing Gabriel Adjustable E's up front and Gabriel air shock out back.*

*A combination of blue, yellow, magenta, orange, purple, red and charcoal graphics will grab the eye of anyone within sight. A chrome-looking "Ranchero" was painted on the tailgate as a finishing touch.*

*A highly detailed and healthy 351 was upgraded with a Crane cam, Offenhauser dual-port intake manifold, Holley 780 carb, reworked heads, dual exhausts and turbo mufflers. Dress-up was assisted by chrome Moroso valve covers, Russell steel braided hoses and a chromed master cylinder.*

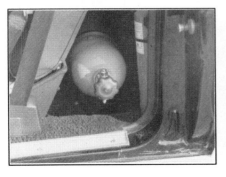

*There are times in the life of every hot rodder when a little more performance is nice. For those occasions, Dirk has a NOS Power Shot nitrous oxide system tucked behind the seat.*

*To keep the engine compartment as clutter free as possible, Dirk relocated the battery to a special place in the cargo bed, hidden beneath the rigid tonneau cover.*

wheels are fitted with P295R-50-15 BFGoodrich Radial T/A's and the front wheels with P245R-60-14 Super GT Radials.

Dirk's Ranchero is anything but all show. Under the hood is a very healthy and highly detailed 351 cid V8. A few of the performance modifications include a Crane cam, Offenhauser dual-port intake manifold with a Holley 780 cfm 4-barrel, reworked heads, and dual exhausts with turbo mufflers. For those times when more than a "little" more performance is needed, Dirk added a NOS Power Shot nitrous oxide system.

The engine compartment is thoroughly detailed. Billet Race Cars is responsible for the aluminum engine compartment panels. Other dress-up items include chrome plated Moroso valve covers, Russell steel braided hoses, chrome plated master cylinder, Edelbrock Ram Flow air cleaner and the Offy intake was polished.

The automatic has been beefed up with the addition of a Thompson 2500 rpm stall-speed torque converter and a TransGo reprogramming kit. The transmission is shifted by a B&M Quick Click shifter. The 9-inch Ford rearend now houses 4.11:1 gears for snappy acceleration.

Dirk wanted his Ranchero at pavement scraping level, so he enlisted the talents of Dean Napier at Dino's Custom Lowering for a thorough lowering job. Gabriel Adjustable "E" shocks were added to the front and Gabriel air shocks were added to the rear. Dirk then had the Ford factory anti-roll bars chrome plated to dress up the underside of the pickup.

The finishing touch was the addition of a bed cover from Gaylord's Custom Tops. Dirk has built one of the nicest custom Rancheros we've ever seen. Rancheros have a unique character all their own, and with examples like Dirk McConnell's around to set the trend, we expect to see more in the future.

*Relatively stock interior features the addition of a Grant GT steering wheel to keep the fingers happy during long hours on the road.*

BY JIM CLARK

# HYBRID HAULER

**Vehicle: 1954 Ford F-100**
**Owner: Jim Longworth — Tacoma, Washington**

Custom F-100s are usually a combination of more than all their stock components. Items from a variety of other vehicles are added or substituted for existing components. The finished vehicle that is produced is a hybrid consisting of the best of both, harmoniously assembled into an updated custom hauler.

This 1954 Ford F-100 belonging to Jim Longworth of Tacoma, Washington illustrates this concept very well. It retains a stock appearance through the utilization of original sheet metal, but that's where the factory influence ends. The rest is pure custom. The drivetrain underwent the most change, with installation of a '69 Ford 390 cu.in. V8 and C-6 automatic trans. Engine mods include: 406 high-performance heads, 428 CJ cam, 9.5:1 pistons, Holley intake with Holley 650 cfm 4-barrel and dual exhaust.

Out back is a '69 F-100 Spicer power-lock rearend (3.55:1) mated to a '69 LTD driveshaft. Front suspension is from a '67

*Don't be fooled by the stock appearance of this sedate looking '54 F-100, because the factory sheetmetal is just about all that is original. The rest is pure custom.*

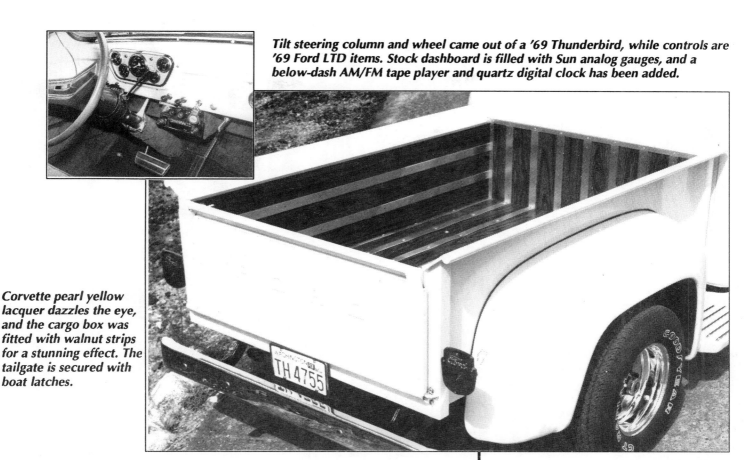

*Tilt steering column and wheel came out of a '69 Thunderbird, while controls are '69 Ford LTD items. Stock dashboard is filled with Sun analog gauges, and a below-dash AM/FM tape player and quartz digital clock has been added.*

*Corvette pearl yellow lacquer dazzles the eye, and the cargo box was fitted with walnut strips for a stunning effect. The tailgate is secured with boat latches.*

*Down in the weeds in the front, Jim's F-100 rides on the front suspension from a '67 Chevelle. Rear suspension is from a '69 Ford F-100 with power-lock differential. ET mags are fitted with Goodyear GT radials.*

*Beneath the hood resides a '69 Ford 390 V8, followed by a C-6 automatic transmission. Engine modifications include 406 high-performance heads, 428 CJ cam, 9.5:1 pistons, Holley intake topped by a Holley 650 cfm 4-barrel.*

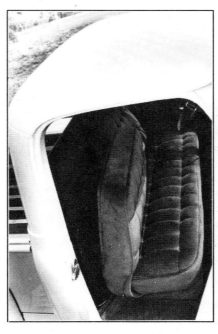

*Bench seat was borrowed from an International Scout, then custom upholstered to match the door panels and headliner in brown waffle pattern velvet.*

Chevelle, still married to the original frame. Brakes are also taken from the same source. ET-mags are fitted with Goodyear GT radials, GR 60-14 up front and LR 60-15 rear.

A number of interior components have been borrowed from a '69 T-Bird. These include: column shifter, tilt-column and wheel. Controls are from a '69 LTD. Rocky Peters of Parkland Upholstery in Tacoma covered the International Scout bench seat, door panels and headliner in brown velvet waffle pattern. The stock dash has an insert with a full set of Sun analog gauges. It's joined by a tape-player and quartz digital clock.

Corvette pearl yellow acrylic lacquer covers the completely stripped sheet metal. The bed has been fitted with walnut strips and the gate secured by boat latches.

The reward for all of these efforts has been a host of awards including the Pacific Division ISCA class champion honors. It's more than a show truck though, it regularly makes the weekend outings for F-100s throughout the West. Definitely a classic hybrid.

BY JIM CLARK

# SUPERCLEAN 'CAMINO

*Vehicle: 1965 Chevrolet El Camino*
*Owner: Chuck McConnell — Redlands, California*

**C**huck McConnell of Redlands, California needed a transportation vehicle, so when he heard about a '65 El Camino available for the paltry sum of $175, he couldn't pass it up. While it did need work, it was in running condition and represented quite a bargain as the basis for some pretty solid transportation. Chuck went right out and snapped it up.

The car did serve well as an everyday driver and stayed in basically the same condition for over six years. In the seventh year though, the decision was made that the little El Camino would become something better than an everyday beater... much better. It took a year of hard work to change the thrashed 'Camino into the beautiful machine that Chuck drives today.

Out came the smoking powerplant, and in its place went a '66 Corvette 327 complete with an early model Z/28 cam and valvetrain, and a Z/28 pan, pickup, and windage tray. Chuck also added an Edelbrock C4B manifold with a 600 cfm carb, Hedman Headers, and Mallory ignition. The entire engine and engine compartment have been decked out with lots of fresh black and white paint, gold accenting, and plenty of chrome for a show appearance.

The powerful engine couples to a wide ratio Muncie M21 tranny with an 11-inch diaphragm clutch. Other drivetrain modifications include heavy-duty universal joints and a 12-bolt rearend out of a '66 El Camino. Stopping power is provided by drum brakes in the rear and front discs, which were scavenged from a later-model El Camino. Traction action is handled superbly by Cragar S/S wheels and BFGoodrich T/A radials at all four corners.

Since Chuck wanted a subtle custom

*A lot of effort has gone into making this '66 El Camino a very smooth, subtle custom. Upon close inspection, one can note the incredible amount of attention-to-detail paid everywhere.*

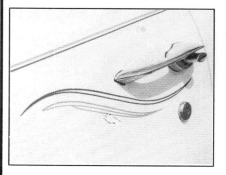

*Two-tone brown pinstriping is found throughout to accent the bright Corvette White paint job. The pinstriping was applied by none other that Chuck's boyhood hero, Ed "Big Daddy" Roth.*

*Beneath a handsome saddle brown tonneau cover rests an equally detailed cargo bed area done in gray Zoletone paint. A lift-up compartment has been custom-built into the front part of the bed.*

The stock, and rather tired, El Camino mill was replaced with a reworked and detailed Corvette 327 powerplant. Lots of fresh paint, chrome, and detailing can be found beneath the hood.

Chuck replaced the stock seat with a bench seat from a later model El Camino, and then had it reupholstered in saddle brown velour and vinyl. Headliner, dash pad, and door panels also match.

The instrument cluster has been blacked out for a nice look, and then accented with a column-mounted Sun tach and a leather GT steering wheel.

The rear quarter panels have been punched out some 2-1/2 inches to accommodate wider wheels and tires, the body has been dechromed, and the Chevy insignia has been eliminated from the tailgate. All are subtle touches that the custom buff can certainly appreciate.

Above- Chuck has retained the stock radio but has plans for a Kenwood stereo system in the near future. Note the Sun oil pressure and water temperature gauges that have been flush-mounted in the dash.

appearance in the rear, he flared out the rear quarter panels approximately 2-1/2 inches and added slightly wider wheels and tires here. He also removed all the chrome trim around the fenderwells, took off the body emblems and filled in the holes, and eliminated the Chevy insignia on the tailgate. Jack Maxim of Yucaipa, California applied the Corvette White acrylic enamel, while Ed "Big Daddy" Roth did the two-tone brown pinstriping.

To enhance the bright white machine, Chuck blacked out the Camino's grille and added black Tornado side mirrors on each door. The bumpers were rechromed, and all remaining chrome and stainless steel has either been hand or machine polished for a new appearance. Beneath the saddle brown tonneau cover, which is the handiwork of Tracy Ramirez, rests a nicely-detailed cargo bed section painted in two tone Zoletone truck paint. A lift-up compartment has been built into the front part of the bed.

Inside the cab we find a '66 El Camino bench seat that has been reupholstered in saddle brown velour and vinyl. The seat, along with the matching headliner, dash pad, and door panels, were also handled by Tracy Ramirez. Brown low-pile carpeting covers the floor area to accent the handsome upholstery. Among the many additions in the cab are a Grant GT leather steering wheel, a Hurst shifter, and Sun auxiliary instrumentation.

Chuck McConnell had definitely reworked a former "beater" into something really special. It has taken a lot of time and no doubt a large chunk of cash, but the end result is certainly a fine, subtle custom that anyone would be proud to own.

**BY JIM CLARK**

**R**on and Kathy Mangus of Bloomington, California are the proud owners of this highly detailed 1956 Ford F-100, which has more than earned the right to bear its custom license plates, "1 Tuff '56." It's tough and it's trick at every corner.

The pickup has quite an interesting history behind it, as it was purchased brand new by Kathy's father and served faithfully as Kathy's transportation all during high school. Then, when Ron and Kathy married, her father handed over the pink slip and the customizing began. Since the pickup was still needed to serve as an everyday workhorse, though, the custom work was done in stages so it could remain a regular daily driver for the couple.

Among other things, the truck has served well as a showcase for Ron's skills as a trimmer and auto upholsterer at Quality Auto Upholstery in Bloomington. His handiwork is evident throughout, from the custom bra and rear tonneau cover to the interior appointments.

The pickup has received many mechanical transplants including the addition of Chevelle power steering, a Camaro rearend, and a Ford 302 engine backed by a C-4 trans. This powerplant is highly detailed and boasts features such as a Crane cam and lifters, Edelbrock manifold, Carter carburetor, Moroso valve covers and air cleaner, and lots of chromed parts. The engine compartment is further enhanced by orange paint, a brass radiator, chromed fan shroud, and stainless steel braided lines and hoses. A nice touch is also added by a chromed fire extinguisher that is mounted to a fenderwell beneath the hood. All wiring is nicely tied and routed cleanly in sheathing.

*Another trick boasted by this truck is the custom rear tonneau cover, also made by the owner, Ron Mangus, at Quality Auto Upholstery. Beneath the cover, one finds a detailed bed of oak planks and chromed strips.*

# ONE TUFF '56

*Vehicle: 1956 Ford F-100*
*Owners: Ron and Kathy Mangus — Bloomington, California*

*This '56 Ford F-100 is custom throughout with attention to detail evident at every corner. Note the custom-made vinyl front bra, a bit of the owner's handiwork as an upholsterer.*

*Plenty of chrome is found throughout on this truck, including the taillights, running boards, mirrors, grille, bumpers, and emblems.*

*Beneath the hood rests a Ford 302 V8 replete with lots of chrome and high-performance goodies. Other mechanicals include a Ford C-4 trans, Chevelle steering column, and Camaro rearend.*

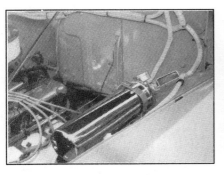

*This chromed fire extinguisher, which is mounted just forward of the firewall on the fenderwell, is just one of the many chrome appointments that brighten up this truck's engine compartment.*

*Another nice touch found inside is a pair of auxiliary gauges mounted in a chromed underdash housing. Note, too, the chromed emergency brake handle and steering column mount.*

*Ron also dealt his touch to the interior with some upholstery magic consisting of brown velour on the seat, headliner, and visors. Plush brown carpet covers the floorboard.*

*Below- On the inside, we find an interior boasting orange-painted metalwork and even more chrome. Note the underdash-mounted AM/FM/cassette and leather LeCarra steering wheel.*

Gathering real attention for this truck is a brilliant orange enamel paint job applied by Bill Smith of Rialto, California. The paint is accented with multi-color pinstriping by Bobby Kossey. As if this weren't enough, shimmering highlights are provided at seemingly every point by chromed running boards, grille, bumpers, taillights, and mirrors courtesy of MJB Chrome in Rialto. Chromed Cragar wheels, 15x10-inch in the rear and 15x7-inch in the front, combined with Winston radial meats and a 3-inch front drop, give this truck a formidable street stance that can't be beat.

On the inside, every piece of metal is either painted orange or chromed, just like the outside. Ron upholstered the bench seat in brown velour and then followed suit by doing the headliner and visors to match. Brown floor carpeting and a brown leather LeCarra steering wheel from R.C. Enterprises finish off this decor nicely. Adding a touch of class are a pair of auxiliary gauges mounted in a chromed housing and an underdash-mounted AM/FM/cassette stereo deck.

It has taken about $6,000 and many years of effort to bring Ron and Kathy's F-100 to the pristine shape it's in now, but it has all been worthwhile. The truck has nabbed top honors in its class at the Fontana Days car show in their area, and will no doubt glean many more trophies at future outings. In between, though, this sharp F-100 will do its everyday job well by providing just about the best everyday transportation anyone could ask for.

**BY JIM CLARK**

*photos by Robert K. Smith*

# DRAGSTRIP TERROR

*Vehicle: 1948 Chevy Pickup*
*Owner: Doug McIntyre*

**V**intage pickups are most often admired by appreciative auto enthusiasts at close range. They sport custom paint, upholstery and detail work on a par with other types of custom vehicles, but are powered by a highly detailed workhorse type powerplant. This '48 Chevy is different though. It garners its share of awards, sweepstakes to best-in-show, but still holds its own out on the strip.

Doug McIntyre has owned the pickup since '72. It was bought from friend Paul De Mello, who has helped on occasion with the modifications over the years. Those modifications have been extensive. The truck was disassembled and the front section of the new frame replaced. A frame clip from the front of a '71 Camaro is welded on in place of the stock front suspension. At the rear a 9-inch Ford posi-traction assembly with 4.57:1 gears attaches via coilover shocks and a 4-bar setup.

Doug wanted to get more performance than was available from the 283 Chevy V8 and Powerglide combo in the truck. What he ended up with is a powertrain that turned this vintage hauler into a dragstrip terror. Pushing this relative heavyweight through the 1/4-mile in the 12-second range in excess of 100 mph.

It's based on another version of the small block Chevy V8. This being a 350 with a host of modifications, including a .030 overbore, TRW pistons with full-floating pins, roller cam and lifters, angled-plug heads, and Hilborn injection. Exhaust exits through aluminized headers and a custom dual

*Sweet and clean, this very nicely done '48 Chevy looks tame enough from the outside (almost like something grandpa would have driven), but it's a real dragstrip terror, turning the 1/4-mile in the 12-second range in excess of 100 miles per hour.*

*A peek under the hood shows why the early post-war pickup is such a hot ride. The Chevy 350 V8 has been overbored .030, stuffed with TRW pistons, a roller cam, and topped with Hilborn injection.*

Fat tires and a coilover-suspended Ford 9-inch with posi-traction make for a quick getaway. BFG rubber measures 295/60-15 in back, mounted to 10-inch Enkei wheels. Custom dual exhaust is visible just forward of the rear axle.

Located in the indoor/outdoor carpeted bed is the battery, moved to that position to make room for more engine under the hood.

At the rear of the cargo bed is the fuel cell, positioned over the rear axle to add a bit more to the traction department.

A '77 Cadillac Coupe DeVille split-back seat offers plenty of comfort to driver and passenger. Doug cut down the seat riser for this installation, then had the seat upholstered with vinyl and plush fabric.

A LeCarra steering wheel fits nicely atop a '76 Chevy van column. Gauges are Stewart-Warner and Mallory, and the tach is from AutoMeter.

system. The big V8 is backed by a street and strip Turbo 400 trans and 3500 stall-speed converter. Most of the mechanical work was done by the owner, while the frame work was performed by Al Simon of Fontana, California.

Credit for the spectacular Porsche Red paint and superb bodywork goes to Dave Totten of Classic Lacquer Co., in Anaheim. Work on the truck has been performed over a period of 15 years. Though subtle, the work on the body includes countless hours of detailing.

All body seams were filled, hood nosed, cowl vents filled, tailgate smoothed and the chains removed. Below the gate, a pair of custom taillights were fabricated. Highlighting the red exterior is blue striping by Herb Martinez. Inside the bed, a pair of small wheel-tubs had to be added to accommodate the wide wheel and tire combo. The rears are 10-inch wide Enkei fitted with 295/60-15 BFGoodrich T/A Radials. Matching 7-inch wide Enkei and 235/60-15 T/A's reside up front.

Also located in the indoor/outdoor-carpeted bed are the battery and fuel cell, positioned at the rear for traction. Stainless strips and a tonneau cover finish it off.

The interior of the cab received the same level of attention as the rest of the truck. Vinyl covers the door panels and custom headliner. Doug cut down the seat riser and installed a '77 Coupe DeVille split-back seat, outfitted in vinyl and plush fabrics.

Steering is handled via a LeCarra wheel atop a '76 Chevy van column. Below the seat, a Pioneer stereo is mounted, which feeds a set of Pioneer coaxial speakers. Gauges and tachometer fitted into the dash are from Stewart-Warner, AutoMeter and Mallory.

On the street or off, this vintage hauler is a top performer. Doug and a host of friends, Rocky Strickland in particular, have spent a lot of time and effort on the truck, and the results speak for themselves.

# CLASSIC HAULER

**BY JIM CLARK**

*Photos by Robert K. Smith*

*Vehicle: 1957 Chevy*
*Owner: Dan Drabant — Camarillo, California*

**W**hat could be more satisfying to this Customer Service Manager than completing the refurbishing of his brilliant India Red '57 Chevy pickup? Not much, we suspect, as it is one of the nicest we have seen in a long time.

Owner Dan Drabant of Camarillo, California acquired the vehicle from his parents, who had bought it for $900 in 1962. Dan invested $4000 dollars and much of his spare time over a 4-year period to bring it to its present condition. A great deal of the work went into rebuilding the drivetrain and restoring the truck to its original condition.

The stock 283 Chevy V8 and 4-speed Hydramatic trans were rebuilt then installed in the truck, which was newly painted by Ken Ford of BJ's Auto Body in Camarillo. Steve Sanford of Carter Prepaint in Chatsworth applied the striping.

Inside the cab, new paint was shot in the same color of red and new instrumentation was acquired to replace the worn originals. A red-tinted bubble speedometer cover replaces the glass cover. Mounted in the dash is a Jensen AE 518 stereo tape system feeding a pair of Pioneer TS 8 speakers. In place of the Chevy steering wheel Dan has installed an oak-rimmed Superior wheel.

Departing slightly from the restoration theme, he had Eric Thorsen cover the stock bench seat in 2-inch pleated oxford vinyl with a matching insert in the headliner. The original wheels also were replaced by polished 8x15 Indy slot mags fitted with G70-15

*There is something about the classic styling of the '57 Chevy pickup that immediately attracts truck lovers. Believe it or not, this one was originally bought for $900, then another $4000 and 4 years were spent to bring it to its present condition.*

*Basic restoration was done to the body, but then this is a style that doesn't need any modification to make it look dynamite. Pos-A-Traction tires surround 8x15 Indy slot mags with center knock-offs.*

The cargo box was restored, using wood for the flooring. Needless to say, this is one pickup that isn't going to be hauling gravel or anything else that could damage the bed.

The cargo box side step says it all, "Don't even think of stepping here." This is the kind of truck that demands the respect of spectators.

and L70-15 Torque Twister Pos-A-Traction tires. Center knockoffs have Chevy emblems in their centers.

Four years of effort have paid off for Dan, now that his truck is completed. He does more than display it though, it is driven to events like the Nationals in Ogden, Utah and the National Chevy-GMC Truckin' Club, of which he is a member. This is certainly the way to go trucking in style.

Following the concept of simple and inexpensive upgrades, the original bench seat was covered with 2-inch pleated oxford vinyl, with a matching insert in the headliner.

Basically stock interior features a few minor changes, such as the oak-rimmed Superior steering wheel, and a dash-mounted Jensen sound system that plays through Pioneer speakers. A red-tinted bubble covers the speedometer pod.

The stock Chevy 283 V8 and 4-speed Hydra-matic transmission were rebuilt and installed, delivering ample power and retaining the nostalgia influence of a resto-rod.

BY JIM CLARK

# SUPER SKATE

**Vehicle: 1970 Chevy**
**Owner: Roger Sharp — Phoenix, Arizona**

**W**hy would you build a radical pickup with a wing and ground effects style fairing? To have something different, if you are Roger Sharp of Phoenix, Arizona. This is not the first vehicle that he has built which fits this category. Roger has put together three fine street rods ('27-T roadster, '30-A pickup and '31 Ford Vicky), before building this unusual pickup.

Super Skate began its years of service as a daily driver for Roger's business, the Truck Stop in Phoenix. But, sooner or later any vehicle owned by an automotive enthusiast will fall prey to some kind of custom treatment. For Roger's '70 Chevy short bed pickup, the racing theme was selected.

The most noticeable of the modifications are the Webster's Auto Body 6-1/2 inch top chop, rear wing mounted in the bed and the ground-effects skirts made by S&S Custom Truck Parts. Sheetmetal and tubing were used to create the front air dam and 1-1/2 inch steel molded flares. The tailgate and gap below were also covered with sheetmetal panels.

Louvers have been punched extensively into many areas of the truck, including the tailgate and rear lower panel, ground-effects side skirts, hood, rear wing, glove box door, and various trim panels in the engine compartment. The louvered theme was also carried through on the acrylic instrument cluster cover, head and taillights and hood scoop inlet cover.

Porsche Red enamel was flawlessly applied by Custom Mania, with pinstriping by JAK of Mesa, Arizona. The bumpers, grille surround and bed area have been done in flat black, with

*Man alive! This truck screams "hot rod" all the way from the hood scoop to the ground effects skirts to the tail-mounted wing. And if that isn't enough, check out the rear tires and mean, low stance.*

*Among the most noticeable of body modifications is the 6-1/2 inch top chop, nicely executed for a smooth, low appearance.*

*A bed-mounted wing is a real eye catcher when combined with the rest of the ground effects fairings and skirts. The tailgate has been liberally punched with louvers, following the theme established elsewhere on the body.*

*Louvered headlight covers and license plate shield enhance the horizontal lines of the bar grille, and carry the louver theme even farther.*

*More louvers are located on the hood, and the scoop gives immediate indication that this is a high-performance truck.*

*Below- Power is supplied by a small block Chevy engine, equipped with a Crane cam, Accel dual-point ignition, 4-barrel carb, and Cyclone headers.*

*Simple and clean interior places function above form, however the louvered theme has carried over here. Stewart-Warner instruments and a Super Sun tach relay vital signs. ARA air conditioning system keeps things cool, and a Wink mirror gives a clear view to the rear.*

the round tube grille painted bright red.

To achieve its radical rake, '70 Chevy Impala spindles and disc brakes with cut coils were installed up front. Coils were retained in the rear, fitted with Gabriel air shocks. Wide 14x15 Cragar SST's carrying 33x19.50-15LT Mickey Thompsons in the rear, and American 4-1/2x15 slotted mags shod with P195/75R15 Firestones account for most of the rake.

Power is presently supplied by a Chevy small block V8 equipped with a Crane cam, Accel dual-point ignition, 4-barrel carburetor, and Cyclone headers. A heavy duty 3-speed transmission with Hurst shifter and 12-bolt Chevy rearend complete the drivetrain. This mild setup was chosen in order to retain the mild manners required for this daily driver. We understand that a real killer drivetrain is in the works.

Inside the cab, things have been kept simple and functional. Black Nycrush fabric and vinyl cover the bench seat, equipped with a fold down center armrest. Additional instrumentation includes a Super Sun Tachometer and Stewart-Warner oil and temperature gauges. Robert's AM/FM cassette stereo system and CB radio are fitted into the dash above the ARA air conditioning system. An Izumi custom wheel, Wink mirror and etched windows finish the in-cab modifications.

BY JIM CLARK

# IMPY ONE

**Vehicle: 1974 Chevy**
**Owner: John Impellizeri — West Covina, California**

*One look at John Impellizeri's '74 Chevy is enough to convince anyone why hot rod trucks are so popular. A machinist by trade, John's craftsmanship shows up nicely in the work he did on this half-ton.*

When John "Impy" Impellizeri from West Covina, California decided to build a personal hauler, he didn't mess around. John is a machinist by trade, and his craftsmanship shows in his daily transportation. John purchased the '74 Chevy half-ton Super Cheyenne for $4000. Three years of hard work, and another $10,000 later, John has one of the slickest pickups around.

Though the outside of John's pickup received a subtle, tasteful custom treatment, the drivetrain is strictly serious business. John started fresh in the engine compartment with a 1970 350 cid 4-bolt main block. The engine was built from the crank up by Chuck's Engines in LaPuente, California.

The crank was blueprinted, Chevy pink stripe LT-1 rods installed with J&E 7.5:1 pistons, and everything in the lower end was balanced. A Clay Smith cam, chrome-moly push rods, solid lifters, Clay Smith springs and retainers make up the valvetrain. The heads are '65 461 castings that have been ported, polished, cc'ed, and TRW valves were added by Chuck's Engines.

John added Doug Thorley alumicoat headers and Sonic Turbo mufflers with large diameter exhaust tubing and a crossover pipe to handle the volume of exhaust gases this engine pumps out. Up top, a Hampton 6-71 blower running a 10% overdrive ratio is bolted to a Weiand intake manifold. Two Holley 600 cfm 4-barrels fed by a Holley Blue fuel pump regulated at 7-1/2 psi supply fuel to the stout small block. A Mr. Gasket Pro Scoop is bolted on top of the carbs, housing a K&N air cleaner.

The ignition system consists of an Allison electronic ignition, Mallory Pro wires and Autolite spark plugs. With such a heavy investment in the engine, John didn't want to leave anything to chance, so a Nascar high volume oil pump was added along with a Hayden oil cooler and a Corvette 5-1/2 quart chrome plated oil pan.

*Lowered, louvered, and riding on a mean stance, this West Covina cruiser has all the right elements to turn heads. Darkly tinted glass adds an air of mystery.*

John had the Turbo 350 transmission beefed up with the help of a 2500 rpm stall-speed torque converter and a B&M shift kit. The driveshaft has been shortened to 54-1/4 inches by Driveline Service in Whittier, California. The stock rearend was replaced with a 12-bolt positraction Chevy rearend with 4.11:1 gears. Putting all that power to the ground are a set of homemade ladder bars and John added Moroso springer type wheelie bars just in case it ever hooks up.

The half-ton has been lowered at all four corners. In the front, John cut two full turns off a pair of big block Chevy pickup coils. The rear was lowered by relocating the axle to the other side of the leaf springs. Gabriel Adjustable "E" shocks are used in the front and Gabriel air shocks control the rear ride height.

BFGoodrich Radial T/A's, P265-50-15's in the front and P295-50-15's

Lowering at all four corners was accomplished by cutting two full turns out of the front coils and relocating the rear axle above the leaf springs.

A set of Moroso springer type wheelie bars are in place, just in case things ever really hook up. The truck runs a 12-bolt rearend with 4.11:1 ratio for quick getaways.

A 350 cid 4-bolt engine was balanced and blueprinted using pink stripe LT-1 rods and J&E 7.5:1 pistons, a Clay Smith cam, and other goodies. A Hampton 6-71 blower sits atop a Weiand manifold, fed by a pair of Holley 600 cfm 4-barrels. Let us say, this puppy will run!

Chromed Zenith wire wheels are wrapped by BFGoodrich Radial T/A's for quick traction. Suspension is assisted through the turns by a set of chrome plated GM anti-roll bars.

in the rear, are mounted on chromed Zenith wire wheels. The front wheels are 7.5x15's and the rears are 10x15's. To keep the pickup flat in the turns, John bolted up a set of chrome plated GM anti-roll bars.

As you can see, John prefers a tastefully customized exterior to a wild showpiece. The body has been cleaned up by shaving the door handles, removing and filling all the emblems and trim pieces. The tailgate skin has been louvered and a hole was cut in the hood by John Anderson of Bellflower, California for the hood scoop.

Steve's Paintin' Place, also in Bellflower, is responsible for the beautiful paint job. Over the deep gloss black basecoat, candy blue, turquoise and purple stripes were added to the lower body. Just enough to make the pickup really stand out.

The interior is also clean and functional. Stock carpet was replaced with '79 Cadillac Seville plush black carpet, and the seats and door panels were upholstered in a high quality black velour material by Ed Lopez of West Covina. Stewart-Warner gauges have been added behind the dash and a large Mallory tachometer is mounted on the steering column to monitor what is going on in the engine compartment. John added a Grant GT wood steering wheel to get a better feel of the road. The sound system consists of an Audiovox stereo cassette deck with Panasonic and Kenwood speakers.

The finishing touch was a dark smoked window tinting job by Ideal, highlighted with window etching from Glass Axe in West Covina. John must be mighty proud of his '74 half-ton, we can't think of a much nicer means of daily transportation.

*Clean and functional interior features Stewart-Warner instruments and a large Mallory tach. Grant GT wood steering wheel adds driver comfort, while a sound system combining Audiovox, Panasonic and Kenwood components pumps out the tunes.*

BY TODD KAHO

# THE SHELBY TOUCH

*Vehicle: 1985 Dodge D-150*
*Owner: Carrol Shelby*

**C**arrol Shelby doesn't put his name on anything you could call ordinary. So why should his personal pickup be any different? We can assure you, after driving Carrol's '85 Dodge D-150, it's anything but ordinary.

Now that the legendary Shelby magic is at work under the Pentastar banner, instead of the blue oval, Chrysler is once again earning a reputation as a performance car company. It's not surprising then, when Carrol decided to put together his personal hauler, it not only had to look great, but it had to be fast. We think you'll agree, the pickup on these pages meets both of these priorities in the traditional Shelby style.

The body and paintwork is the product of Chrysler's styling studio in Detroit. From the massive chrome plated front bumper, to the slick hinged-in-the-middle rigid bed cover, all the bodywork is one-off custom work. Notice how the clean front chin spoiler blends around the sides of the truck into a ground effect style lower body treatment. There are numerous detail touches that make the D-150 a show quality piece, but it's a daily driver for Carrol.

The paint is styled after the scheme used on the Shelby Charger. The brilliant blue and silver graphic treatment demands attention, yet it is clean enough to be tasteful. Fat Goodyear Eagle ST radials are

*Carrol Shelby's personal pickup has been treated to some refinements that boost both the exterior impact and the performance. After all, Carrol Shelby wouldn't drive anything that could be regarded as ordinary.*

*A rigid bed cover protects anything that is hauled in the carpeted cargo box from the elements, and is hinged in the middle to make access easier. Massive roll bar plays host to four driving lights, a pair of air horns, and a CB antenna.*

Beneath the chromed bumper/brush guard combination is a chin spoiler that wraps around to blend with the side ground effects treatment. Note the special mesh grille.

Two pair of exhaust tips peek out from below the rear step bumper, hinting at the kind of performance that is lurking under the hood. A set of fat Goodyear Eagle ST Radial rubber puts the traction on the ground.

Left- The CS logo is prominently embroidered into the headrests of the high-back performance bucket seats which replaced the stock bench. Between the seats is a trick little console featuring a pull-out drink holder and plenty of extra storage space. There's also a dash-mounted tachometer for keeping track of what's happening under the hood.

A balanced and blueprinted MoPar 360 cid V8 was put together using Direct Connection performance parts. The block was O-ringed, 9.5:1 pistons and a performance camshaft added. Cast iron W2 heads replaced stock units. A Holley intake and 600 cfm Holley 4-barrel were added. Spark is delivered by a Chrysler ECU "Gold Box" ignition. Hooker headers and a free-flow exhaust system allow the potent V8 to breath easily

mounted on factory Dodge alloy wheels to retain the Dodge identity.

The styling studio also did a number on the inside of the pickup. The blue and silver motif was used here as well. High-back performance bucket seats replace the stock bench, and sport headrests stitched with the CS logo. Between the seats is a trick little console featuring a pull-out drink holder from the T-115 and plenty of extra storage space. There's also a dash-mounted tachometer, hinting that there is something other than a slant six in the engine compartment.

Popping the hood won't disappoint, Shelby Performance Center did their part with a balanced and blueprinted 360 cid V8. The 360 has been completely reworked using Direct Connection performance parts. The block was O-ringed, 9.5:1 DC pistons and a performance camshaft added. Then stock heads were replaced with cast iron W2 heads. A Holley intake and 600 cfm Holley four-barrel have also been added. Spark is supplied to the healthy MoPar by a Chrysler ECU "Gold Box" ignition. Hooker headers and a free-flow exhaust system allow the potent V8 to breath properly. The automatic transmission has been reworked to handle the extra power, with the addition of a shift kit installed by Overbey Transmission in La Habra, California. Shelby Performance Center dynoed the powertrain and found it produced 350 honest tire-burning horsepower.

When Carrol puts his boot in it, the pickup is capable of some startling performance. 0-60 takes just 7.74 seconds, and the quarter mile is covered in 16.3 seconds, with a trap speed of 87.8 mph.

When your name is Carrol Shelby, you've earned the right to drive any-thing your heart desires. Carrol really likes to drive this pickup home at night. After driving it for ourselves, we don't blame him a bit. The Shelby pickup is fast and fun. Now let's see, where did we put the Direct Connection catalog....

**ROD & KUSTOM**

## REMOTE CONTROLS

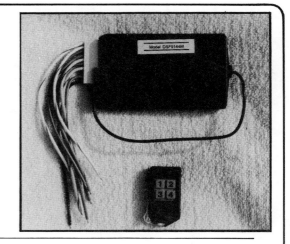

*Ball's remote controls are a 4-channel, 4-mode system with the Rod & Kustom Car builder in mind. This system was designed for our industry and not the burglar alarm companies.*

This system will work on power windows, door actuators, solenoids, trunk releases, and switch lights off and on. It will also work with hydraulics for raising and lowering chassis.

$145.00 EACH

## POWER WINDOW KITS

O.E.M. STYLE

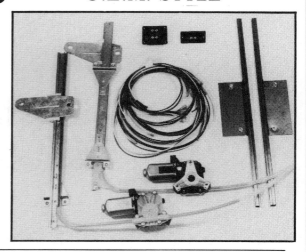

Ball's power windows feature a center lift with a "Z" channel support to stop any window teetering going up or down.

This O.E.M. system is very fast and easy to install with only four mounting locations. The system uses five wire GM switches or Ball's switches with or without indicator lights. We also offer window channel for mounting glass.

Kit A: 2 Regulators
(1 right & 1 left)
**$249.95**

Kit B: Full Window Kit Features:
3 switches, 1 full wiring harness, 2 bottom window channels, 2 window regulators **$319.95**

---

Over 10,000 SOLD!

*(Model Opened for Display)*

## BALL'S ACTUATORS

Ball's actuators are the best actuators money can buy for opening door latches and trunk lid latches.

We have a variety of switches available from momentary buttons to magnet and remote switching.

We guarantee our motor to have more power than any other motor or solenoid available today!

**PRODUCT FEATURES**
1) Waterproof
2) Nylon pinion
3) High speed micro motor
4) 3/4" of travel – push or pull
5) Aluminum secondary gears
6) Mounting holes
7) Built-in clutch, motor returns to neutral position after being activated

$38.95 *each*

IF YOU'RE INTO RODS & KUSTOMS
**YOU'VE GOTTA HAVE**

Phone:
**(219) 457-2880**

# ROD & KUSTOM

11875 S.R. 13 North • Syracuse, IN 46567

# TO STREET ROD OR TO RESTORE

**Either way...** If you're the type who sees treasure, not trash in this 1936 Ford Pick-Up, seen recently in a Florida field, then Daytona Mig, with their twelve different MIG welders, five TIG welders, six Plasma cutters, complete line of restoration books, accessories, consumables and a staff of car enthusiasts is your one stop shop, whether you choose to street rod or restore!

**160 AMP MODEL #850**

## Shop MIG Welders

160 AMP
180 AMP
200 AMP
240 AMP

**CALL FOR PRICES!**

## Plasma Cutters

35 AMP
50 AMP
70 AMP
90 AMP
120 AMP
150 AMP

**CALL FOR PRICES!**

**35 AMP HIGH FREQUENCY MODEL #931**

## Precision TIG Welders

**NEW!**

### Model 16 P

The new TIG 16 P is a full featured TIG. Equipped with AC/DC, high frequency, square wave. It is the smallest, most professional TIG welder made. It welds steel, stainless, chrome moly, aluminum & many exotic metals.

With five different TIGs to choose from, Daytona MIG has the right one for you. Also available: 100,160,200,250 amp.

## Combi MIG

- Uses flux-core wire
- Model #888
- 110VAC/130AMP Output

# DAYTONA MIG

**SEE US AT:**
STREET ROD NATS
SPRING CARLISLE ID 37-40
FALL CARLISLE 0173-176
FALL HERSHEY Greenfield GAM 96-100

**SHOWROOM AT:**
1821 HOLSONBACK DRIVE
DAYTONA BCH., FLA 32117

**ALL OUR PRODUCTS HAVE:**
- ONE YEAR WARRANTY & 5 DAY MONEY-BACK GUARANTEE
ASK ABOUT OUR EXCLUSIVE TRADE UP PROGRAM
If at any time you wish to trade in, or up to another unit we will take your old unit in trade

## ORDERS: 800-331-9353

**SERVICE:** (904) 274-1245
**FAX:** (904) 274-1237

  MasterCard  U P S  C O D  VISA

BY JOHN LEE

# STUDE STUDY

*Vehicle: 1950 Studebaker*
*Owner: Randy Truhlsen — Blair, Nebraska*

**S**tudebaker Brothers Manufacturing Co. got its start in the mid-1800's building farm wagons, and later in the century was the world's largest builder of horse-drawn vehicles. Henry and Clem Studebaker entered the motorized vehicle field in 1902, and their company continued to build trucks right through 1964, two years before the demise of the Studebaker automobile.

The 2R Series introduced the first truck restyling after the war in 1949. It was an attractive package in its pudgy way, and a number of them have been hot rodded and customized over the years.

Earlier models were powered by the small 169 cid flathead six and can really stand a power transfusion. The light trucks were offered with a 224 cid, 140-hp OHV V8 in 1955. In good condition, this mill can still be an adequate performer, especially with the 3-speed overdrive transmission. But repair parts are difficult to find, and hop-up equipment is all but nonexistent.

A swap to a dependably modern small block, therefore, is a smart move. Builder Gene Paist chose the plentiful 400 cid Chevy when converting this '50 Stude half-ton, now owned by Randy Truhlsen of Blair, Nebraska. To make the swap easier, he used the whole front subframe from a late Camaro, which allowed him to lower the front end and provided disc brakes and power steering, too.

The rearend also came from the Camaro, and late Z/28 spoke wheels are mounted all around with Goodyear Eagle GT radials. A 400 Turbo trans is used along with the stock engine. A Cadillac provided the tilt column with

*With a bit of attention to the right details, this '50 Studebaker half-ton became a sleek mild custom. The rounded shape lends itself to smoothing by removal of trim and door handles. Faint pink flames lick the fenders, announcing that this truck is a hot rod.*

*Down-in-the-weeds stance was achieved by a combination of Camaro front subframe and rearend, which deliver a car-like ride and improved handling.*

Front of the truck was left pretty much stock, with the exception of the flames and the fact that the bumpers were painted body color. But beneath the mild mannered pickup body is a lot of chassis and powertrain modification. Although not visible here, a front subframe from a late Camaro was installed to lower the nose, provide improved ride/handling, power disc brakes and power steering.

Cradled on the Camaro subframe, is a relatively stock late model 400 cid Chevy V8, backed up by a TH400 automatic transmission. Plenty of steam for the old Stude.

column gear selector and a custom wood-rimmed steering wheel.

Gauges from a '64 Ford pickup were mounted in the dash, and seating is on a Ford split bench finished in brown velour.

While the front remains stock except for some trim removal, the rear got the custom treatment in the form of Ford pickup taillights mounted on the ends of the bed sides, and a tailgate cover stamped with an X for strength. The panel below the bed is stock, something other pickups of the era didn't have. Paist painted the bumpers to match the rest of the truck, which is light pink with darker pink flames.

There are still a few of these Studebakers around, and as you can see, they make neat hot rod haulers!

The rear received some special treatment in the form of Ford taillights which were installed in the ends of the bed sides, and a tailgate cover, stamped with an X for strength. Late Z/28 spoke wheels are surrounded by Goodyear Eagle GT radials.

# SOURCES

**A-l Racing Parts**
770 Route 28, Box 7S
Middlesex, NJ 08846
(201) 968-2323
Mustang II Suspension Parts

**Aldan Shock Absorbers**
646 E. 219th St.
Carson, CA 90745
(213) 834-7478
Coil-Over Shocks

**Bitchin' Products**
9392 Bond Ave.
El Cajon, CA 92021
(619) 449-2837
Street Rod Sheet Metal Products

**Borgeson Universal Company**
1050 S. Main St., Dept HRMx
Torrington, CT 06790
(203) 482-8283
Steering Universal Joints and Shafts

**Butch's Rod Shop**
2853 Northlawn Ave.
Dayton, OH 45439
(513) 298-2665
Suspension Components, Accessories

**Dennis Carpenter Reproductions**
PO Box 26398
Charlotte, NC 28221-6398
(704) 786-8139
Ford Reproduction Parts

**Centech, Inc.**
Box 139, RD 2
Perkiomenville, PA 18074
(215) 287-6707
Wiring Kits & Accessories

**Coachworks of Yesteryear**
P.O. Box 651
Oakland, FL 34760
(407) 877-0344
Reproduction Body Parts

**Conte Enterprises**
28002 ll0th Ave. E.
Graham, WA 98338
(206) 847-4886
Independent Front Ends

**Dixie Truck Works**
9233 Sandburg Ave.
Charlotte, NC 28213
(704) 549-1267
Replacement Chevy Body Panels

**Fairlane Company**
210 E. Walker St. MX
St. Johns, MI 48879
(517) 224-6460
Fiberglass Parts

**Fatman Fabrications**
8621 Fairview Road, Hwy 218
Charlotte, NC 28227
(704) 545-0369
IFS Kits, Front End Components

**Gibbon Fiberglass Reproductions**
P.O. Box 490
Gibbon, NE 68840
(800) 833-8019
Fiberglass Reproduction Body Parts

**Golden State Pickup Parts**
PO Box 1019, Dept TSP
Santa Ynez, CA 93460
(806) 886-2020
Chevy Truck Parts

**Heavy Chevy Truck Parts, Inc.**
PO Box 860, Dept TS
Siloam Springs, AR 72761
(501) 524-9575
Chevy Truck Parts

**Hot Rod and Custom Supply**
1020 SE 12th Ave.
Cape Coral, FL 33990
(813) 574-7744
Ford Flathead Parts

**Bruce Horkey Cabinetry**
Rt. 4, Box l88X
Windom, MN 58101
(507) 831-5625
Truck Bed Parts, Fiberglass

**Martz Chassis Engineering**
508 East Pitt Street, Dept X
Bedford, PA 15522
(814) 623-9501
Independent Front Ends

**Patrick's**
PO Box 648
Casa Grande, AZ 85222
(602) 836-1117
Vintage Speed Equipment, Truck Parts

**PBI Inc.**
562 W. Ely Street
Alliance, OH. 44601
(216) 821-2852
Ford Twin I-Beam Dropped Axles

**Perfect Performance Products, Inc.**
8851 W. Freeway, Suite 114
Ft. Worth, TX 76116
(8I7) 244-8898
Universal Wiring Assemblies

**Ron Francis Wire Works**
167 Keystone Road
Chester, PA 19013
(215) 485-1937
Wiring Kits

**Sanderson Headers**
202 Ryan Way
S. San Francisco, CA 94080
(415) 583-6617
Exhaust Headers

**Joe Smith Automotive**
3070 Briarcliff Road, NE
Atlanta, GA 30329
(404) 634-5157
Ford Parts

**SoCal Pickups, Inc.**
6321 Manchester Blvd.
Buena Park, CA 90621
(714) 994-1400 or (213) 941-4693

**Specialty Power Windows**
Route 2, Goodwyn Road
Forsyth, GA 31029
(912) 994-9248
Power Window Kits

**Stovebolt Engine Co.**
PO Box 166
Corbett, OR 97019
(503) 695-2571
Chevy/GMC 6-Cyl. Engines

**Street & Performance**
Route 5, #1 Hot Rod Lane
Mena, AR 71953
(501) 394-5711
Chevy/Ford Fuel Injection, Accessories

**Randy Truhlsen**
Rt. 2
Blair, NE 68008
(402) 426-5405

**Vintage Air**
10305 I-35 N.
San Antonio, TX 78233
(512) 654-7171
Air Conditioning/Heating Systems

**Bill Walski Fiberglass**
6202 SW 55th Ct.
Davie, FL 33314
(305) 587-5557

**Weedetr Street Rod Components**
1355 Vista Way, Unit X
Red Bluff, CA 96080
(916) 527-2040
Ford Suspension Parts

**Western Chassis and Component**
230 Dunworth
Visalia, CA 93291
(209) 625-1248
Truck Chassis Lowering Parts

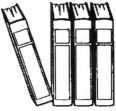

Our name is ............

We sell parts for......

We make .................

We do it at discounted prices so real hot rodders can have....................

# REAL
# HOT
# RODS

Everything from chrome goodies to performance machine work to traditional T kits, to glass bodies, to chassis to .... well, you get the idea.

**REAL HOT RODS ARE DRIVEN!**

**REAL HOT RODS**
**Airport Industrial Park**
**P.O. Box 748**
**Driggs, ID 83422**
**(208) 354-8137**

At **REAL HOT RODS** we can get you on the road to hot rodding fun at prices you can afford.